To Malcolm Walker with many thanks for your most appreciated help.

The Metropolitan Opera on Record

A Discography of the Commercial Recordings

Second Edition

Frederick P. Fellers

THE SCARECROW PRESS, INC.
Lanham • Toronto • Plymouth, UK
2010

Published by Scarecrow Press, Inc.
A wholly owned subsidiary of The Rowman & Littlefield Publishing Group, Inc.
4501 Forbes Boulevard, Suite 200, Lanham, Maryland 20706
http://www.scarecrowpress.com

Estover Road, Plymouth PL6 7PY, United Kingdom

British Library Cataloguing in Publication Information Available

Library of Congress Cataloging-in-Publication Data
Fellers, Frederick P.
  The Metropolitan Opera on record : a discography of the commercial recordings / Frederick P. Fellers. — 2nd ed.
     p. cm.
  Includes bibliographical references and index.
  ISBN 978-0-8108-7664-4 (cloth : alk. paper)
  1. Metropolitan Opera (New York, N.Y.)—Discography. 2. Operas—Discography. I. Title.
  ML156.4.O46F4 2010
  016.7821026'6—dc22   2010012489

♾™ The paper used in this publication meets the minimum requirements of American National Standard for Information Sciences—Permanence of Paper for Printed Library Materials, ANSI/NISO Z39.48-1992.

Printed in the United States of America

To the Memory of

Max Rudolf
and
Rose Bampton

Contents

Acknowledgments

Most of the research for the recordings of the Metropolitan Opera Chorus and Orchestra made between 1906 and 1972, which normally give no information about recording dates and recording locations on the published recordings, took place in the early 1980s in what were then the archives of CBS Records and RCA Records. (Since then these names have changed several times, and both have now become one archive as situations evolve. In this discography these archives will be referred to by the names of the companies as they were at the time the recordings were made as the Victor Archives and the Columbia Archives). One could not have asked for more help and kindness than was given by Bernadette Moore and Jerry Thomas at RCA for the Victor Archives material and Tina McCarthy at CBS for the Columbia Archives material.

Special thanks is gratefully given to Max Rudolf and Rose Bampton who provided much knowledge that could not be obtained elsewhere and who took considerable time to answer many questions. It is difficult to truly express just how helpful Maestro Rudolf was in this project. He wrote and telephoned with excellent information and never hesitated to share his time. There were three ways in which he shared his knowledge. Of greatest importance was that he had kept copies of schedules and other documents so that he alone could provide the exact date and location of the Ravel concerto session with Wittgenstein, and similarly he was able to provide not only the exact date of the Metropolitan Opera Club recording of *Le Nozze di Figaro* which happened on 15 November 1955, but even additional information that was not needed for this discography such as the date for the rehearsal of this recording which had taken place on 13 November 1955. Secondly he also had strong memories of events during recording sessions and some of these are mentioned in the discography. Finally of lesser importance was that Maestro Rudolf sometimes mentioned possibilities. As an example of this he thought a couple of the sessions for the Metropolitan Opera Club recordings might have been made at the Columbia Studios rather than at the Metropolitan Opera House where information found in the Metropolitan Archives indicates they were made. Since there is so very little exact information to be found about this series, these possibilities are given along with information to the contrary. It was also a pleasure to exchange a number of letters with Rose Bampton concerning the anonymous recordings made in 1940 in some of which she participated and in some of which her husband, Wilfred Pelletier, conducted. She was very kind to look over the lists of dates and singers and to agree or in some cases disagree with what had been written. In spite of the fact that information in the Victor archives states that three of the nine sessions took place in Philadelphia's Academy of Music, she was quite firm in her belief that all of the sessions took place in New York's Town Hall. A bit of guilt is felt in perhaps pushing her on this point, but she never wavered in her belief that she made all her recordings in New York and not in Philadelphia. An example of her correspondence on this point will be found in the section about this series in the *Introduction*.

It will always be a most happy memory to remember the great help given by Robert Tuggle, Director of the Metropolitan Opera Archives. All of the information found in the archives that has benefited this discography was solely because of his skill and kindness. Without his knowledge and assistance, this work would be much, much the poorer.

The orchestra manager of the Metropolitan Opera, Robert Sirinek, was most helpful in providing the dates for the recording sessions of the 1980s and 1990s. This amplified the information given by the recording companies.

David Hamilton was very helpful in giving much good advice and sharing information.

Many thanks are also gratefully given to Samuel Brylawski, Georgia Cravey, Daniel Paradis, Malcolm Walker, Lawrence F. Holdridge, Robert Warren, Jr., Barbara Sawka, Susan Stinson, Ronald Dethlefson, Ross Laird, Giv Cornfield, George Spitzer, David Canfield, Ross Allen, Michael H. Gray, Frederick Roffman, Christopher Gibson, Lawrence Downey, and Mary R. Sive.

Renée Camus of Scarecrow Press is sincerely thanked for much good advice and for many improvements to this discography. It was a pleasure to see how her suggestions brought much-needed clarity.

Introduction

This discography lists all the commercial sound recordings made by the Metropolitan Opera Chorus and Orchestra, with and without soloists, from 1906 through 1998. (New Metropolitan Opera releases after 1998 were devoted to video recordings.) While some later reissues on various labels are given when known, no claim is made that all such reissues are listed. It is the aim of this discography to list all issues by the original recording companies who were responsible for making and selling these recordings. The main section is a chronological listing of recording sessions. Indices of composers, titles and artists refer back to each item recorded. Ironically, because of the vast difference in methods of recording from the first to the last session, it is often easier to be specific about exactly what was recorded at a certain moment in time ninety years ago than twenty years ago. This permits the earlier listings to often be more detailed than later ones. During most of the 78 rpm era, it was very difficult to alter the two to five minutes of sound that comprised one side of a disc, while today minute bits of sound can easily be added, moved or deleted as required. These differences are reflected in the way the discography is organized. For example, with the 1947 recording of *La Bohème,* it is simple to indicate the exact recording date for each of the twenty-six sides that comprised the original 78 rpm release of the set. However, for the 1959 recording of *Macbeth,* it is not possible to show exactly which section of the opera was recorded on each recording date, although the exact recording dates for the work as whole are known. Of course, whenever it is possible to clearly give the exact date for any section of a recorded work, that is done.

The history of commercial recordings of ensembles of the Metropolitan Opera begins with a certainty that probably no longer exists and a possibility that now cannot be proven. The certainty refers to the Leeds & Catlin cylinders and the possibility to the New York Grand Opera Chorus discs. During the acoustical period of recording, when recordings were made by singing or playing into a recording horn without any electrical amplification, a series of recordings clearly labeled as being made by the Metropolitan Opera Chorus began in 1910. A few years later, also during the acoustical period, recordings were made by the Metropolitan Opera House Orchestra. The first electrical recordings of the orchestra were made by Brunswick in 1925. From 1927 through 1930, Victor made a remarkable series of recordings with Giulio Setti directing the Metropolitan Opera Chorus and Orchestra with some of the Metropolitan's and Victor's leading singers. The Great Depression caused very little to be recorded in the 1930s. In 1940, condensed versions of twelve popular operas were released anonymously with labels reading *"The World's Greatest Operas."* The musicians making these recordings probably had connections with the Metropolitan Opera. From 1941 through 1954, the Metropolitan Opera recorded for Columbia. In 1947 Columbia's recording of the Metropolitan Opera's performance of an English version of *Hänsel und Gretel* was the first complete commercial opera recording ever made in the United States. During the 1950s, RCA Victor recorded three complete operas and highlights of two operas. From 1955 through 1957, the Metropolitan Opera in association with the Book-of-the-Month Club recorded nineteen abridged operas. The high cost of recording in the United States caused no commercial Metropolitan Opera recordings to be made in the 1960s. In 1972 Deutsche Grammophon recorded one complete opera and released highlights of the gala honoring Sir Rudolf Bing. In the 1980s and 1990s with the coming of digital recording techniques, a distinguished series of recordings, primarily conducted by James Levine, was made. Each of these categories of the recording history of the Metropolitan Opera is discussed below.

Leeds & Catlin. Probably around 1901 or 1902, the Leeds & Catlin Company made a series of recordings of the Metropolitan Opera House String Orchestra directed by Nahan Franko. Nineteen two minute wax cylinders by these artists were listed in the 1902 catalogue of the company. It is likely that the total number sold of each of these recordings was very limited, and sadly, it is not known if any of these recordings are still in existence. The only proof we now have that any of these titles ever existed is from the 1902 Leeds & Catlin catalogue. All of the listings for the Metropolitan Opera House String Orchestra from that catalogue are listed in the *Additional Recordings* section of the appendix of this discography, because we do not now have a single example of these recordings.

New York Grand Opera Chorus. Between 7 June 1906 and 4 April 1913, the Victor Talking Machine Company recorded a chorus which was named the New York Grand Opera Chorus on the record labels and in the company's catalogues. This name seems to exist only in relationship to these Victor recordings, since there was no New York Grand Opera Company which could have had a chorus with this name. In listening to the chorus in these recordings, one can hear the sound of a specific ensemble that seems to have had a background of working together for some time. It is not the sound of an *ad hoc* group of performers put together for a single occasion. Furthermore, this chorus does not sound as if it employs any of the usual singers that Victor used for their own chorus recordings during this time. Victor's recordings of what the company called the Victor Opera Company, the Victor Chorus, the Victor Male Chorus, the Victor Oratorio Chorus and their Trinity Choir have a very different sound than the recordings of the New York Grand Opera Chorus. For their own chorus recordings, Victor used singers such as Frank C. Stanley, Henry Burr, Harry Macdonough, Corinne Morgan, Elise Stevenson, Reinald Werrenrath and William F. Hooley. The excellent voices of these singers were quite distinctive, and they are no where to be heard on any of the New York Grand Opera Chorus recordings. Unlike the various Victor chorus recordings by their own singers, which were sung in English, the New York Grand Opera Chorus recordings were sung in Italian and French. These recordings sound as if the singers were practiced in these languages and sound nothing at all like native English speakers trying to approximate a foreign tongue. Also the spirit and enthusiasm of the New York Grand Opera Chorus are quite different from the more staid and proper sounding Victor house chorus recordings. One has only to listen to the exuberance of the New York Grand Opera Chorus in their recording of the "Toreador Song" with Emilio de Gogorza to imagine singers who were used to performing this music on the stage. They do not sound like singers who were only being employed in a recording studio to read and perform music, no matter how well they technically accomplished it.

The March 1907 catalogue of *Victor Red Seal Records* has this announcement of the first recordings of the New York Grand Opera Chorus: "The Victor offers something new to the public. Four fine records of favorite opera choruses by one of the greatest operatic singing organizations in the world. The work of this chorus was one of the features of the past season and the ensemble was pronounced the best heard in years. The difficulties to be overcome in the recordings of these numbers were very great, but the Victor has been equal to the task and the result is now offered to the public."

Of course, just because advertising copy speaks of the chorus as if it were an established organization means little in itself, and it in no way proves this chorus to be the Metropolitan Opera Chorus. However, if this were only a pick-up chorus of regular Victor singers as were used in their common black label popular recordings, why did this group rate being released on Victor's prestigious and more expensive series of Red Seal records which was reserved for the world's most prominent artists including the singers of the Metropolitan Opera? More to the point, why was the line becoming increasingly blurred between recordings labeled New York Grand Opera Chorus and those labeled Metropolitan Opera Chorus?

Here is a résumé of the Victor recording sessions that employed the New York Grand Opera Chorus. The first session on 7 June 1906 had two recordings released: the "Porter's Song" from *Martha* with the solo part sung by Emilio de Gogorza, and the "Soldiers' Chorus" from *Faust* recorded on a ten inch disc. Both were sung in Italian. The second session on 8 June 1906 had one recording released: "Scorrendo uniti" from *Rigoletto*. The third session on 11 June 1906 had two recordings issued: the "Toreador Song" from *Carmen* with Emilio de Gogorza as soloist and the chorus "Gli aranci olezzano" from *Cavalleria Rusticana*. The labels of the "Toreador Song" credited the New York Grand Opera Chorus, but the Victor catalogues, which had initially also credited the New York Grand Opera Chorus were changed, and by May 1915 and afterwards, the Victor catalogues listed the Metropolitan Opera Chorus for this title. This is a change that had to have been done for a purpose. The simplest thing would have been to have left catalogue listings exactly as they were each time the catalogue was updated.

The chorus from *Cavalleria Rusticana* was always credited to the New York Grand Opera Chorus, but a curious event happened at a recording session on 4 April 1913. This title was remade on that day at a session that was officially credited as a recording session of the Metropolitan Opera Chorus. The two other titles that were made that day were released as Metropolitan Opera Chorus recordings. This 1913 remake of the chorus from *Cavalleria Rusticana* was released as being made by the New York Grand Opera Chorus even though the recording files indicate it was made by the Metropolitan Opera Chorus. This remake from 1913 was released on the same record number, 64048, as the 1906 recording. It should be noted that from time to time Victor re-recorded a title when they thought they could do a better job either artistically or mechanically. As long as the accompaniment remained the same, each time the piece was re-recorded by the *same* artist, the same matrix number, which was assigned as the recording was first being made, would continue to be used, but with a different take number for each new try. Victor would then release the newer recording with the same record number as the older one. The only thing that changed was the take number, and in most cases the public would not know that a newer recording replaced the older one. For example, there are a series of Victor recordings by Melba that she recorded in 1907, and which she remade in 1910. The originals and remakes have the same matrix numbers and the same record numbers. However, the take numbers were higher for the later recordings. For these 1906 and 1913 recordings of the *Cavalleria Rusticana* chorus which both appeared on record number 64048 and which both had the matrix number of B-3452, the only thing that changed was the take number with the 1906 recording having a take -3 and the 1913 recording having a take -6. The important thing to remember here is that when Victor used the same matrix number for later recordings, it was only done when the re-recordings involved the *same* artists. If the later re-recording employed different performers, it was Victor's practice to assign a completely new matrix number and to begin the series of take number back at take -1. Having these 1906 and 1913 recordings use the same matrix number, implies that Victor considered the New York Grand Opera Chorus and the Metropolitan Opera Chorus to be the same artists.

On 6 January 1910 the first Victor session was held that was officially credited to the Metropolitan Opera Chorus on the labels: the "Miserere" from *Il Trovatore* with Alda and Caruso. Eleven days later on 17 January 1910, there was another Metropolitan Opera Chorus session held in which three recordings were made. Two of these were duets from *Faust* sung by Farrar and Journet which were issued on discs with the labels clearly crediting the Metropolitan Opera Chorus and the third was of Journet singing "Le veau d'or" from *Faust* but with no name given for the chorus. A year would pass before Victor would again record either the Metropolitan Opera Chorus or the New York Grand Opera Chorus.

Three connected recording sessions on 19 and 20 January and 17 February 1911 provide a number of possible connections between these two differently named choruses. The session on 19 January 1911 produced one issued recording, "Écoute-moi bien" from *Faust* in which Antonio Scotti was accompanied by what was called only Grand Opera Chorus on the record label. There was also one unissued recording, "La Kermesse" from *Faust*, and only one take was made of it. On the next day, 20 January 1911, three titles were recorded and all three were unissued: (1) two takes were made of a new re-recording of the earlier New York Grand Opera Chorus recording of the "Soldiers' Chorus" from *Faust*, but this time it was made as a longer recording on a twelve inch disc instead of a ten inch disc and sung in the original French instead of an Italian translation, (2) take -2 of "La Kermesse" from *Faust*, and (3) takes -1 and -2 of Costa's song "Luna Nova" with Antonio Scotti as soloist. The recording book in the Victor archives credits the session of 17 February 1911 to the New York Grand Opera Chorus, and it completes the attempts made at the titles from the sessions of the 19th and the 20th of the preceding month. During the 17 February 1911 session, three works were recorded: (1) takes -3 and -4 of "La Kermesse" from *Faust* with the third take being chosen for issue, (2) take -3 of the new longer French version of the "Soldiers' Chorus" from *Faust* which was issued, and (3) takes -3 and -4 of Costa's "Luna Nova" with the fourth take chosen to be issued. The two selections from *Faust* were issued with labels and catalogues crediting the recordings to the New York Grand Opera Chorus. The story was different for "Luna Nova." It was first issued with labels reading N. Y. Grand Opera Chorus. However, labels on later pressings were changed and clearly show the Metropolitan Opera Chorus, and this is for exactly the same recording. The Victor catalogues also list the Metropolitan Opera Chorus for "Luna Nova." Raymond Sooy, who began work for the Victor Talking Machine Company in 1903 and who worked for the company for more than thirty years, was possibly the recording engineer, or recorder as Victor named the position, for these three sessions in January and February 1911. In his memoirs, which seem to have developed from his diary, he has this entry for the first session on 19 January 1911, "The first recording engagement of the Metropolitan Grand Opera Chorus from the Metropolitan Opera Company of New York."[1] Of course, as we have seen, this date was not the actual first recording of the Metropolitan Opera Chorus. Perhaps he meant it was the first time he had operated the recording machinery for a recording session employing this ensemble, but he clearly connects the chorus to the "Metropolitan Opera Company of New York" and, interestingly, he uses the word "Grand" in the title which Victor used in connection with the New York Grand Opera Chorus but never in connection with the Metropolitan Opera Chorus.

As was mentioned above, the last session that used the name New York Grand Opera Chorus was that of 4 April 1913 which produced three issued recordings. The recording book in the Victor Archives shows that the Metropolitan Opera Chorus was used on this date, and the Metropolitan Opera Chorus was credited on the labels of the issued recordings of the choruses from *Les Huguenots* and *Die Zauberflöte*. However, the remake of the chorus from *Cavalleria Rusticana* was issued, as we have seen, as being recorded by the New York Grand Opera Chorus.

So to sum up, we have a session officially credited to the Metropolitan Opera Chorus that also produced a recording with the name New York Grand Opera Chorus. We have sessions credited to the New York Grand Opera Chorus that produced recordings with the name Metropolitan Opera Chorus. And we have instances in which the Victor catalogues and labels were changed to list Metropolitan Opera Chorus that had earlier listed New York Grand Opera Chorus for the *same* recordings. It does not seem possible that all these variances can simply be casual mistakes. The published Victor catalogues, supplements and various books were compiled with great care, and errors were exceedingly rare and quickly corrected. Also of interest is that we have the writings of a Victor employee who may have actually operated the recording equipment during the sessions that were connected with the New York Grand Opera Chorus' name in January and February 1911, and he refers to the first of these three recording sessions as the "first recording engagement of the Metropolitan Grand Opera Chorus from the Metropolitan Opera Company of New York."

One other possible connection should be mentioned. Among the thrilling excerpts of live performances at the Opera House that Metropolitan Opera librarian Lionel S. Mapleson made on wax cylinders between 1901 and 1904 is a recording of the "Soldiers' Chorus" from *Faust* from the performance of 14 February 1903. Although the soloists sang their parts in the original French during this season, the Metropolitan Opera Chorus sang their parts in an Italian translation as was the custom at that time. Three years later on 7 June 1906 when the New York Grand Opera Chorus made their Victor recording of the "Soldiers' Chorus" from *Faust*, it was sung in the same Italian translation as that the Metropolitan Opera in 1903. It is also interesting to hear how similar the timbre is of the choruses in both recordings.

This is pure speculation and unless some old contract should ever be discovered to prove or disprove it, it may be that the Victor Talking Machine Company entered into an agreement with the Metropolitan Opera to use its name on their recordings, and the first instance of this happening was the 6 January 1910 recording of the "Miserere." Perhaps the other chorus recordings were made at a lesser cost because the Metropolitan Opera's name was not used, and that later an agreement was made authorizing the use of the Metropolitan Opera's name. If this be true, it could explain how de Gogorza's 1906 "Toreador Song" could first be listed with the New York Grand Opera Chorus and then have later catalogues show the Metropolitan Chorus for the same recording, and how Scotti's "Luna Nova" first appeared with labels listing the New York Grand Opera Chorus and then was quickly changed to the Metropolitan Opera Chorus. It does not seem likely that the Metropolitan Opera would permit its name to be used unless there was a specific agreement authorizing its use especially if the use of their name was by a high profile company like Victor which was busy recording many of the singers at the Metropolitan Opera. It may even be that during most of these years, Victor had a contract with the Metropolitan Opera that gave Victor the exclusive use of the Metropolitan's name for recordings. In any case, several of the New York Grand Opera Chorus recordings are somehow linked to the Metropolitan Opera Chorus, and from actual listening to the style and performance characteristics of all these recordings, it does not seem possible that any of them could have been made by the usual Victor staff recording vocalists. It seems that the case can be made that the New York Grand Opera Chorus *may* have been the Metropolitan Opera Chorus, and that is about as close as one can get without any more documentation being made available.

The acoustical recordings of the Metropolitan Opera Chorus. From 6 January 1910 through 27 July 1917, the Metropolitan Opera Chorus made a series of recordings for Victor primarily in accompaniment to various soloists. There were just four strictly chorus recordings released. It is not always possible to determine the name of the conductor since the Victor files do not always indicate this. It was unusual during these years to find the name of the conductor given on the labels as Gaetano Scognamiglio's was for the quartet and quintet from *Un Ballo in Maschera*. Most of the Victor recordings in this discography before 1916, which do not have a conductor listed, were probably conducted by Walter B. Rogers (1865-1939) who was then Victor's house conductor, and who directed well over one thousand recordings during his years at Victor. It is not likely that any of the Victor acoustical recordings used the orchestra of the Metropolitan Opera. In fact almost all of the Victor labels used until 1914 clearly state "accompaniment by Victor Orchestra," and it was surely the Victor Orchestra that played for all these Victor recordings even after 1914 when Victor labels no longer mentioned the name of their own orchestra when it was used in accompaniment to soloists.

Sometime between 1908 and 1913 five recordings of the Metropolitan Opera House Chorus were issued on U.S. Everlasting Indestructible cylinders. It is also reported that fourteen discs were recorded by Edison on 19 December 1910 in which the Metropolitan Opera House Chorus was directed by Giulio Setti, but these recordings were never issued. The Metropolitan Opera House Chorus was used in an 11 January 1921 Columbia recording of "Pescator, affonda l'esca" from *La Gioconda* sung by Stracciari, which did not indicate the name of the chorus on the record label, but which did list the Metropolitan Opera Chorus in catalogues and in company files. There was also an unissued Brunswick recording made on 19 April 1924 with Michael Bohnen. There is the probability that the Metropolitan Opera Chorus was used on a number of recordings for different companies during these years without any credit being given. The reason for this anonymity may be due to exclusive contracts or to the amount of money companies were willing to pay.

The acoustical recordings of the Metropolitan Opera House Orchestra. Beginning in 1916 for the Columbia Graphophone Company and in 1917 for the Victor Talking Machine Company, both companies began to make a series of recordings by leading American orchestras. Columbia began with the Chicago Symphony Orchestra, the Cincinnati Symphony Orchestra and the Philharmonic Orchestra of New York, and Victor began with the Boston Symphony Orchestra and the Philadelphia Orchestra. After many years in which the emphasis was on vocal recording, technical improvements in the acoustical recording process permitted the recording companies to look to a field that had been generally avoided—that of symphonic recordings.

The first recordings of the Metropolitan Opera House Orchestra in the World War I era were probably made by Pathé with the orchestra under the direction of Gennaro Papi. The exact date of the recording session is unknown, because the Pathé files are believed to have been destroyed. This much is known however. The Pathé recordings were released in October 1918, and Columbia's first session of an exclusive agreement began on 8 March 1918. The Pathé recordings were probably made after the last recordings of the Metropolitan Opera Chorus for Victor on 27 July 1917 and before the first Columbia session on 8 March 1918, but there is no way of proving this. The Pathé recordings were unlike those for Victor and Columbia and could not be played on a Victor or Columbia machine without a special attachment. Victor and Columbia discs required the use of a steel needle which vibrated sideways or laterally in the record groove. Pathé's discs were played by a sapphire stylus that vibrated vertically or in a hill and dale fashion in the grooves. It was Pathé's practice to make the original recording on a large cylinder which was probably of excellent quality, but this recording was then copied to a disc, and there had to be some degradation of sound in the copying process.

Columbia announced the beginning of their exclusive agreement to record the Metropolitan Opera House Orchestra in the July 1918 supplement of Columbia Records when the first recordings were offered for sale. Although he is not named, it appears to be Artur Bodanzky standing in front of the orchestra in the photograph that is above these words in the supplement:

First Metropolitan Opera Records

With five of the greatest orchestras in America all playing beneath Columbia standards it remained only to secure the most élite and exclusive organization in the musical world—the Orchestra of the Metropolitan Opera of New York. This orchestra, which has sat before the famous curtain for so many years and given the greatest performances of opera in history, has admitted Columbia tone only can do full justice to their supreme standards. It is with pride that needs no apology we announce the Metropolitan Opera Orchestra exclusive Columbia artists. Listening to the interpretation of this orchestra, it seems we feel the very atmosphere from the sacred walls of the historic opera house. As we listen to the melodies of the *Faust Ballet* it seems as if the lights grow dim, the curtain rises and we hear the music as only it is played by the Metropolitan Orchestra. In the *Adagio* is all the wondrous tone of this orchestra which for so many years has satisfied the most musical of all the musical audiences of the world.

And even today so much can be felt about the tenor of the time in just reading the advertising copy. The Columbia sessions in March and April 1918 were directed by Artur Bodanzky, and those in December 1919 by Giuseppe Bamboschek. The last two Columbia sessions in April 1922 do not give the name of the conductor, and it is difficult to explain the anonymity. It is possible that the orchestra might have been led by a Columbia house conductor or by a Metropolitan Opera conductor who could not be listed on a Columbia label because that conductor was already an exclusive artist for a rival company. If there be any truth in this second supposition, one good candidate would be Gennaro Papi who had conducted the orchestra in the recordings for Pathé and who would shortly begin a new series of recordings of the Metropolitan Opera House Orchestra for Vocalion records and who was an exclusive artist for Vocalion. It is also interesting to note that one of the titles in these last Columbia sessions, the "Zampa Overture," was also the first title released in the new series directed by Papi for Vocalion.

The last series of acoustical recordings of the Metropolitan Opera House Orchestra was made for the Aeolian Company's Vocalion label under the direction of Gennaro Papi. Unlike the black shellac used by other companies, Vocalion records made a visual impression with their red color. Eight titles were recorded *circa* 1923 and 1924, but since the company's files have apparently not survived, it is impossible to give exact dates. In the fall of 1924, the Vocalion label was sold to the Brunswick-Balke-Collender Company.

The first electrical recordings for Brunswick. With the purchase of Vocalion, Brunswick records apparently inherited the recording agreement with the Metropolitan Opera House Orchestra and Genarro Papi, because the Brunswick catalogue of 1927 lists them as exclusive Brunswick artists, but only four titles were recorded before the agreement ended. These titles were among the first electrical recordings Brunswick made, and the "Prelude" to *Cavalleria Rusticana* recorded on 8 April 1925 is probably the earliest electrical recording that Brunswick issued, and it remained in the catalogue for well over a decade. Brunswick's Light-Ray process of electrical recording, unfortunately, was prone to distortion and was replaced after a couple of years by the Western Electric system that was used by Victor and Columbia so these first electrical recordings are not as good sounding as contemporary electrical recordings made by Victor and Columbia.

      Giulio Setti directing the Metropolitan Opera Chorus and Orchestra for Victor. In the twenty-two recording sessions Giulio Setti directed for Victor from 26 October 1927 through 17 April 1930, some of the most brilliant commercial recordings involving the Metropolitan Opera of the 78 rpm era were made. It would be difficult not to succeed with artists such as Giovanni Martinelli, Giuseppe De Luca, Ezio Pinza, Beniamino Gigli, Amelita Galli-Curci, Louise Homer, Rosa Ponselle, Maria Jeritza, Lawrence Tibbett, Marion Telva and Giacomo Lauri-Volpi. For the first time both the Metropolitan Opera's Chorus and Orchestra were employed together in recordings, and as it had for many years, Victor had under contract many of the leading singers of the opera company. Everything came together very nicely. Giulio Setti has perhaps not been given sufficient credit for the success of these Victor recordings, where all is accomplished in just the proper way in always bringing the greatest credit to the singers and the works. Setti was probably involved in most of the acoustical Victor recordings of the 1910s as chorus master and was given label credit as a supporting singer in the rôle of Roderigo in Pasquale Amato's 10 December 1911 recording of "Inaffia l'ugola!" from *Otello*. Angelo Bada also received label credit for singing his customary rôle of Cassio. In some of the many recordings Setti was involved in, there was the need for a very short passage, perhaps only one or two words, to be sung by a secondary singer. Probably many of these occasions were handled by an anonymous chorus member or two. It seems that Giulio Setti himself has filled in on a number of times besides those listed in the Victor files. For example the voice of the singer who sings the few words of Ruiz in Martinelli's 17 November 1927 performance of "Di quella pira" is credited in the files as being sung by Setti as was the 1911 *Otello* scene. The aging of the voice in the two recordings is also plausible for it belonging to Setti, who was forty-two years old in the 1911 recording and fifty-eight years old in the 1927 one. The other occasions, when it is suspected that Setti also sang a few words, are indicated in the discography. The reader of the discography is free to ignore these points if the reader does not also hear the similarity.

      Recordings in the 1930s. The Great Depression put an end to Victor's extensive recordings under Giulio Setti's direction. From the last Setti session in 1930 until May 1939, there were only two discs released, and both were recorded in 1934. In one of these, the Metropolitan Opera House Male Chorus and an orchestra accompanied Grace Moore, who sang two songs from her popular motion picture *One Night of Love*. This was recorded for Brunswick and was conducted by Wilfred Pelletier, who also conducted the other disc of more imposing substance for Victor in which the Metropolitan Opera Orchestra accompanied Lawrence Tibbett in arias from two of his contemporary successes, *Merry Mount* and *Emperor Jones*. An unusual aspect of this disc considering the difficult economic times and perilous state of the recording industry, and almost amounting to a luxury, was that it was first issued with a sheet of paper with detailed synopses of both operas and the points at which the recorded arias appeared in the plots. Then in two sessions in May 1939, Pelletier directed an abridged recording of *Otello* highlighted by memorable performances by Giovanni Martinelli and Lawrence Tibbett. Tibbett also participated in two scenes from *Simon Boccanegra* with other artists and, in a rather strange juxtaposition, two patriotic songs.

      "The World's Greatest Operas" recordings. In May and June 1940 nine recording sessions were held in which excerpts from twelve popular operas were made. The technical quality of the recordings, made by Victor, was excellent, but when they were released, Victor's name was nowhere to be seen and only "World's Greatest Operas" was printed on the labels. The performances were often very good indeed, but the labels did not list any artists' names. The finished recordings sold well and were later repackaged in various ways and were transferred to 45 rpm and 33⅓ rpm. Some were even in the active catalogue eighteen years later. Charles O'Connell, who supervised the recording sessions for Victor, wrote the following in his 1947 book *The Other Side of the Record*.

      A few years ago Victor was asked to produce certain recordings of both opera and symphonic works for a certain agency normally not connected in any way with the business of recorded music. These records were to be produced under a special label, and no indication given of the identity of the performers or of the producer. The symphonic records actually were made by personnel of the NBC Symphony, the Philharmonic Symphony of New York, the orchestra of the New Friends of Music, and of the Philadelphia Orchestra. The conductors were Eugene Ormandy, Fritz Reiner, Artur Rodzinski, Fritz Stiedry, Alexander Smallens, Wilfred Pelletier, Hans Wilhelm Steinberg, and Charles O'Connell. For the operatic records it was necessary to engage a company of artists capable of doing both German and Italian opera. This was accomplished with the very important co-operation of Wilfred Pelletier, conductor of the Metropolitan, and I engaged Pelletier, Smallens, and Hans Wilhelm Steinberg to conduct the opera records. The whole job had to be done very economically, and therefore it was necessary to employ in them singers of real ability but not necessarily with great names; in a word, singers who would sing for very little money. It was in the course of assembling these that I became acquainted with Eleanor Steber, Norman Cordon, and Leonard Warren, and as a result of their performances I quickly engaged them for Victor Red Seal records. They have since very emphatically justified my belief in them.[2]

From the Victor files, Michael H. Gray has provided the best discography of these sessions. It was printed in both the *ARSC Journal* and in *Le Grand Baton.* As Mr. Gray's work so clearly shows, the Victor files indicate everything they normally would for other contemporary recordings with one exception. For the opera recordings, the record cards and session sheets in the archives do not provide any artists' names except for the sessions of 25 and 26 June 1940 when names are added. At the top of the session sheets, where the artists' names would normally be given, is written the name of an organization no music lover would ever have heard of, the PUBLISHERS SERVICE SYMPHONY ORCHESTRA. Nowhere in any official documentation is anything ascribed to the Metropolitan Opera.

At this point it is necessary to pause, because what has been written so far is all that can be said with no chance of contradiction from the original documentation before any possible Metropolitan Opera connections are mentioned. It is not surprising that from the time the recordings were first released, listeners would wonder and speculate about the artists. Mr. Gray's discography mentions several of these early lists of possible singers.

One of the first reference works in print that mentions the name of the Metropolitan Opera in connection with these recordings is to be found in *The World's Encyclopædia of Recorded Music* published in 1952. It credits the excerpts from *Carmen* to "Joan Peebles (M-S), R. Jobin (T), L. Warren (B), Metropolitan Opera Cho. & Orch.— Pelletier." For *Faust* it lists only, "E. Steber (S), A. Tokatyan (T), N. Cordon (Bs)," for *Lohengrin* it lists only, "R. Bampton, A. Carron, etc.," and for *Tristan und Isolde* it lists only, "R. Bampton (S), A. Carron (T), L. Summers, etc." All of the other titles from "The World's Greatest Operas" series are credited to anonymous artists which was exactly the only listings that any of the recordings themselves provided. It would be difficult to speculate about how specific names became known to the editors of *The World's Encyclopædia of Recorded Music*. On the other hand, it would be difficult to listen to the recordings and, especially because they are so well recorded, to not be able to pick out specific artists such as the distinctive voices of Rose Bampton, Arthur Carron, Eleanor Steber, Leonard Warren and Raoul Jobin.

Rose Bampton was contacted by the compiler of this discography in the early 1980s to ask about the recordings and the participants. She kindly looked over the casts and agreed about the major participants. She also wrote that the accompanying musicians were made up of "Met people" as she put it. This makes sense because as Charles O'Connell wrote that the "whole job had to be done very economically," it would be logical to employ musicians who were already very familiar with the music so that time would not be spent in extensive rehearsing. O'Connell also wrote about engaging a company of artists for the operatic recording, and that it "was accomplished with the very important co-operation of Wilfred Pelletier, conductor of the Metropolitan." Rose Bampton, of course, was the wife of Maestro Pelletier, and she may have known somewhat more about these recordings than other participants. In any case, it was also likely she would have recognized various members of the chorus and orchestra even if she knew absolutely nothing about the series as a whole and would have recognized "Met people." If the chorus and orchestra were essentially that of the Metropolitan Opera, it may have been they were hired as individuals in the same way as when O'Connell described some of the symphonic recordings being made by "personnel of the NBC Symphony" instead of being made by the "NBC Symphony." It was, no doubt, cheaper to hire "personnel of the NBC Symphony" instead of the "NBC Symphony," and the result was probably very similar.

Rose Bampton was quite firm in holding one belief that is in contrast to the paper files in the Victor Archives, and this concerns the locations of the recording sessions. Here is a list of the dates and locations of the sessions as stated in the written documentation:

26 May 1940	Academy of Music, Philadelphia
27 May 1940	Academy of Music, Philadelphia
28 May 1940	Town Hall, New York City
30 May 1940	Town Hall, New York City
31 May 1940	Town Hall, New York City
5 June 1940	Town Hall, New York City
17 June 1940	Academy of Music, Philadelphia
25 June 1940	Town Hall, New York City
26 June 1940	Town Hall, New York City

Rose Bampton sang in the three sessions that were ascribed to Philadelphia, but she stated that all the sessions took place in New York's Town Hall. In an exchange of letters when the point was pressed again if it just might be possible that she may have not remembered the locations correctly, she replied with the following. This is a portion of her letter of 2 August 1983, and with the exclamation points it may show how convinced she was of her belief:

(Regarding the recordings of Tristan, Tannhauser, and Lohengrin, I do not recall that they were made it [in] Philadelphia!! Also Aida, Pagliacci, Faust, and Carmen!! I think everything was made in Town Hall.)

When Eleanor Steber, who sang in the session of 17 June 1940 that is stated to have taken place in Philadelphia, was asked by David Hamilton to give the location of the sessions, she too said that she was certain all the sessions took place in Town Hall and not in Philadelphia.[3]

    If the documentation is perfect and both Rose Bampton and Eleanor Steber are wrong, it makes it possible that the sessions held in Philadelphia may have used an orchestra and chorus of musicians from Philadelphia instead of the musicians that Wilfred Pelletier would have co-operated in possibly securing from the Metropolitan Opera. On the other hand, in the first three decades of the twentieth century, it was common practice for musicians from New York City to take the train to Camden, New Jersey, to record in Victor's studios there. Also if the documentation is perfect and the sessions of 26 and 27 May were in Philadelphia and the next session on 28 May was in New York, it presents a rather cumbersome picture of all the bulky and heavy recording equipment, engineers and soloists being taken from a location in Philadelphia that was remote from established Victor studios where they had operated for two days, and then being quickly disassembled and reassembled the next day in New York at a different remote location. That certainly would not be impossible, but it seems cumbersome at the least, and to what end? In the second session on 27 May the excerpts from *Tristan und Isolde* were completed, and excerpts from both *Tannhäuser* and *Lohengrin* were begun. According to the documentation, the *Tannhäuser* and *Lohengrin* excerpts were then both concluded on the next day, 28 May, in a different hall ninety or so miles away. Listening to the *Tannhäuser* and *Lohengrin* excerpts officially made in different halls, it is difficult to hear any differences in the sound between the two halls, one of which has a thousand seats more than the other. Another comparison in sound can be made when one listens to the recording of the fifty-five anonymous musicians on 26 May 1940, which Victor documentation puts in the Academy of Music in Philadelphia, playing the "Prelude" to *Tristan und Isolde*, and then listens to the same music in the Victor recording of 1937 in which this music is played by Leopold Stokowski and the Philadelphia Orchestra in the same hall. This comparison provides very few similarities, but then the size of the orchestras was probably different, and more importantly, there is next to nothing this side of celestial spheres that sounds as glorious as Leopold Stokowski and the Philadelphia Orchestra did when playing Wagner in the 1930s.

    If the documentation is wrong and both Rose Bampton and Eleanor Steber remembered correctly where they were, what possible cause could there be for such an error in the printed files? The most likely cause is simply an error on the part of the person typing the sheet. Looking at all the information on the sheets which lists groove pitch, identification of machines, publishers, timings of record sides, whether or not a wax was played back on the spot, and timings of selections along with titles, matrix and take numbers, it does not seem possible that the sheet could have been typed on the spot as the session was taking place. It is difficult to imagine that Fred Lynch, John Crawford or any other Victor engineer of the time, would have a noisy typewriter with them and would have time to type session sheets. It was just too intricate and required almost everything to be finished before anything could be typed. At the Columbia Archives there are still to be found handwritten and typed sheets for the same sessions from this same time period. It seems most likely that the same thing happened at Victor with the engineers noting in long hand what they were doing as they accomplished it, and then taking the handwritten sheets back to the home office, where a clerk would type up all this information—a clerk who would probably be typing far away from where the session actually took place, and who would probably throw away the handwritten sheet after the information was typed. Earlier typed sheets in the Victor Archives from many years before, list New York and Camden recording sessions on the same piece of paper, which of course, would not be possible to accomplish as it was being done. Another far-fetched possibility would be that the locations were deliberately entered in error for some accounting or billing purpose. Only a very few people would ever see this information. This is not information that could be seen by everyone as it was with the information in the Victor catalogues, where for many years there was a printed plea for the public to contact the Victor Catalogue Editor in Camden, New Jersey, to let him know if there were any mistakes. No, this information was private, and it was seen by very few people. If something would be wrong, only these few people would know or care.

In this discography the sessions that the official documentation places in Philadelphia will be entered with a question mark for the location. The reader may, of course, place them in whichever location seems correct for that reader. It is difficult to believe that both Rose Bampton and Eleanor Steber would not know where they were or for them to have any reason to say something they knew to be untrue, and it is also difficult to believe the documentation is incorrect, but mistakes are surely to be found wherever fallible humans are involved. It is reasonable to assume we do not know.

In this discography these nine sessions are entered with question marks for the artists except for the last two sessions when names were entered in the files. To emphasize that we can be sure about these two dates, these artists names are underlined in these instances. There is no official listing for these recordings to have been made by the Chorus and Orchestra of the Metropolitan Opera. It is more likely that the sessions were accomplished with "personnel" of the Metropolitan Opera.

Since all these operas were clearly identified as "condensed versions," it is no surprise that there are sometimes small cuts in the music chosen for recording. Sometimes the cuts were of just a few measures, while at other times a verse of an aria was omitted. When the original recordings were transferred to 33⅓ rpm for the Camden series, additional little cuts were sometimes made. This was probably done for timing reasons to get all the selections from one opera onto one side of a 33⅓ rpm disc. The Parade Record Company reissued *The World's Greatest Operas* recordings in two versions—with and without narration by Milton Cross. Parade also issued some little 45 rpm excerpts that might have only one side or a side and a half from the original series on one side of a 45 rpm disc. Noting their popularity and long years of service, these anonymous recordings had to have had a great influence on many listeners.

The Columbia recordings of 1941-1954. Columbia began recording the Metropolitan Opera Orchestra again in 1941 in a Bastille Day recording session in which Lily Pons sang excerpts from her success at the Opera House in *La Fille du Régiment.* After the recording ban hiatus from August 1942 to November 1944 caused by the strike of the musicians' union, Columbia recorded the Metropolitan Opera Chorus in December 1944, but not the Metropolitan Opera Orchestra, in scenes from *Boris Godunov.* This was soon followed by a number of fine recordings of various excerpts featuring both the Metropolitan Opera's Orchestra and Chorus. One session provides a bit of mystery in wondering why it was kept under wraps for so many years. On 29 May 1945 in Carnegie Hall, Helen Traubel with the Metropolitan Opera Orchestra directed by Ernst Knoch recorded nine selections. She was in wonderful voice and the recording was technically excellent, but nothing was released on 78 rpm. Four titles were released on an Odyssey disc in 1972, and one more escaped on a Sony CD in 1999. In listening to these and test pressing of the other titles from this session, it is difficult to guess what might have been the cause for holding them back.

In March 1947 the Metropolitan Opera signed a contract to record exclusively for Columbia, and in June of that year *Hänsel und Gretel* became the first complete opera recording to have been made in the United States. Over the next seven years nine more complete operas and many excerpts were made by Columbia. If there was a single problem with the arrangement, it was that many of the Metropolitan Opera's leading singers were under contract to RCA Victor. Columbia and the Metropolitan Opera might have wished to have cast some recordings with other singers who were exclusively recording for RCA Victor, but even with this restriction, many wonderful recordings were made with many treasured performances made permanent.

RCA Victor recordings in the 1950s. RCA Victor recorded excerpts from *Un Ballo in Maschera* in 1955 which commemorated the debut of Marian Anderson. Later in 1958 and 1959 with complete recordings of *Vanessa, Il Barbiere di Siviglia* and *Macbeth*, and with excerpts from *Samson et Dalila*, RCA Victor made some distinguished recordings, most of which have remained in the catalogues almost constantly. The excerpts from *Samson et Dalila* should be better known. The cost of recording in the United States caused RCA Victor to stop making complete opera recordings in the U.S. on a regular basis and to move most of their complete opera activities to Europe.

The Metropolitan Opera Record Club recordings of 1955-1957. The Metropolitan Opera entered into an agreement to record and distribute operas with the Book-of-the-Month Club. As they were advertised, all of the nineteen operas were "Abridged for Home Listening"—some slightly and others greatly. The first ones were recorded at the Metropolitan Opera House but the technical quality of the recording varied between very good and less so. There are still letters of complaint in the Metropolitan Opera Archives from the public to the Metropolitan Opera concerning what the writers felt to be less than the best technical standards. Columbia was hired for their expertise to record the remaining operas, but no mention was ever made on the discs or elsewhere that Columbia was doing the actual recording. Columbia did excellent work in their studios, but one wonders if they could have done even better work in the Opera House itself. Some of the operas, including ones recorded by Columbia, were later released by RCA Victor and sold to the general public with, of course, absolutely no mention made that Columbia was involved—even as a hired hand. The files in the Victor Archives refer to the source being tapes provided by the Book-of-the-Month Club. One wonders if RCA Victor ever knew that they were selling recordings that had been made by Columbia. The original master tapes and all of the recording documentation are now missing. The exact recording dates that are known came from what can be found in the Metropolitan Opera Archives and from what Max Rudolf was able to provide. In the absence of all the recording dates, these abridged operas are arranged alphabetically followed by the Ravel *Concerto* recording for which there is also no official documentation. These 1955-1957 recordings cover item numbers 647 through 727.

Again, as with the earlier exclusive recording contract begun with Columbia in 1947, there had to be times that certain artists could not be used because they were under exclusive contract with other companies. It now seems a bit odd that *Die Fledermaus, Hänsel und Gretel, Madama Butterfly* and *La Bohème* would be chosen as titles for this series since all these operas were still for sale in Columbia's active catalogue in performances recorded by the Metropolitan Opera just a few years before. In a letter of 20 September 1983, Max Rudolf wrote to the compiler of this discography: "When we recorded *Carmen, Figaro,* and *Il Trovatore,* these operas were in the current repertoire and, therefore, did not require special preparation. *Hansel and Gretel* needed extra work prior to the recording sessions, not only because this work was then outside the repertoire, but due to the choice of a different translation (John Gutman's) which had to be learned." While some of the performances are what might be described as good standard performances, there are also a number of gems to be found here. In 2006 the Metropolitan Opera Guild issued a three compact disc set of highlights from the Metropolitan Opera Record Club recordings which were expertly transferred from the original 33⅓ rpm long playing discs. The set also contains a valuable essay by Paul Gruber telling the history of these recordings with information about the artists who recorded them.

Deutsche Grammophon in 1972. After thirteen years of no commercial recordings, Deutsche Grammophon recorded two in 1972. A single disc of highlights from the Metropolitan Opera Gala Honoring Sir Rudolf Bing was issued, and a recording of the new production of *Carmen* was made. *The Carmen Chronicle: the Making of an Opera* by Harvey E. Phillips has a section of the book dealing with the recording sessions.[4]

The digital recordings. The rich treasury of recordings made available in the 1980s and 1990s, primarily conducted by James Levine, requires no comment. It is only necessary to look at the titles and artists involved to appreciate their value.

Only one recording session from this period appears not to have been released: a Central Park Gala with Pavarotti scheduled for Decca on 16 June 1991. This may have been connected with a public outdoor concert five days earlier that was interrupted and cancelled because of rain. When a different Pavarotti Central Park concert was issued two years later, it did not employ artists of the Metropolitan Opera.

A note on the compilation of this discography. It was the goal to acquire copies of every released title in as many formats as possible. However it was not possible to obtain the five cylinders that comprise item numbers 12 through 16, so these titles are given as listed in the U. S. Everlasting Records catalogues and have not been verified. Also the two discs that are listed as items 59, 113 and 114 proved elusive. This means it was not possible to determine the playing speeds of these discs, although the speed of item 59 is probably the same as that of the two other released titles from this session. Without a copy of the disc that is listed as items 113 and 114, it was also not possible to find out their matrix numbers since there are no company files remaining for Vocalion. With these exceptions, every other released title in this discography has been verified.

Notes

1. Raymond Sooy, "Memoirs of My Recording and Traveling Experiences for the Victor Talking Machine Company, 1898-1925," *The David Sarnoff Library*, http://www.davidsarnoff.org/soo.html (18 Oct. 2009).
2. Charles O'Connell, *The Other Side of the Record* (New York: Alfred A. Knopf, 1947), 329-330.
3. David Hamilton, "A Metropolitan Opera Discography," ARSC Journal, vol. XVI, no. 3 (1984), 59.
4. Harvey E. Phillips, *The Carmen Chronicle: the Making of an Opera* (New York: Stein and Day, 1973).

Arrangement and Explanation

The main listing is arranged chronologically by recording session. Each recorded work is given an item number to facilitate indexing. The indices of composers, titles and artists refer back to the item numbers in the main chronological listing of recording sessions. All notes about any aspect in the discography are placed immediately following whatever is to be commented upon. There is no separate section of notes and comments. For example, if a title is commented upon, these remarks follow the title, or if the catalogue number is commented upon, these remarks follow the catalogue number and so forth. It is the goal of this discography to make all information understandable without needing to memorize various abbreviations or requiring a search in several places to get a full picture.

Here is an outline or framework showing the arrangement of information in a typical session as shown in this discography. It is followed by an explanation of each part.

Session date; Session location.
[Primary source of information.]

Item #. **COMPOSER: *Title.***
>>> *Artists performing this selection.*
>>>>>> matrix number
>>>>>>>> *speed of original recording*
>> *Form of release*   **Company name and Number** / release dates

Session dates and location. For the recordings in this discography made before 1972, it was necessary to get this information from the recording company archives if they were still in existence. Recordings made after 1972 had this information on the published recording, and the recording sessions are arranged by this published information. It is not always possible to determine the location of each recording session.

Primary source of information. To be sure, information for each item came from multiple sources, but this is the source of the basic information. In most cases for the recordings made before 1972, the primary source was the archives of the recording companies. The recordings made after 1972 had the recording dates and locations on the issued recordings. In many cases for recordings made in the 1980s and 1990s, it was possible to give additional and more specific recording dates from information in the files at the Metropolitan Opera. This additional information is given in this primary source of information note, while the main session date listed directly above it, is given exactly as it is stated on the published recording.

Item number. Each work listed is given a consecutive item number to facilitate indexing and cross referencing.

Titles. The form of title as used in this discography is based on the principles of uniform titles as used by the Library of Congress but with a number of modifications. The names of works that were written using the Roman alphabet are given in the original language of the composition and as first used by the composer. Thus *Der Fliegende Holländer* is used and not *The Flying Dutchman*. Definite and indefinite articles are always used. Smaller sections of complete works such as arias, duets, scenes, acts, overtures, preludes, etc., are listed in a common form of the title of that section following a dash and the name of the complete work. Examples are *Aïda—Celeste Aïda* and *Le Nozze di Figaro—Overture*. Giving the name of the complete work first emphasizes its importance and makes it easy to see the most important part of the title. Using a dash to unite the complete work and a section of that work unifies the title, instead of having it in several parts. Variant titles are sometimes given: *Mignon—Légères hirondelles. ("Swallow Duet")* and *Faust—Chœur des Soldats. ("Soldiers' Chorus")*. The result is that titles appear almost exactly as they did for decades on Victor labels, and this may be a comfort for many, such as the compiler of this discography, who are comforted by the familiar. Titles of works that were written using the Cyrillic alphabet are given in the common forms used in the West. If the work is not sung in the original language, that is indicated.

Artists. The names of the artists involved in the recording are given here as they appeared on the original release along with other artists whose names may not have always been given on the published recordings. An example of an additional name is indicating that Fausto Cleva was an assistant in some of the recordings in 1929 and 1930. Cleva's name was not given on the record labels, but it was clearly shown in the company files, so that is indicated here. In regards to the name of the Metropolitan Opera Orchestra, the name of the orchestra is given as it appeared on the original release. There is a variety of possibilities, and here are most of the variant names:

Metropolitan Opera House Orchestra
Metropolitan Opera Orchestra
Orchestra of the Metropolitan Opera Association
Orchestra of the Metropolitan Opera Association of New York City
Orchestra of the Metropolitan Opera Association, New York
Members of the Metropolitan Opera Orchestra
The MET Orchestra
Metropolitan Opera House String Orchestra.

Matrix. During the 78 rpm era, recordings were usually made on a wax blank. It was necessary to identify this original recording, and the number assigned to the recording as it was being made is usually called the matrix number. The matrix number might or might not appear on the discs that were on sale to the public, but it is vital to truly identifying a particular recording. There is usually no connection between the matrix number and the catalogue or order number that would later be assigned to a recording when it was placed on sale to the public.

Many of the matrix numbers in this discography are followed by take numbers. Take numbers refer to the number of attempts that were made to record the matrix. For example, when the *Zampa—Overture* was being recorded by Columbia on 12 April 1922, it was assigned a matrix number of 98022. Three takes or attempts were made to record this overture with the second take being chosen to be put on sale. In the discography the matrix and take numbers are shown in this manner with the take chosen for publication underlined: **98022 -1 -2 -3**. The completed matrix and take number for this recording would be 98022-2. The take is usually separated from the matrix number with a dash. In this discography, all take numbers are preceded with a dash to make clear that they are take numbers and no other numbers.

Victor matrix numbers, as used in the years covered in this discography, begin with a letter prefix. In the years 1906 through 1917, B was used for ten inch discs and C for twelve inch discs. In the years 1927 through 1930, BVE was used for ten inch discs and CVE for twelve inch discs. In the years 1934 through 1940, BS was used for ten inch discs and CS for twelve inch discs. Some Victor recordings (discography items 17, 19, 40) after initially being released pressed from the original masters were later available in copied versions that were made by an acoustical process that is indicated on the released discs with an S/8 instead of a take number. It is not clear today exactly what the meaning of the S and the 8 could be. These transcribed discs have a somewhat poorer sound than the originals. Perhaps this copying process was done when it was necessary to have a new master made because of wear of the original master during record production, and when it was not possible to arrange a new recording session with the artists. The Victor recordings made between 1934 and 1940 in this discography were made with two recording machines operating simultaneously. This meant that for the first take, the recording made on the first machine was marked take -1, and the recording of this first take made on the second recording machine was marked take -1A. The second take made on the two machines provided take -2 and take -2A. If it was later necessary to electrically copy a take to raise or lower the volume or perhaps correct some cutting problem, those copied takes were given a suffix of "R" as in takes -1R or -2R.

The *circa* 1923/1924 Vocalion recordings in the discography show the matrix numbers that appeared on the published discs that have been examined. Since there appear to be no company files remaining, it is not possible to determine unissued matrix numbers or even unissued titles. It appears Vocalion assigned a separate matrix number each time a new attempt was made to record a composition and did not use take numbers.

Similarly the 1924 and 1925 Brunswick recordings were given a separate matrix number for each take. **E15577 E15578 E15579 E15580** means there were four takes or attempts made to record this title, which is item 118 in the discography, and the second attempt was issued. When the 1934 Brunswick titles were made, Brunswick was using a separate letter for each take.

The Columbia recordings of 1941 and for the next nine years or so, until tape recording began to be used, were originally recorded on lacquers revolving at 33⅓ rpm and were later copied to 78 rpm for sale to the public. Several recordings could be put on each lacquer. It is not possible to give take numbers for these Columbia recordings although matrix numbers appear on each disc. Columbia matrices beginning with the letters CO were ten inch discs, and those beginning with XCO were twelve inch discs. When Columbia produced the first modern 33⅓ rpm long playing recordings for sale to the public beginning in 1948 and went back to their original lacquer masters to make new copies, their new versions often revealed sound that was greatly improved over what had been offered at the old speed.

Since matrix numbers that appear on 33⅓ rpm long playing discs were assigned long after the original recordings were made and have little meaning, they are omitted.

Speed. One staggers through a mine field with both eyes shut when the subject of the correct speed of 78 rpm discs comes up. It is generally agreed that until roughly the early 1930s when 78.26 rpm became standard, recording speeds varied although the companies said they were exact. Phonographs had speed adjustments, and the record speed could easily be adjusted. Here, from a Columbia record sleeve from the same period as their 1918 and 1919 recordings of the Metropolitan Opera House Orchestra, is what Columbia gave as the speed of their recordings:

SPEED OF COLUMBIA RECORDS—80

Columbia records are uniformly recorded at a speed of 80 revolutions per minute.

We cannot too strongly impress upon our patrons the fact that to obtain the best results in reproduction, the instrument upon which the record is being played should be running at exactly that speed. The most reliable means of insuring this is to pin a small piece of white paper on the turntable of the instrument. Then, using the second hand of your watch as a guide, regulate the machine so that the turntable makes 20 revolutions to 15 seconds. The revolutions may easily be counted by keeping track of the paper on the turntable.

However for the recordings to be played back in the proper key, almost all of the Columbia discs must be played back at speeds above 80 rpm—some slightly, while the "Grand March" from *Aïda* (item 94) demands 84.51 rpm.

Victor had this statement in their November 1913 catalogue and similar statements were in most of their catalogues year after year:

All Records Should Be Played at a Speed of 78

Every Victor record is recorded at this speed and therefore requires a speed of seventy-eight to reproduce it properly.

Set the regulator so that the turntable of your Victor revolves seventy-eight times per minute, *and never change it* unless for some special purpose, as when using records for dancing to suit the exact taste of the dancers. And don't depend entirely on the regulator, but test the speed occasionally by placing a slip of paper under the edge of the record, *and while it is playing*, count the number of times the paper revolves in one minute.

You will, of course, meet the man who insists on turning the regulator of his Victor up and down, thus changing the speed with each record he plays. *Don't imitate him—he is wrong.* Only at a speed of seventy-eight can you hear the actual tones of the singer just as they were recorded.

But many Victor recordings actually were recorded around 76.59 rpm or thereabouts, and Caruso's 1911 recording of "Di' tu se fedele" from *Un Ballo in Maschera* is recorded at 75 rpm. Other speeds are commonly found. In the March 1917 supplement of *New Victor Records*, there is a two page article that tells about visiting with Caruso as he listened to a new Victor record of his voice for the first time. The unnamed author states that Mr. Child, the Director of the Victor Talking Machine Company's laboratory, invited the author to call on Caruso. These three paragraphs are telling:

> In a beautiful apartment, hung halfway between Broadway and the heavens, Caruso stepped over to a handsome walnut Victrola and started the new record, and—we watched.
>
> With the opening notes, he moved quickly to a piano and struck a chord. The least bit of a nod of his head showed that he found pitch correct, and then slowly he paced the floor, lips moving slightly, as he followed the record, tone by tone.
>
> Eyebrows, the quick Caruso smile and eloquent shoulders, passed judgment on every word, every phrase, every slight nuance. Once, listening to a high note sung pianissimo, he even made a gleeful "face," for Caruso the boy is never very far away from Caruso the artist; and the Victrola had caught to the utmost, the artist's *intention* as well as his marvelous tone.

It is interesting that the first thing Caruso did when playing the new record was to go to the piano to check the pitch. Caruso surely had an excellent Victrola in perfect mechanical order. If he had followed Victor's official statements on the speed of Victor records, he would already have had the speed regulator set at 78, and he would have followed Victor's stern admonition to *"never change it."* If the first thing Caruso did when hearing the opening notes of a recording, was to check the pitch to make sure it was correct, then that may have been his usual practice when playing a recording. It appears that Caruso, Victor's most prestigious artist, was likely to be acting in the same way as the man whom Victor warned the public not to imitate. It is clear that if the pitch was not correct, Caruso would have corrected it. It is fascinating that this would be in a Victor publication.

Suggested speeds are given for each recording in this discography through 1930. The compiler of this discography will not state that these are the only correct speeds for each recording. When well known authorities like Aida Favia-Artsay and William R. Moran have given different speeds for the same recording, it would be foolish and presumptuous for this writer to contradict them even in their differences. This writer will only state that the speeds given here are the speeds he uses when playing each recording because the given speeds sound to be correct and on pitch for each selection. The speeds given here are those found on the stroboscope used by the writer. If the reader has a slightly different stroboscope that lists 76.60 rpm instead of 76.59, that difference is unlikely to be noticed.

Recordings made after 1930 do not have speeds indicated because these can be assumed to be at 78.26 rpm in almost all cases. One late 78 rpm disc does have a suggested speed given, and that is for Eleanor Steber's recording of "Ernani, involami" from *Ernani* recorded on 17 August 1950. Through what has to have been a processing error, some or perhaps all of the 78 rpm copies that were sold have to be played at 72.73 rpm. There is no problem with the 33⅓ rpm edition.

Form of release. The forms of each release are given below the listing of artists, matrix numbers and suggested speeds. *78 rpm* refers to all the early coarse grooved disc recordings that might actually need to be played at speeds between 70 and 85 revolutions per minute (rpm). *4 min. cylinder* refers to cylinder recordings that must be played on a cylinder machine that can play four minute cylinders, as opposed to two minute cylinders. *45 rpm* refers to the seven inch microgroove discs that are played at 45 rpm. *33⅓ rpm* refers to ten and twelve inch microgroove discs that are played at 33⅓ rpm. _Open Reel Tape, 4 Track, 7 ½ ips._ refers to stereophonic tape which uses two tracks when the reel of tape is played in one direction and two other tracks when the tape is turned over and played the other direction. It is recorded at seven and one half inches per second. _Cassette_ refers to the enclosed tape cartridge that plays at one and seven-eighths inches per second. _CD_ refers to compact discs.

Company name and Number. This refers to the recording company name and catalogue number on each release that a purchaser would use to order a particular title. All recordings in this discography list the name as given on the label printed on the published recording, except for two major companies of the 78 rpm era. The United States company that began as the Victor Talking Machine Company kept recordings in its catalogue for many years under the same catalogue number, but the name of their records on their labels changed several times. When Farrar and Journet's recording of the first part of the "Church Scene" from _Faust_ was released in 1910, the labels read **Victrola Record 89035**. By 1918 labels for this recording stated it was **Victrola 89035**. Scotti's recording of "Luna Nova" was first issued in 1911 with labels reading **Victrola Record 88290**. By 1916 the labels used on this recording read **Victor 88290**. When Pinza and Martinelli's recording of the "Temple Scene" from _Aïda_ was first released in 1929, the labels stated it was **Victrola 8111**. But by 1939 the labels read **Victor 8111**. And if a new copy of the same recording were purchased in 1949, the labels would say that it was now **RCA Victor 8111**. During these years of 1929, 1939, and 1949, the name of the recording company given on the label varied along with the label name as it changed from Victor Talking Machine Company, to RCA Manufacturing Company, Incorporated, to RCA Victor Division of Radio Corporation of America.

Therefore there are these possible label names for this company depending on when the labels were printed and on the ownership structure:

> **Victor**
> **Victor Record**
> **Victrola**
> **Victrola Record**
> **RCA Victor**

All 78 rpm recordings in this discography made by this company use the name **Victor**.

The other major company of the 78 rpm era that presents a challenge is the Gramophone Company. They reissued Metropolitan Opera recordings in Europe and other parts of the world that were originally recorded by Victor in the United States. This company, frequently referred to as His Master's Voice (HMV), and its sister companies employed a rich variety of possible names often with the same catalogue number.

When the Gramophone Company issued Gigli and Pinza's 1927 recording of "Tu che a Dio" from _Lucia di Lammermor_ in their international series, it was on **His Master's Voice DB 1229** on records pressed in England. It was on **Disque "Gramophone" DB 1229** on records pressed in France, but was also later **La Voix de Son Maître DB 1229** in France. (Deutsche Grammophon, which recorded the 1972 Metropolitan Opera recordings, is not connected to HMV).

Depending on the country where the recordings were manufactured or intended to be sold, the names on the labels included the following:

> **His Master's Voice**
> **Disco "Grammofono"**
> **La Voce del Padrone**
> **Schallplatte "Grammophon"**
> **Disque "Gramophone"**
> **Disque pour Gramophone**
> **La Voix de Son Maître**
>   _etc._

All 78 rpm recordings in this discography issued by this company use the name **HMV**.

Sets of multiple discs have the album number in bold type with the numbers of individual discs in the set, when known, following in parentheses: **Columbia MOP-30** (13011/26-D). When a selection takes up only one side or so in a set, as when a single aria is referenced in a set with several arias, the album number is first given in bold type followed by the number of the individual record in that set in parentheses which contains the aria in question: **Columbia M-691** (72134-D). When sets of multiple discs were released in two versions, one in manual sequence and one in automatic sequence to be used on record changers, that is indicated with the type of sequence following the record number in italics: **Columbia OP-27** (12810/22-D) _manual sequence_ and **Columbia MOP-27** (12823/35-D) _automatic sequence._

Recordings made before 1958 can be assumed to be monophonic. Recordings made in 1958 and 1959 were released in both monophonic and stereophonic editions. This is indicated in italics following the record number: **RCA Victor LM-6138** *mono* and **RCA Victor LSC-6138** *stereo*. All later recordings released on 33⅓ rpm discs can be assumed to be stereophonic.

When release dates could be determined from company files for original issues, this information is given following the record numbers. When the date of release and the date the recording was cut from the catalogue are known, it is shown this way: **released May 1921 to 16 July 1925**. When only the release date is known and no cut date is to be found, it is shown this way: **released 27 September 1929 to ?**. When the release date is not known, but the date the recording was cut is known, it is shown this way: **released from ? to 1920**.

For many compact disc reissues of earlier recordings, a release date is given that comes from the copyright date—either the © or the ℗ date—on the published item. While this is not always exact, it is usually close to the release date.

United States releases are listed first. Non-United States releases follow.

In the first part of the discography during the 78 rpm era and slightly beyond when it was relatively simple to know exactly what was recorded each day, it is sometimes necessary to interrupt the chronological sequence to gather together information from earlier sessions when these multiple earlier sessions come together in the issuance of a single title. An example of this can be seen in regards to the complete recording of *Faust*. The sessions of 21, 23 and 25 May 1951 are listed in the regular sequence of sessions. Following this last session on 25 May 1951, there is a section marked by borders, just as this paragraph is marked, which momentarily interrupts the sequence. This section with borders has all of the information brought together from the earlier sessions. It gives all the artist information along with all the release information. Also in this "bordered" section is given the information about individual selections that were released from the entire work. As another example, there are "bordered" sections during the sessions of May and June 1940 when parts of several different operas were being recorded during each session. As soon as the last part of an opera has been recorded, a "bordered" section gives all the information about that recording brought together in one place. In the last part of the discography there is no need for these "bordered" interruptions of the chronological sequence, because the contemporary methods of recording do not lend themselves to easily showing exactly what was recorded on each day.

The Recording Sessions

Session of 7 June 1906.
[Information from Victor archives and Fagan & Moran's *The Encyclopedic Discography of Victor Recordings* (1986).]
The New York Grand Opera Chorus may have been the Metropolitan Opera Chorus.

1. **GOUNOD:** *Faust—Le veau d'or.* (chorus in Italian)
   Emilio de Gogorza, New York Grand Opera Chorus & Orchestra - Walter B. Rogers.
   matrix: **B-3447 -1 -2**
   Not released by Victor.

2. **FLOTOW:** *Martha—Lasst mich euch fragen.* (in Italian as *"Chi mi dirà"*) *("Canzone del Porter" "Porter Song")*
   Emilio de Gogorza, New York Grand Opera Chorus & Orchestra - Walter B. Rogers.
   matrix: **B-3448 -1 -2** (Take -1 used for Canada; take -2 for USA)
              speed: 80.89 rpm
   <u>*78 rpm*</u>   **Victor 64051** / released September 1906 to 1909

3. **BIZET:** *Carmen—Chanson du Toréador.* *("Toreador Song")*
   Emilio de Gogorza, New York Grand Opera Chorus & Orchestra - Walter B. Rogers.
   matrix: **C-3449 -1 -2**
   Not released by Victor. This was re-recorded during the session of 11 June 1906.

4. **GOUNOD:** *Faust—Chœur des Soldats.* (in Italian as *"O gloria cinta d'allor, d'allor"*) *("Soldiers' Chorus")*
   New York Grand Opera Chorus & Orchestra - Walter B. Rogers.
   matrix: **B-3450 -1 -2 -3**
   As a ten inch disc sung in Italian, this work was recorded during this session and that of 11 June 1906. As a twelve inch disc sung in French, takes were made on 20 January 1911 and 17 February 1911.

speed: 80.89 rpm

<u>*78 rpm*</u>   **Victor 64047** / released August 1906 to 1912. [Label gives beginning of text as *"Deponiam il brando"* (*"Déposons les armes"* in the original French), but this earlier section is not recorded.]

<u>Session of 8 June 1906.</u>

[Information from Victor archives and Fagan & Moran's *The Encyclopedic Discography of Victor Recordings* (1986).] **The New York Grand Opera Chorus may have been the Metropolitan Opera Chorus.**

5. **VERDI:** *Il Trovatore—Squilli, echeggi la tromba guerriera.* *("Soldiers' Chorus")*
    New York Grand Opera Chorus & Orchestra - Walter B. Rogers.
        matrix: **B-3451 -1 -2**
    Not released by Victor. This was re-recorded during the session of 11 June 1906.

6. **MASCAGNI:** *Cavalleria Rusticana—Gli aranci olezzano.* *("Blossoms of oranges")*
    New York Grand Opera Chorus & Orchestra - Walter B. Rogers.
        matrix: **B-3452 -1 -2**
    Not released by Victor. This was re-recorded during the sessions of 11 June 1906 and 4 April 1913. Takes from both recording dates were issued under the same number: 64048. Even though the recording book in the Victor archives states that the 1913 re-recording was made by the *Metropolitan Opera Chorus*, the record labels and catalogues still gave *New York Grand Opera Chorus*.

7. **VERDI:** *Rigoletto—Scorrendo uniti.*
    New York Grand Opera Chorus & Orchestra - Walter B. Rogers.
            matrix: **B-3453 -1 -<u>2</u> -<u>3</u>** (Take -2 used for USA; -3 for Canada)
                speed: 76.59 rpm
    <u>*78 rpm*</u>   **Victor 64049** / released September 1906 to 1920

<u>Session of 11 June 1906.</u>

[Information from Victor archives and Fagan & Moran's *The Encyclopedic Discography of Victor Recordings* (1986).] **The New York Grand Opera Chorus may have been the Metropolitan Opera Chorus. The first item recorded during this session, the *"Chanson du Toréador,"* always had New York Grand Opera Chorus listed on the labels and in *The Victor Book of the Opera*. Early Victor catalogues also listed New York Grand Opera Chorus, but starting with the May 1915 catalogue of Victor Records through the 1923 catalogue, this recording was credited to the Metropolitan Chorus.**

8. **BIZET:** *Carmen—Chanson du Toréador.* *("Toreador Song")*
    Emilio de Gogorza, New York Grand Opera Chorus & Orchestra - Walter B. Rogers.
        matrix: **C-3449 -3 -<u>4</u>**
    This had previously been recorded during the session of 7 June 1906. Those takes had not been released.
                speed: 76.59 rpm
    <u>*78 rpm*</u>   **Victor 74046** / released August 1906 to 1909
                Victor 88178 / released May 1909 to 1925

HMV 032031
HMV DB 625
Victor 26000

9. **GOUNOD:** *Faust—Chœur des Soldats.* (in Italian as *"O gloria cinta d'allor, d'allor"*) (*"Soldiers' Chorus"*)
  New York Grand Opera Chorus & Orchestra - Walter B. Rogers.
   matrix: **B-3450 -4**
  Not released by Victor. As a ten inch disc sung in Italian, a take from the session of 7 June 1906 was issued rather than this one. As a twelve inch disc sung in French, this was later re-recorded during the sessions of 20 January 1911 and 17 February 1911.

10. **VERDI:** *Il Trovatore—Squilli, echeggi la tromba guerriera.* (*"Soldiers' Chorus"*)
  New York Grand Opera Chorus & Orchestra - Walter B. Rogers.
   matrix: **B-3451 -<u>3</u> -4**
  This had previously been recorded during the session of 8 June 1906, but those takes were not released.
    speed: 76.59 rpm
 78 rpm   **Victor 64050** / released September 1906 to 1920. [From around 1908 until about 1914, record labels stated "accompaniment by Victor Orchestra."]

11. **MASCAGNI:** *Cavalleria Rusticana—Gli aranci olezzano.* (*"Blossoms of oranges"*)
  New York Grand Opera Chorus & Orchestra - Walter B. Rogers.
   matrix: **B-3452 -<u>3</u> -4**
  This was previously recorded during the session of 11 June 1906, but those takes were not issued. Take -3 from this session was first released on Victor 64048. This title was recorded again during the session of 4 April 1913 and take -6 from that session was also issued on Victor 64048 replacing take -3 made during this session. Both issued takes were issued under the same number: 64048. Even though the recording book in the Victor archives states that the takes made on 4 April 1913 of this title were made by the *Metropolitan Opera Chorus*, the record labels and catalogues still gave *New York Grand Opera Chorus.*
    speed: 76.59 rpm
 78 rpm   **Victor 64048** / released August 1906 to ? [From around 1908 until about 1914, record labels stated "accompaniment by Victor Orchestra."]

Session(s?) of ca. 1908-1913.

[Information from Duane D. Deakins' *U. S. Everlasting Records* (May 1961) and Major H. H. Annand's *The Catalogue of the United States Everlasting Indestructible Cylinders 1908-1913* (Second edition, September 1973).]
The U. S. Phonograph Company of Cleveland, Ohio, produced indestructible (*i.e.,* non-wax) black celluloid cylinders from 1908 through 1913 under the name "U. S. Everlasting." The recording date(s) of the titles listed below is not known.

12. *La Zingarella.* (perhaps **VERDI:** *La Traviata—Coro delle Zingarelle.*)
  Metropolitan Opera House Chorus.
 4 min. cylinder **U.S. Everlasting 21137**

13. *Coro dei Mattadori.* (perhaps **VERDI:** *La Traviata—Coro dei Mattadori.*)
   Metropolitan Opera House Chorus.
   4 min. cylinder   **U.S. Everlasting 21140**

14. *Vieni a Guerriero.* (perhaps **VERDI:** *Aïda—Vieni, o guerriero vindice*)
   Metropolitan Opera House Chorus.
   4 min. cylinder   **U.S. Everlasting 21141**

15. **WAGNER:** *Lohengrin—Treulich geführt.* *("Brautchor" "Bridal Chorus")*
   Metropolitan Opera House Chorus.
   4 min. cylinder   **U.S. Everlasting 21257**

16. **WAGNER:** *Tannhäuser—Pilgerchor.* *("Pilgrims' Chorus")*
   Metropolitan Opera House Chorus.
   4 min. cylinder   **U.S. Everlasting 21258**

Session of 6 January 1910; New York City.

[Information from Victor archives.]

17. **VERDI:** *Il Trovatore—Miserere.*
   Frances Alda, Enrico Caruso, Metropolitan Opera Chorus & Orchestra - Walter B. Rogers.
   matrix: **C-8506 -2 -3**   (Take -1 had been recorded on 27 December 1909 without the Chorus. The take -3 master was transcribed on 1 November 1915 to make a new master. Records pressed after this date were marked with an **S/8** where the take number is usually given. The transcribed versions have a somewhat poorer sound than the original. The first pressings of 89030 listed below were from the original take -3 master while later pressings used the S/8 copy.)
   speed: 76.59 rpm

   78 rpm   **Victor 89030** / released January 1910 to ?   [Until about 1914, the labels credited "accompaniment by Victor Orchestra." Some pressings of this record, as for other titles of the same period, have a *descriptive back label* on the blank side which gives a translation of the text and description of the scene.]
   Victor 8042 / released 28 July 1923 to ?
   HMV 2-054007
   HMV DK 119
   DGG 78518
   45 rpm   **RCA Victor WCT-4**
   33⅓ rpm   **RCA Victor LCT-1003** / released 29 December 1950 to 1 September 1956
   Murray Hill 920328
   CD   **RCA Victor 60495-2-RG** / released 1990 to ?
   Naxos 8.110719 / released 2001 to ?
   Gala GL 304

Session of 17 January 1910; New York City.

[Information from Victor archives and Fagan & Moran's *The Encyclopedic Discography of Victor Recordings* (1986).]

18. **GOUNOD:** *Faust—Quand du Seigneur le jour luira. ("Scène de l'Église, part 2")*
   Geraldine Farrar, Marcel Journet, Metropolitan Opera Chorus & Orchestra - Walter B. Rogers.
   matrix: **C-8559 -1 -2**
   speed: 78.26 rpm

   78 rpm   **Victor 89037** / released April 1910 to ? [Until about 1914, the labels credited the "Victor Orchestra."]
                 Victor 8021 / released 25 May 1923 to 1928
                 HMV 2-034008
                 HMV DK 109
   Cassette   **MET 513-C** / released 1991 to ?
   CD   **MET 513-CD** / released 1991 to ?

19. **GOUNOD:** *Faust—Seigneur, daignez permettre à votre humble servante.*
   ("Scène de l'Église, part 1")
   Geraldine Farrar, Marcel Journet, Metropolitan Opera Chorus & Orchestra - Walter B. Rogers.
   matrix: **C-8560 -1** (The take -1 master was transcribed on 4 December 1914 to make a new master. Records pressed after this date were marked with an **S/8** where the take number is usually given. The transcribed versions have a somewhat poorer sound than the original. The first pressings of 89035 listed below were from the original take -1 master while later pressings used the S/8 copy.)
   speed: 78.26 rpm

   78 rpm   **Victor 89035** / released April 1910 to ? [Until about 1914, the labels credited the "Victor Orchestra."]
                 Victor 8021 / released 25 May 1923 to 1928
                 HMV 2-034009
                 HMV DK 109
   Cassette   **MET 513-C** / released 1991 to ?
   CD   **MET 513-CD** / released 1991 to ?

20. **GOUNOD:** *Faust—Le veau d'or.*
   Marcel Journet, Metropolitan Opera Chorus & Orchestra - Walter B. Rogers.
   matrix: **B-3166 -2** (Take -1 had been recorded on 8 March 1906 without the chorus and was released as Victor 64036. Take -2 from this session was also issued under the same Victor catalogue number. Takes -3 and -4 would be recorded during the session of 19 January 1912 and take -4 from that session would also be released under the same Victor catalogue number of 64036.)
   speed: 78.26 rpm

   78 rpm   **Victor 64036** [The Metropolitan Opera Chorus is not listed on the record labels or in the catalogues. During the two years or so that take -2 was available on 64036, the labels credited the "Victor Orchestra."]
                 HMV 7-32001
                 HMV DA 167
   33⅓ rpm   **Heritage XIG 8010**
   CD   **EMI Classics 50999 206267 2 3** / released 2009 to ?

Session of 19 December 1910.

[Information from an article in the *New Amberola Graphic* of January 1992, p. 4, *"Random Notes Concerning Edison Recording Artists,"* by Ray Wile.]

This article reports that fourteen discs were recorded on this date but titles are not given.

21.-34. **COMPOSERS?—*Titles?***
> *Metropolitan Opera House Chorus - Giulio Setti.*
> *Not released by Edison.*

Session of 19 January 1911.

[Information from the *Encyclopedic Discography of Victor Recordings Project* through the kind assistance of Mr. Samuel Brylawski. It must be noted that in the first volume of John R. Bolig's *The Victor Red Seal Discography* (2004) the date of the first item in this session is given as 20 January 1911.]

The Grand Opera Chorus may have been the Metropolitan Opera Chorus. Victor employee Raymond Sooy noted that this session was: "The first recording engagement of the Metropolitan Grand Opera Chorus from the Metropolitan Opera Company of New York." Please see the *Introduction* for more about this and other sessions under *New York Grand Opera Chorus*.

35. **GOUNOD: *Faust—Écoute-moi bien.*** *("Death of Valentine" "Morte di Valentino")*
> *Antonio Scotti, Grand Opera Chorus & Orchestra.* [An unknown soprano sings the few words of Siebel and Marguerite at the beginning.]
> > matrix: **C-9827 -1**
> > *speed: 77.42 rpm*

<u>78 rpm</u>	**Victor 88282** [Until about 1914, record labels stated "accompaniment by Victor Orchestra."]
	HMV 2-032001
	HMV DB 668

36. **GOUNOD: *Faust—La Kermesse.*** *("Vin ou bière")*
> *New York Grand Opera Chorus & Orchestra.*
> > matrix: **C-9828 -1**

> *Not released by Victor.* This was re-recorded during the session of 20 January 1911, but that take was not released. It was recorded again during the session of 17 February 1911, and a take from that session was issued.]

Session of 20 January 1911.

[Information from Fagan & Moran's *The Encyclopedic Discography of Victor Recordings* (1986) and from the *Encyclopedic Discography of Victor Recordings Project* through the kind assistance of Mr. Samuel Brylawski.]

The New York Grand Opera Chorus may have been the Metropolitan Opera Chorus.

37. **GOUNOD: *Faust—Chœur des Soldats.*** *("Soldiers' Chorus")*
> *New York Grand Opera Chorus & Orchestra.*

matrix: **C-3450 -1 -2**

Not released by Victor. As a ten inch disc sung in Italian, this had previously been recorded on 7 June 1906 and 11 June 1906. At this session and the one on 17 February 1911, this was recorded as a twelve inch disc sung in French. The take recorded on 17 February 1911 was issued.

38. **GOUNOD:** *Faust—La Kermesse. ("Vin ou bière")*
   New York Grand Opera Chorus & Orchestra.
   matrix: **C-9828 -2**

Not released by Victor. [This was first recorded during the session of 19 January 1911, but that take was not released. It was recorded again during the session of 17 February 1911, and a take from that session was issued.]

39. **COSTA:** *Luna Nova. ("The New Moon" "Canzone Marinaresca" "Neapolitan Song")*
   Antonio Scotti, Chorus & Orchestra. [The name of the chorus is not indicated in the *Encyclopedic Discography of Victor Recordings Project* database.]
   matrix: **C-9831 -1 -2**

Not released by Victor. [This was re-recorded during the session of 17 February 1911, and a take from that session was issued.]

Session of 17 February 1911; New York City.

[Information from Victor archives and Fagan & Moran's *The Encyclopedic Discography of Victor Recordings* (1986).] **The New York Grand Opera Chorus may have been the Metropolitan Opera Chorus. The recording book in the Victor archives attributes this session to the New York Grand Opera Chorus.** *"New York Grand Opera Chorus"* **does appear on the record labels and in the Victor catalogues for the first two items.** *"Metropolitan Opera Chorus"* **is given in the catalogues for the third item. Some labels for the third item give** *"Metropolitan Opera Chorus"* **and some give** *"New York Grand Opera Chorus"* **for the exact same recording.**

40. **GOUNOD:** *Faust—La Kermesse. ("Vin ou bière")*
   New York Grand Opera Chorus & Orchestra. [An unknown voice sings the lines allotted to Wagner.]
   matrix: **C-9828 -3 -4** (The take -3 master was transcribed on 23 November 1915 to make a new master. Records pressed after this date were marked with an **S/8** where the take number is usually given. The transcribed versions have a somewhat poorer sound than the original. The first pressings of 74213 listed below were from the original take -3 master while later pressings used the S/8 copy.)
   This had been recorded during the sessions of 19 and 20 January 1911, but those takes were not issued.
   speed: 76.59 rpm

78 rpm   **Victor 74213** / released May 1911 to January 1920. [Until about 1914, the labels credited "accompaniment by Victor Orchestra." Some pressings of this record, as for other titles of the same period, have a *descriptive back label* on the blank side which gives a translation of the text and description of the scene.]

41. **GOUNOD:** *Faust—Chœur des Soldats. ("Soldiers' Chorus")*
   New York Grand Opera Chorus & Orchestra.
   matrix: **C-3450 -3**

As a ten inch disc sung in Italian, this had previously been recorded on 7 June 1906 and 11 June 1906. At the sessions of 20 January 1911 and this one, the work was recorded as a twelve inch disc sung in French.
   speed: 76.59 rpm

78 rpm   **Victor 74214** / released May 1911 to January 1920. [Until about 1914, the labels credited "accompaniment by Victor Orchestra." Some pressings of this record, as for other titles of the same period, have a *descriptive back label* on the blank side. Besides giving a translation of the text, this descriptive back states, "The latter part of this famous number, on a 10-inch record, has been in the Victor catalogue for some years, but is now offered for the first time in complete form. As will be seen, the first part, hitherto omitted, is one of the most attractive portions."]

42. **COSTA:** *Luna Nova. ("The New Moon" "Canzone Marinaresca" "Neapolitan Song")*
    Antonio Scotti, Metropolitan Opera Chorus (on some labels) or New York Grand Opera Chorus (on some labels) & Orchestra. (Metropolitan Opera Chorus is shown in the Victor catalogues.)
          matrix: **C-9831 -3 -4**
    This had been first recorded during the session of 20 January 1911, but those takes were not issued.
                  speed: 76.59 rpm
    78 rpm   **Victor 88290** / released May 1911 to 1920
                HMV 2-052037

Session of 19 November 1911.
[Information from Victor archives.]

43. **VERDI:** *Un Ballo in Maschera—Di' tu se fedele. ("Barcarola")*
    Enrico Caruso, Metropolitan Opera Chorus (Giulio Setti, director) & Orchestra.
          matrix: **B-11270 -1 -2**
                  speed: 75 rpm
    78 rpm   **Victor 87091** / released December 1911 to May 1923. [Until about 1914, the labels credited the "Victor Orchestra."]
                Victor 512 / released 1923 to ?
                HMV 7-52025
                HMV DA 102
    45 rpm   **RCA Victor WCT-35**
    33⅓ rpm   **RCA Victor LCT-1034** / released 14 December 1951 to ?
                RCA Red Seal ARM1-3570
                Murray Hill 920328
    CD   **RCA Victor 60495-2-RG** / released 1990 to ?
                RCA Victor Red Seal 74321 63469 2 / released 1999 to ?
                RCA Victor Gold Seal 09026-61242-2
                Naxos 8.110721 / released 2001 to ?
                MET 525-CD
                Nimbus NI 1742
                Nimbus NI 1794
                Nimbus NI 7803

Session of 10 December 1911.

[Information from Victor archives.]

Giulio Setti sings briefly on the last two items listed here. He may have also been the orchestra and/or chorus director for all the works recorded during this session.

44. **MASCAGNI:** *Cavalleria Rusticana—Il cavallo scalpita.*
    Pasquale Amato, Metropolitan Opera Chorus & Orchestra.
        matrix: **B-11282 -1**
            speed: 76.59 rpm

<u>78 rpm</u>   **Victor 87097** / released April 1912 to 1920. [Until about 1914, the labels credited the "Victor Orchestra."]
            HMV 7-52023
            HMV DA 504
<u>Cassette</u>   **MET 512-C** / released 1991 to ?
<u>CD</u>   **MET 512-CD** / released 1991 to ?

45. **PONCHIELLI:** *La Gioconda—Pescator, affonda l'esca.* *("Barcarola")*
    Pasquale Amato, Metropolitan Opera Chorus & Orchestra.
        matrix: **B-11283 -1 -2**
            speed: 76.59 rpm

<u>78 rpm</u>   **Victor 87093** / released February 1912 to 1923. [Until about 1914, the labels credited the "Victor Orchestra."]
            Victor 539 / released 7 June 1923 to 1928
            HMV 7-52024
            HMV DA 126
<u>Cassette</u>   **MET 524-C** / released 1994 to ?
<u>CD</u>   **MET 524-CD** / released 1994 to ?
            Nimbus NI 7897

46. **VERDI:** *Otello—Inaffia l'ugola!* *("Brindisi")*
    Pasquale Amato, Angelo Bada, Giulio Setti, Metropolitan Opera Chorus & Orchestra.
        matrix: **C-11284 -1 -2**
            speed: 76.59 rpm

<u>78 rpm</u>   **Victor 88338** / released February 1912 to 1920. [Until about 1914, the labels credited the "Victor Orchestra." Setti's name was misspelled on the first printing of the labels as "Cetti." This was soon corrected.]
            HMV 2-054026
            HMV DK 110
<u>Cassette</u>   **MET 514-C** / released 1992 to ?
<u>CD</u>   **MET 514-CD** / released 1992 to ?

47. **VERDI:** *Rigoletto—Povero Rigoletto!*
    Pasquale Amato, Angelo Bada, Giulio Setti, Metropolitan Opera Chorus & Orchestra.
        matrix: **C-11349 -1**
            speed: 76.59 rpm

78 rpm	**Victor 88340** / released November 1912 to 1923. [Until about 1914, the labels credited "accompaniment by Victor Orchestra." Some pressings of this record, as for other titles of the same period, have a *descriptive back label* on the blank side which gives a translation of the text and description of the scene.]
	Victor 6041 / released 25 May 1923 to 1930
	HMV 2-052057
	HMV DB 158
CD	**Nimbus NI 7897**

Session of 15 January 1912; New York City.
[Information from Victor archives.]

48. **DONIZETTI:** *La Favorita—Splendon più belle in ciel.*
   Marcel Journet, Metropolitan Opera Chorus & Orchestra.
       matrix: **C-11457 -1 -2**
           speed: 76.59 rpm

78 rpm	**Victor 74273** / released April 1912 to January 1920. [Until about 1914, the labels credited "accompaniment by Victor Orchestra." Some pressings of this record, as for other titles of the same period, have a *descriptive back label* on the blank side. Besides giving a translation of the text and description of the scene, this descriptive back states, "The noble voice of Journet is shown to great advantage in the solo, while the choral responses make the record a highly impressive one."]
	HMV 2-052167
	HMV DB 615
	HMV 882
33⅓ rpm	**Sociedade Brasileira de Discos Historicos JALP & JAL 7002**

49. **WAGNER:** *Lohengrin—Mein Herr und Gott.* (*"Königs Gebet"*)
   Marcel Journet, Metropolitan Opera Chorus & Orchestra.
       matrix: **C-11458 -1 -2**
   Not released by Victor.

50. **MEYERBEER:** *Les Huguenots—Pour cette cause sainte.* (in Italian as *"La causa è santa"*)
   (*"Bénédiction des Poignards" "Blessing of the Swords" "Gloire au Grand Dieu vengeur"
   "D'un sacro zel l'ardore"*)
[There has been a variety of titles given to this recording. Victor labels first gave the title as "Benediction des Poignards," then later as "Benedizione de' Pugnali," and finally as "Benediction of the Poignards." The Victor catalogues consistently used "Bénédiction des Poignards" with and without the acute accents. From the first edition in 1912 through the seventh edition in 1924 of *The Victor (Victrola) Book of the Opera* the title was always given as "Benediction of the Swords," with a musical example of "the noble strain of the *Benediction"* in an Italian translation as "D'un sacro zel l'ardore." "D'un sacro zel l'ardore" was also used as the title on the HMV labels. However Journet and the Metropoltian Opera Chorus do not sing this Italian translation, which was also printed in the 1896 Rullman libretto as the "London Edition," but instead clearly sing the Ricordi Italian translation which uses the words "La causa è santa" and not "D'un sacro zel l'ardore."]
   Marcel Journet, Metropolitan Opera Chorus & Orchestra.
       matrix: **C-11459 -1 -2**

speed: 76.59 rpm

78 rpm **Victor 74275** / released April 1912 to ? [Until about 1914, the labels credited "accompaniment by Victor Orchestra." Some pressings of this record, as for other titles of the same period, have a *descriptive back label* on the blank side which gives a translation of the text and description of the scene.]

Victor 6173 / released 18 June 1923 to ?

HMV 2-032009

HMV DB 307

51. GOUNOD: *Faust—Choral des épées.*

Pasquale Amato, Marcel Journet, Metropolitan Opera Chorus & Orchestra. (The recording book in the Victor archives does not list a conductor, but *The Victor Book of the Opera* lists "Giulio Setti, Director" for this title. He may have been the director of the chorus or of both the chorus and orchestra. It also sounds as if it is Setti who sings the one word of Wagner "Holà.")

matrix: **C-11460 -1 -2**

speed: 76.59 rpm

78 rpm **Victor 89055** / released April 1912 to May 1923. [Until about 1914, the labels credited "accompaniment by Victor Orchestra." Some pressings of this record, as for other titles of the same period, have a *descriptive back label* on the blank side. Besides giving a translation of the text and description of the scene, this descriptive back states, "This is a remarkably fine reproduction, the men's voices being rich and sonorous, and the dramatic feeling intense."]

Victor 8003 / released 25 May 1923 to 1928

HMV 2-034014

HMV DK 101

Cassette **MET 513-C** / released 1991 to ?

CD **MET 513-CD** / released 1991 to ?

Nimbus NI 7897

Session of 19 January 1912; New York City.

[Information from Victor archives and Fagan & Moran's *The Encyclopedic Discography of Victor Recordings* (1986).]

52. GOUNOD: *Faust—Le veau d'or.*

Marcel Journet, Metropolitan Opera Chorus & Orchestra - Walter B. Rogers.

matrix: **B-3166 -3 -4** (Take -1 had been recorded on 8 March 1906 without the chorus. Take -2 was recorded during the session of 17 January 1910 and was issued under the same single sided catalogue number (64036) as take -4 from this session.)

speed: 77.42 rpm

78 rpm **Victor 64036** [The Metropolitan Opera Chorus is not listed on the record labels or in the catalogues. Until about 1914, the labels credited "accompaniment by Victor Orchestra."]

Victor 695 [The Metropolitan Opera Chorus is not listed on the record labels or in the catalogues.]

53. **MEYERBEER:** *Robert le Diable—Valse Infernal.* [Journet sings in French while the Metropolitan Opera Chorus sings in Italian]

Marcel Journet, Metropolitan Opera Chorus & Orchestra - Walter B. Rogers.

matrix: **C-11473 -1 -2**

speed: 77.42 rpm

78 rpm   **Victor 74282** / released May 1912 to ? [Until about 1914, the labels credited "accompaniment by Victor Orchestra." Some pressings of this record, as for other titles of the same period, have a *descriptive back label* on the blank side which gives a translation of the text and description of the scene, and states "Journet gives an impressive rendering of the utterances of the fiend, *Bertram,* while the chorus of demons, supposed to proceed from the Cavern of Satan, is strikingly sung by the Opera Chorus."]

Victor 6176 / released 18 June 1923 to ?

HMV 032278

HMV DB 310

33⅓ rpm   **Sociedade Brasileira de Discos Historicos LPG 5**

CD   **International Record Collectors' Club IRCC-CD 800**

Nimbus NI 7894

Marston 53009-2 / released 2009 to ?

Session of 22 March 1912; New York City.

[Information from Victor archives.]

54. **GOMES:** *Il Guarany—Senza tetto.*

Pasquale Amato, Metropolitan Opera Chorus & Orchestra.

matrix: **B-11784 -1 -2**

speed: 77.42 rpm

78 rpm   **Victor 87105** / released July 1912 to March 1917. [Until about 1914, the labels credited "accompaniment by Victor Orchestra."]

Victor 940 / released 25 July 1923 to January 1930

HMV 7-52027

55. **BIZET:** *Carmen—Les voici ... Si tu m'aimes.* [Although the record label and Victor catalogues state that this is sung in Italian as *Se tu m'ami,* it is actually sung in the original French]

Margarete Matzenauer, Pasquale Amato, Metropolitan Opera Chorus & Orchestra.

matrix: **C-11785 -1 -2**

speed: 77.42 rpm

78 rpm   **Victor 89061** / released July 1912 to November 1915. [Record labels credit "accompaniment by Victor Orchestra." Some pressings of this record, as for other titles of the same period, have a *descriptive back label* on the blank side. Besides giving a translation of the text and description of the scene, this descriptive back states, "After the depressing close of the third act, the spirited chorus which opens Act IV is most welcome . . . This number is full of lovely melodies and is one of the most beautiful records of the *Carmen* series."]

HMV 034158

Opera Disc 77508

33⅓ rpm   **RCA Victor LCT-6701** / released May 1955 to ? [The first half of this recording in which the Metropolitan Opera Chorus sings is omitted on this transfer.]

Session of 7 June 1912; New York City.
[Information from Brooks & Rust's *The Columbia Master Book* (1999).]
The Metropolitan Opera Chorus is credited in Brooks & Rust's *The Columbia Master Book* for the first work listed for this session. The Metropolitan Opera Chorus is not listed on the labels for any of these recordings. The reason for this is not clear. Perhaps there was an exclusive contract with Victor for the name of the Metropolitan Opera.

56. **DONIZETTI:** *La Favorita—Splendon più belle in ciel.*
    Cesare Alessandroni, Metropolitan Opera Chorus as "Grand Opera Chorus" & Orchestra.
        matrix: **19923 -1**
                speed: beginning at 77.42 and ending at 75 rpm
    78 rpm   **Columbia A1218**

57. **PUCCINI:** *Tosca—Te Deum.*
    Cesare Alessandroni, Metropolitan Opera Chorus as "Grand Opera Chorus" & Orchestra.
        matrix: **36396 -1 -2**
                speed: beginning at 80 rpm and ending at 76 rpm
    78 rpm   **Columbia A5430**

58. **WAGNER:** *Lohengrin—Treulich geführt.* *("Brautchor" "Bridal Chorus")*
    Metropolitan Opera Chorus as "Columbia Grand Opera Chorus" & Orchestra.
        matrix: **36397 -1**
                speed: beginning at 79.12 and ending at 74.23 rpm
    78 rpm   **Columbia A5414**

Session of 4 April 1913; New York City.
[Information from Victor archives.]

59. **MASCAGNI:** *Cavalleria Rusticana—Gli aranci olezzano.* *("Blossoms of oranges")*
    Metropolitan Opera Chorus as "New York Grand Opera Chorus" & Orchestra.
        matrix: **B-3452 -5 -6**
This was a re-recording of an earlier New York Grand Opera disc made during the session of 11 June 1906. The recording book in the Victor archives shows that the Metropolitan Opera Chorus was employed for the remake, but *New York Grand Opera Chorus* was still used on the labels and in the catalogues. This performance was issued on the same record catalogue number as the 1906 recording.
                speed: [Probably 76.59 but it was not possible to acquire this disc to verify it.]
    78 rpm   **Victor 64048** / released from ? to 1920

60. **MASCAGNI:** *Cavalleria Rusticana—Regina Coeli.*
    Metropolitan Opera Chorus & Orchestra.
        matrix: **B-13079 -1**
Not released by Victor.

61. **MEYERBEER:** *Les Huguenots—Rataplan.* (in Italian) *("Soldiers' Chorus")*
    Metropolitan Opera Chorus & Orchestra.
        matrix: **B-13080 -1 -2**

speed: 76.59 rpm

78 rpm   **Victor 45051** / released July 1913 to ? [Until about 1914, the labels credited "accompaniment by Victor Orchestra."]

62. MOZART: *Die Zauberflöte—O Isis und Osiris. ("Priesterchor")*
Metropolitan Opera Chorus & Orchestra.

matrix: **B-13081 -1 -2**

speed: 76.59 rpm

78 rpm   **Victor 45051** / released July 1913 to ? [Until about 1914, the labels credited "accompaniment by Victor Orchestra."]

Session of 3 April 1914; New York City.
[Information from Victor archives.]

63. VERDI: *Un Ballo in Maschera—La rivedrà nell' estasi.*
Frieda Hempel, Enrico Caruso, Léon Rothier, Andrés Perello de Segurola, Metropolitan Opera Chorus (Giulio Setti, director) & Orchestra - Gaetano Scognamiglio.

matrix: **C-14659 -1 -2**

speed: 77.42 rpm

78 rpm	**Victor 89077** / released August 1914 to May 1923
	Victor 10005 / released 28 May 1923 to 1930
	HMV 2-054052
	HMV DM 103
33⅓ rpm	**RCA Victor LM-2639** / released 16 October 1962 to ?
	RCA Red Seal ARM1-4684
	Murray Hill 920328
	MET 402 / released 1985 to ?
Cassette	**MET 402-C** / released 1985 to ?
CD	**RCA Victor 60495-2-RG** / released 1990 to ?
	RCA Victor Gold Seal 09026-61242-2
	Naxos 8.110726 / released 2002 to ?
	Nimbus NI 1790
	Nimbus NI 7834

64. VERDI: *Un Ballo in Maschera—È scherzo od è follia.*
Frieda Hempel, Maria Duchêne, Enrico Caruso, Léon Rothier, Andrés Perello de Segurola, Metropolitan Opera Chorus (Giulio Setti, director) & Orchestra - Gaetano Scognamiglio.

matrix: **C-14660 -1 -2**

speed: 77.42 rpm

78 rpm	**Victor 89076** / released June 1914 to ?
	Victor 10005 / released 28 May 1923 to 1930
	Victor M-953 (16-5000) / released 26 November 1943 to ?
	HMV 2-054050
	HMV DM 103

45 rpm	**RCA Victor WCT-4**
	RCA Victor ERAT 8 / released 24 December 1953 to 1 September 1956
33⅓ rpm	**RCA Victor LCT-1003** / released 29 December 1950 to 1 September 1956
	RCA Red Seal ARM1-4684
	Murray Hill 920328
CD	**RCA Victor 60495-2-RG** / released 1990 to ?
	Naxos 8.110726 / released 2002 to ?
	MET 525-CD
	Nimbus NI 1790
	Nimbus NI 7834

Session of 16 April 1914; New York City.

[Information from Victor archives.]

For unknown reasons the Metropolitan Opera Chorus is listed on the labels for the first work recorded during this session but not for the second and third works.

65. **WOLF-FERRARI:** *I Gioielli della Madonna—Aprila, o bella.* (*"Serenata Rafaele"* *"Rafaele's Serenade"*)

Pasquale Amato, Metropolitan Opera Chorus & Orchestra.

matrix: **B-14714 -1 -2**

speed: 76.59 rpm

78 rpm	**Victor 87193** / released July 1914 to 1923
	Victor 539 / released 7 June 1923 to 1928
	HMV 7-52058
	HMV DA 126

66. **PUCCINI:** *Tosca—Te Deum.* [The chorus parts marked *con voce parlata* are omitted.]

Pasquale Amato, Metropolitan Opera Chorus & Orchestra. [It sounds as if it is Giulio Setti who sings the four words of Spoletta "Sta bene. Il convegno?"]

matrix: **C-14715 -1 -2**

speed: 76.59 rpm

78 rpm	**Victor 88489** / released September 1914 to 1920. [The Metropolitan Opera Chorus is not listed on the record labels but is listed in *The Victor Book of the Opera*.]
	HMV 2-052094
	HMV DB 637
33⅓ rpm	**Cantilena 6201**
CD	**Nimbus NI 7897**

67. **MEYERBEER:** *L'Africaine—Adamastor, roi des vagues.* (In Italian as *"Adamastor, rè dell' onde profonde"*)

Pasquale Amato, Metropolitan Opera Chorus & Orchestra.

matrix: **C-14719 -1 -2**

speed: 76.59 rpm

78 rpm	**Victor 88490** / released December 1914 to 1920. [The Metropolitan Opera Chorus is not listed on the record labels.]
	HMV 2-052095
	HMV DB 637
CD	**Nimbus NI 7897**

Session of 20 April 1914; New York City.
[Information from Victor archives.]

68. **VERDI:** *La Traviata—Libiamo, libiamo ne' lieti calici.* *("Brindisi")*
   Alma Gluck, Enrico Caruso, Metropolitan Opera Chorus & Orchestra - Giulio Setti. [It is not clear in the Victor recording book if Setti is both chorus and orchestra conductor or only the conductor of the chorus.]
      matrix: **B-14729 -1 -2 -3**
         speed: 76.59 rpm

78 rpm	**Victor 87511** / released December 1914 to ?
	Victor 3031 / released 1923 to ?
	HMV 7-54006
	HMV DJ 100
45 rpm	**RCA Victor WCT-57**
	RCA Victor ERAT 9 / released 24 December 1953 to 1 September 1956
33⅓ rpm	**RCA Victor LCT-1037** / released 1952 to ?
	RCA Vivtor LM-6127 / released 17 February 1956 to 1 October 1958
	RCA Red Seal ARM1-0279
	RCA Red Seal ARM1-4684
	Murray Hill 920328
Cassette	**MET 505-C** / released 1989 to ?
	RCA Victor Gold Seal 09026-68534-4 / released 1996 to ?
CD	**RCA Victor 60495-2-RG** / released 1990 to ?
	RCA Victor Gold Seal 09026-68534-2 / released 1996 to ?
	RCA Victor Red Seal 74321 63469 2 / released 1999 to ?
	RCA Victor Gold Seal 09026-61242-2
	Naxos 8.110750 / released 2003 to ?
	MET 505-CD / released 1989 to ?
	Marston 52001-2 / released 1997 to ?
	Legendary Recordings LR-CD 1011
	Gala GL 304

Session of 16 April 1915; New York City.
[Information from Victor archives.]

69. **VERDI:** *Il Trovatore—Miserere.*
   Emmy Destinn, Giovanni Martinelli, Metropolitan Opera Chorus (Giulio Setti, director) & Orchestra – Walter B. Rogers.

        matrix: **C-15906 -1 -2**
                speed: 77.42 rpm
78 rpm   **Victor 88530** / released August 1915 to ?
               Victor 89119 / released July 1919 to 1923
               Victor 6190 / released 29 June 1923 to ?
               HMV 2-054063
               HMV DB 333
33⅓ rpm   **Camden CDN 5105**
               Sociedade Brasileira de Discos Historicos LPG 4

Session of 19 May 1915; New York City.
[Information from Victor archives.]

70. **BIZET:** *Carmen—Les voici ... Si tu m'aimes.*
     Geraldine Farrar, Pasquale Amato, Metropolitan Opera Chorus (Giulio Setti, director) & Orchestra –
     Walter B. Rogers.
        matrix: **C-16036 -1 -2**
                speed: 78.26 rpm
78 rpm   **Victor 89086** / released October 1915 to 1923
               Victor 8018 / released 25 May 1923 to 1925
               HMV 2-034021
               HMV DK 107
33⅓ rpm   **Camden CAL-359** / released June 1957 to 1 May 1960
CD   **Nimbus NI 7872**

71. **BIZET:** *Carmen—Mais moi, Carmen, je t'aime encore.*
     Geraldine Farrar, Giovanni Martinelli, Metropolitan Opera Chorus (Giulio Setti, director) & Orchestra –
     Walter B. Rogers.
        matrix: **C-16037 -1 -2**
                speed: 78.26 rpm
78 rpm   **Victor 88531** / released October 1915 to July 1919
               Victor 89110 / released July 1919 to May 1923
               Victor 8018 / released 25 May 1923 to 1928
               HMV 2-034024
               HMV DK 107
33⅓ rpm   **Camden CAL-359** / released June 1957 to 1 May 1960
CD   **Nimbus NI 7872**

Session of 8 June 1916; New York City.
[Information from Victor archives.]

72. *La Marseillaise* (Rouget de Lisle).
     Emma Calvé, Metropolitan Opera Chorus (Giulio Setti, director) & Orchestra - Edward King.

matrix: **C-17830 -1 -2 <u>-3</u>**

speed: 75 rpm

78 rpm   **Victor 88570** / released September 1916 to 1923
                Victor 6055 / released 13 June 1923 to 1926
                HMV 2-033063
                HMV DB 162

33⅓ rpm   **Rococo 10**
CD   **Romophone 81024-2** / released 1997 to ?

Session of 7 December 1916; New York City.
[Information from Victor archives.]

73. SAINT-SAËNS: *Samson et Dalila—Vois ma misère, hélas!*
Enrico Caruso, Metropolitan Opera Chorus (Giulio Setti, director) & Orchestra - Josef A. Pasternack.

matrix: **C 18821 <u>-1</u> -2**

speed: 76.59 rpm

78 rpm   **Victor 88581** / released April 1917 to 1923
                Victor 6026 / released 28 May 1923 to 1934
                Victor EM-40 and/or **Victor 15-1039** / released 11 October 1948 to ? [This had two catalogue numbers at the same time. The EM number came from "Heritage Series Record Envelope Masterpiece" which meant it was issued as part of the "Heritage Series," a reissue series, pressed on vinylite and placed inside a shiny foil envelope. 15-1039 was a regular Victor number.]
                HMV 2-032029
                HMV DB 136

33⅓ rpm   **RCA Victor LM-2639** / released 16 October 1962 to ?
                RCA Red Seal ARM1-4914
                MET 101 / released October 1976 to ?
                Murray Hill 920328

Cassette   **MET 101-C**
CD   **RCA Victor 60495-2-RG** / released 1990 to ?
                Naxos 8.110751 / released 2003 to ?
                MET 101-CD

Session of 1 June 1917; New York City.
[Information from Victor archives.]

74. *La Marseillaise* (Rouget de Lisle).
Frances Alda, Metropolitan Opera Chorus (Giulio Setti, director) & Orchestra - Josef A. Pasternack.

matrix: **B-19972 -1 <u>-2</u> -3**

speed: 77.42 rpm

<u>78 rpm</u>   **Victor 64693** / released August 1917 to 1923

                Victor 534 / released 25 May 1923 to 1929

                HMV 7-33034

75. **DONIZETTI:** *Lucia di Lammermoor—Tu che a Dio.*
    Giovanni Martinelli, Metropolitan Opera Chorus (Giulio Setti, director) & Orchestra - Josef A. Pasternack.
    [Some, but not all, of Raimondo's part is sung by an unknown voice; some of the chorus' part is omitted.]
              matrix: **C-19973 -<u>1</u> -2**
              speed: 77.42 rpm
    <u>78 rpm</u>   **Victor 74537** / released November 1917 to ?

                Victor 6189 / released 29 June 1923 to 1928

                HMV 2-052152

                HMV DB 332

76. **DONIZETTI:** *Don Pasquale—Com' è gentil.* *("Serenata")*
    Giovanni Martinelli, Metropolitan Opera Chorus (Giulio Setti, director) with Ted Levy, (piano), and
    Francis J. Lapitino, (harp) - Josef A. Pasternack.
              matrix: **B-19974 -<u>1</u> -2**
              speed: 77.42 rpm
    <u>78 rpm</u>   **Victor 64700** / released September 1917 to 1923

                Victor 734 / released 29 June 1923 to 1929

                HMV 7-52107

                HMV DA 326

    <u>CD</u>   **Nimbus NI 7892/3**

<u>*Session of 27 July 1917; New York City.*</u>
[Information from Victor archives.]

77. *Garibaldi Hymn.*
       Metropolitan Opera Chorus (Giulio Setti, director) & Orchestra - Josef A. Pasternack.
              matrix: **B-20256 -1 -2 -3**
       Not released by Victor although number 45143 had been assigned.

78. *Il Canto degli Italiani.*
       Metropolitan Opera Chorus (Giulio Setti, director) & Orchestra - Josef A. Pasternack.
              matrix: **B-20257 -1 -2 -3**
       Not released by Victor although number 45143 had been assigned.

79. **BORODIN:** *Prince Igor—Chorus of the Tartar Women.* (In Italian) *("Coro di Donne")*
       Metropolitan Opera Chorus (Giulio Setti, director) & Orchestra - Josef A. Pasternack.
              matrix: **B-20258 -<u>1</u> -2 -3**
              speed: 77.42 rpm
    <u>78 rpm</u>   **Victor 45133** / released October 1917 to ?

80. **BORODIN:** *Prince Igor—Chorus of Slaves.* (In Italian) *("Coro e Danza")*
    Metropolitan Opera Chorus (Giulio Setti, director) & Orchestra - Josef A. Pasternack.
    matrix: **B-20259 -1 -2**
    speed: 77.42 rpm
    78 rpm   **Victor 45133** / released October 1917 to ?

81. **MUSSORGSKY:** *Boris Godunov—Pilgrims' Chorus.* (In Italian)
    Metropolitan Opera Chorus (Giulio Setti, director) & Orchestra - Josef A. Pasternack.
    matrix: **B-20260 -1 -2**
    Not released by Victor although number 45138 had been assigned.

82. **MUSSORGSKY:** *Boris Godunov—Coronation Scene.* (In Italian)
    Metropolitan Opera Chorus (Giulio Setti, director) & Orchestra - Josef A. Pasternack.
    matrix: **B-20261 -1 -2**
    Not released by Victor although number 45138 had been assigned.

Session of 1917 or 1918?

[Apparently all Pathé files have been destroyed. The information given here comes from Pathé catalogues and Pathé supplements along with the disc itself.]

These Pathé discs did not have matrix and take numbers similar to the Victor and Columbia recordings of this period. All Pathé discs were first recorded on large master cylinders. Pathé discs were then copied from the master cylinders and were given a disc master number when the master cylinder was copied to make the disc master. For these two recordings, the disc master number begins with the letter E indicating the disc size (which was 11.5 inches) followed by the master cylinder number and ends with a single digit that indicates the sequence of disc masters made for that disc size from the master cylinder. For example, the disc master number for the first work below is E66932-1 and for the second is E66933-1. The release date given is confirmed in the 15 September 1918 issue of *The Talking Machine World.*

83. **TCHAIKOVSKY:** *Marche Slave, Op. 31.* (abridged)
    Metropolitan Opera House Orchestra - Gennaro Papi.
    master cylinder number: **66932**
    speed: 80 rpm
    78 rpm   **Pathé 59059** / released October 1918 to ?

84. **WOLF-FERRARI:** *I Gioielli della Madonna—Act III Intermezzo.*
    Metropolitan Opera House Orchestra - Gennaro Papi.
    master cylinder number: **66933**
    speed: 80 rpm
    78 rpm   **Pathé 59059** / released October 1918 to ?

Session of 8 March 1918; New York City.

[Information from Columbia archives and Brooks & Rust's *The Columbia Master Book* (1999). All takes are not indicated in the files. The takes listed here come from the published discs. A published take -3 assumes there at least must have been unpublished takes -1 and -2 for example.]

85. **PUCCINI:** *Madama Butterfly - Selections.* [No arranger is given on the labels or in the catalogues, but this appears to be the selection arranged by Émile Tavan with several cuts.]
    Metropolitan Opera House Orchestra - Artur Bodanzky.
    matrix: *Side 1* **49331 -1**
    matrix: *Side 2* **49332 -1 -2 -3**
    speed: *80.89 rpm*

    78 rpm   **Columbia A6094** / released April 1919 to 16 July 1925

Session of 12 March 1918; New York City.

[Information from Columbia archives and Brooks & Rust's *The Columbia Master Book* (1999). All takes are not indicated in the files. The takes listed here come from the published discs. A published take -3 assumes there at least must have been unpublished takes -1 and -2 for example.]

86. **PONCHIELLI:** *La Gioconda—Danza della Ore.* (abridged) *("Dance of the Hours")*
    Metropolitan Opera House Orchestra - Artur Bodanzky.
    matrix: **49334 -1 -2**
    speed: *81.82 rpm*

    78 rpm   **Columbia A6118** / released November 1919 to ?

87. **GOUNOD:** *Faust—Ballet Music (Les Nubiennes; Danse antique; Adagio).* *("Dance of the Nubian Slaves; Dance Antique; Adagio")* [Labels show only "Valse" and "Allegretto" on Side 1 and "Adagio" on Side 2.]
    Metropolitan Opera House Orchestra - Artur Bodanzky.
    matrix: *Side 1* **49335 -1**
    matrix: *Side 2* **49336 -1**
    speed: *81.82 rpm for both sides*

    78 rpm   **Columbia A6041** / released July 1918 to 16 July 1925. [Bodanzky's name is omitted on the printing of some labels.]

88. **MEYERBEER:** *Le Prophète—Marche du Couronnement.* *("Coronation March")*
    Metropolitan Opera House Orchestra - Artur Bodanzky.
    matrix: **49337**
    Not released by Columbia.

Session of 15 March 1918; New York City.

[Information from Columbia archives and Brooks & Rust's *The Columbia Master Book* (1999). All takes are not indicated in the files. The takes listed here come from the published discs. A published take -3 assumes there at least must have been unpublished takes -1 and -2 for example.]

89. **BIZET:** *Carmen - Selections (Prelude; Les Toreadors).* [This actually consists of the *Prelude* to the opera with the twenty-eight measures of the fate theme from the end of the *Prelude* played first.]
    Metropolitan Opera House Orchestra - Artur Bodanzky.

matrix: **49344 -1 -2**
speed: 80.89 rpm
78 rpm   **Columbia A6076** / released December 1918 to 16 July 1925

90. **LEONCAVALLO: *Pagliacci - Selections.***
Metropolitan Opera House Orchestra - Artur Bodanzky.
matrix: **49345**
Not released by Columbia.

Session of 26 March 1918; New York City.

[Information from Columbia archives and Brooks & Rust's *The Columbia Master Book* (1999). All takes are not indicated in the files. The takes listed here come from the published discs. A published take -3 assumes there at least must have been unpublished takes -1 and -2 for example.]

91. **VERDI: *Il Trovatore - Selections.*** [This consists of the *Anvil Chorus*, the *Miserere* and *Vivrà! Contende il giubilo.*]
Metropolitan Opera House Orchestra - Artur Bodanzky.
matrix: **49360 -1**
speed: 80.89 rpm
78 rpm   **Columbia A6076** / released December 1918 to 16 July 1925
Columbia 7011-M / released 1925 to ?

92. **JOHANN STRAUSS, II: *Wein, Weib und Gesang, Op. 333.*** (abridged) (*"Wine, Women and Song"*)
Metropolitan Opera House Orchestra - Artur Bodanzky.
matrix: **49361 -1 -2**
speed: 80.89 rpm
78 rpm   **Columbia A6124** / released January 1920 to 16 July 1925

93. **WALDTEUFEL: *Les Patineurs, Op. 183.*** (abridged) (*"The Skaters"*)
Metropolitan Opera House Orchestra - Artur Bodanzky.
matrix: **49362 -1**
speed: 80.89 rpm
78 rpm   **Columbia A6124** / released January 1920 to 16 July 1925

Session of 1 April 1918; New York City.

[Information from Columbia archives and Brooks & Rust's *The Columbia Master Book* (1999). All takes are not indicated in the files. The takes listed here come from the published discs. A published take -3 assumes there at least must have been unpublished takes -1 and -2 for example.]

94. **VERDI: *Aïda—Grand March.***
Metropolitan Opera House Orchestra - Artur Bodanzky.
matrix: **49365 -1**

speed: 84.51 rpm

78 rpm **Columbia A6118** / released November 1919 to ?

Columbia 5089-M

Columbia 7010-M / released 1925 to ?

95. **VERDI:** *Rigoletto - Selections.*
Metropolitan Opera House Orchestra - Artur Bodanzky.
matrix: **49366**
Not released by Columbia.

Session of 10 December 1919; New York City.

[Information from Columbia archives and Brooks & Rust's *The Columbia Master Book* (1999). All takes are not indicated in the files. The takes listed here come from the published discs. A published take -3 assumes there at least must have been unpublished takes -1 and -2 for example.]

96. **VERDI:** *Les Vêpres Siciliennes—Overture.* (abridged)
Metropolitan Opera House Orchestra - Giuseppe Bamboschek.
matrix: **49717 -1 -2**
speed: 80.89 rpm
78 rpm **Columbia A6178** / released May 1921 to 16 July 1925. [Label states *Key of "E" Major.*]

97. **PUCCINI:** *La Bohème - Selections.* [Side 1 arranged by Gaetano Luporini; Side 2 arranged by Émile Tavan.]
Metropolitan Opera House Orchestra - Giuseppe Bamboschek.
matrix: *Side 1* **49718 -1 -2 -3**
matrix: *Side 2* **49719 -1 -2**
speed: 80.89 rpm for both sides
78 rpm **Columbia A6143** / released May 1920 to ?   [Labels state *Key of "F".*]

Session of 13 December 1919; New York City.

[Information from Columbia archives and Brooks & Rust's *The Columbia Master Book* (1999). All takes are not indicated in the files. The takes listed here come from the published discs. A published take -3 assumes there at least must have been unpublished takes -1 and -2 for example.]

98. **DONIZETTI:** *Lucia di Lammermoor - Selections.* [Arranged by Riviere.]
Metropolitan Opera House Orchestra - Giuseppe Bamboschek.
matrix: **49721 -1 -2**
speed: 80.89 rpm
78 rpm **Columbia A6178** / released May 1921 to 16 July 1925. [Label states *Key of "G" Major.*]

99. **GOUNOD:** *Faust - Selections, Part 2.* [Arranged by Moses, *i.e.*, Theodore Moses Tobani.]
    Metropolitan Opera House Orchestra - Giuseppe Bamboschek.
            matrix: **49722 -1**
                  speed: 80.89 rpm
   78 rpm   **Columbia A6167** / released December 1920 to 16 July 1925. [Label states *Key of "F."*]

Session of 17 December 1919; New York City.
[Information from Columbia archives and Brooks & Rust's *The Columbia Master Book* (1999). All takes are not indicated in the files. The takes listed here come from the published discs. A published take -3 assumes there at least must have been unpublished takes -1 and -2 for example.]

100. **GOUNOD**: *Faust - Selections, Part 1.* [Arranged by Moses, *i.e.*, Theodore Moses Tobani.]
    Metropolitan Opera House Orchestra - Giuseppe Bamboschek.
            matrix: **49723 -1**
                  speed: 80.89 rpm
   78 rpm   **Columbia A6167** / released December 1920 to 16 July 1925. [Label states *Key of "F."*]

101. **VERDI:** *La Traviata - Selections.* [Arranged by Theodore Moses Tobani.]
    Metropolitan Opera House Orchestra - Giuseppe Bamboschek.
            matrix: *Side 1* **49726 -1**
            matrix: *Side 2* **49727 -1 -2**
                  speed: 80.89 rpm for both sides
   78 rpm   **Columbia A6149** / released July 1920 to 16 July 1925. [Label of Side 1 states *Key of "E" Minor*; label of Side 2 states *Key of "G" Major.*]

Session of 11 January 1921; New York City.
[Information from Columbia archives and Brooks & Rust's *The Columbia Master Book* (1999).]

102. **PONCHIELLI:** *La Gioconda—Pescator, affonda l'esca.* (*"Barcarolle"*)
    Riccardo Stracciari, Metropolitan Opera House Chorus & orchestra.
            matrix: **79636 -1 -2 -3** (apparently all takes were used)
                  speed: 80 rpm
   78 rpm   **Columbia 79636** / released April 1921 to ? [Even though Columbia catalogues and the Columbia archives credit the Metropolitan Opera Chorus, the labels on this single-sided disc and the double-sided disc listed next merely state *with Male Chorus.*]
                Columbia 33024-D

Session of 12 April 1922; New York City.
[Information from Columbia archives.]
In Brooks & Rust's *The Columbia Master Book* the date for this session is given as 13 April 1922.

103. **HÉROLD:** *Zampa—Overture.* (abridged)
    Metropolitan Opera House Orchestra - [conductor's name not listed].
              matrix: **98022 -1 -2 -3**
                   speed: 78.26 rpm
    78 rpm   **Columbia A6218** / released October 1922 to ?
                   Columbia 7023-M / released 1925 to ?

104. **GOUNOD:** *Faust—Chœur des Soldats.* (arranged for orchestra) *("Soldiers' Chorus")*
    Metropolitan Opera House Orchestra - [conductor's name not listed].
              matrix: **98023 -1 -2 -3**
                   speed: 78.26 rpm
    78 rpm   **Columbia A6224** / released January 1923 to ?
                   Columbia 7011-M / released 1925 to ?

Session of 13 April 1922; New York City.
[Information from Columbia archives.]
In Brooks & Rust's *The Columbia Master Book* the date for this session is given as 14 April 1922.

105. **BORODIN:** *Prince Igor—Polovtsian Dances.* (abridged)
    Metropolitan Opera House Orchestra - [conductor's name not listed].
              matrix: **98024 -1 -2 -3**
                   speed: 78.26 rpm
    78 rpm   **Columbia A6218** / released October 1922 to ?   [Title on label reads: *"Prince Igor from 'Prince Igor.'"*]

106. **WAGNER:** *Tannhäuser—Einzug der Gäste.* *("Fest-Marsch" "Entrance of the Guests")*
    Metropolitan Opera House Orchestra - [conductor's name not listed].
              matrix: **98025 -1 -2 -3**
                   speed: 78.26 rpm
    78 rpm   **Columbia A6224** / released January 1923 to ?
                   Columbia 5089-M
                   Columbia 7010-M / released 1925 to ?

Session(s?) of ca. 1923-1924.
[There are no company files available for these recordings made by The Aeolian Company which appeared on their Vocalion label. The recordings are arranged in the order of their release. The release dates are those given in issues of *The Talking Machine World.* Information from Arnold's *The Orchestra on Record, 1896-1926* (1997) and from the published recordings.]

107. **HÉROLD:** *Zampa—Overture.*
    Metropolitan Opera House Orchestra - Gennaro Papi.

matrix: *Side 1* **11388**
matrix: *Side 2* **11392**
> *speed: 77.42 rpm for both sides*

78 rpm   **Vocalion 35022** / released August 1923 to ?

---

108. **WOLF-FERRARI:** *I Gioielli della Madonna—Act III Intermezzo.*
     Metropolitan Opera House Orchestra - Gennaro Papi.
              matrix: **10821**
> *speed: 75 rpm*

78 rpm   **Vocalion 35025** / released February 1924 to ?
              Aco F33057 [released in the U.K. with the *nom du disque* "Albany Symphony Orchestra"]
              Beltona 5014 [released in the U.K. with the *nom du disque* "Sutherland Orchestra"]

---

109. **MASSENET:** *Scènes Pittoresques—Angélus.*
     Metropolitan Opera House Orchestra - Gennaro Papi.
              matrix: **12035**
> *speed: 75.78 rpm*

78 rpm   **Vocalion 35025** / released February 1924 to ?
              Aco F33057 [released in the U.K. with the *nom du disque* "Albany Symphony Orchestra"]
              Beltona 5016 [released in the U.K. with the *nom du disque* "Langham Symphony Orchestra"]

---

110. **ROSSINI:** *Il Barbiere di Siviglia—Overture.*
     Metropolitan Opera House Orchestra - Gennaro Papi.
              matrix: *Side 1* **12647**
              matrix: *Side 2* **12649**
> *speed: 75.78 rpm for both sides*

78 rpm   **Vocalion 35032** / released May 1924 to ?
              Vocalion K-05119

---

111. **KETÈLBEY:** *In a Monastery Garden.*
     Metropolitan Opera House Orchestra with male chorus - Gennaro Papi.
              matrix: **13028**
> *speed: 76.59 rpm*

78 rpm   **Vocalion 35038** / released July 1924 to ?
              Aco F33072 [released in the U.K. with the *nom du disque* "Albany Symphony Orchestra"]
              Beltona 5013 [released in the U.K. with the *nom du disque* "Sutherland Orchestra"]

---

112. **GRANADOS:** *Goyescas—Intermezzo.*
     Metropolitan Opera House Orchestra - Gennaro Papi.
              matrix: **13032**
> *speed: 76.59 rpm*

78 rpm   **Vocalion 35038** / released July 1924 to ?
              Vocalion K-05199

113. **VERDI:** *Aïda - Selections.*
    Metropolitan Opera House Orchestra - Gennaro Papi.
        matrix: [It was not possible to acquire a copy of this disc to find out this number.]
        speed: [It was not possible to acquire a copy of this disc to determine this.]
   78 rpm   **Vocalion 35046** / released November 1924 to ?
          Vocalion K-05135

114. **PUCCINI:** *La Bohème - Selections.*
    Metropolitan Opera House Orchestra - Gennaro Papi.
        matrix: [It was not possible to acquire a copy of this disc to find out this number.]
        speed: [It was not possible to acquire a copy of this disc to determine this.]
   78 rpm   **Vocalion 35046** / released November 1924 to ?
          Vocalion K-05135

Session of 19 April 1924, A.M.; New York City.
[Information from Ross Laird's *Brunswick Records* (2001).]

115. **WEBER:** *Der Freischütz—Victoria, Victoria! ("Lied des Kilian")*
    Michael Bohnen, Metropolitan Opera Chorus & orchestra.
        matrix: **12922 12923 12924**
   Not released by Brunswick.

Session of 8 April 1925, P.M.; New York City.
[Information from Columbia archives and Ross Laird's *Brunswick Records* (2001).]

116. **MASCAGNI:** *Cavalleria Rusticana—Prelude.*
    Metropolitan Opera House Orchestra - Gennaro Papi.
        matrix: **XE15472 XE15473**
        speed: 77.42 rpm
   78 rpm   **Brunswick 50067** / released October 1925 to ?
          Brunswick 48-L

117. **MASCAGNI:** *Cavalleria Rusticana—Intermezzo.*
    Metropolitan Opera House Orchestra - Gennaro Papi.
        matrix: **XE15474** (This take was used for this title as well as a take from the session of 17 April 1925 for different pressings of Brunswick 50067 according to Laird. Please see also the session of 17 April 1925.)
        speed: 77.42 rpm
   78 rpm   **Brunswick 50067** / released October 1925 to ?
          Brunswick 47-L

Session of 17 April 1925, A.M.; New York City.
[Information from Columbia archives and Ross Laird's *Brunswick Records* (2001).]

118. BIZET: *Carmen—Act III Entr'acte.*
  Metropolitan Opera House Orchestra - Gennaro Papi.
          matrix: **E15577 <u>E15578</u> E15579 E15580**
              speed: 77.42 rpm
  78 rpm   **Brunswick 15106** / released January 1926 to ?
                    Brunswick 44-L

119. BIZET: *Carmen—Act IV Entr'acte.*
  Metropolitan Opera House Orchestra - Gennaro Papi.
          matrix: **E15581 E15582 <u>E15583</u>**
              speed: 77.42 rpm
  78 rpm   **Brunswick 15106** / released January 1926 to ?
                    Brunswick 45-L

120. MASCAGNI: *Cavalleria Rusticana—Intermezzo.*
  Metropolitan Opera House Orchestra - Gennaro Papi.
          matrix: **XE15584 XE15585** (A take from this session as well as the take from the session of 8
          April 1925 was used for different pressing of Brunswick 50067 for this title according to Laird.
          Please also see the session of 8 April 1925.)
              speed: 77.42 rpm
  78 rpm   **Brunswick 50067** / released October 1925 to ?
                    Brunswick 48-L

Session of 26 October 1927, 2:30 to 5:00 P.M.; Liederkranz Hall, NYC.
[Information from Victor archives.]

121. MASCAGNI: *Cavalleria Rusticana—Regina Coeli.*
  Metropolitan Opera Chorus & Metropolitan Opera House Orchestra - Giulio Setti.
          matrix: **CVE-40665 -1 -2**
  Not released by Victor. This was re-recorded during the session of 17 November 1927 and a take from
  that session was released.

122. LEONCAVALLO: *Pagliacci—Son qua!*
  Metropolitan Opera Chorus & Metropolitan Opera House Orchestra - Giulio Setti.
          matrix: **BVE-40666 -1 -2**
  Not released by Victor. This was re-recorded during the sessions of 7 November 1927 and 17 November
  1927. The 17 November 1927 performance was released. (In Dr. Bolig's *Victor Discography Series*, he indicates that take -2 was also released on Victor 4028.)

Session of 7 November 1927, 2:30 to 4:45 P.M.; Liederkranz Hall, NYC.
[Information from Victor archives.]

123. **MOZART:** *Die Zauberflöte—O Isis und Osiris. ("Priesterchor")*
    Metropolitan Opera Chorus & Metropolitan Opera House Orchestra - Giulio Setti.
        matrix: **BVE-40698 -1 -2 -3**
            speed: 78.26 rpm
    78 rpm   **Victor 4027** / released 27 January 1928 to ?

124. **MASCAGNI:** *Cavalleria Rusticana—Gli aranci olezzano. ("Blossoms of oranges")*
    Metropolitan Opera Chorus & Metropolitan Opera House Orchestra - Giulio Setti.
        matrix: **CVE-40699 -1 -2**
            speed: 78.26 rpm
    78 rpm   **Victor 9150** / released 30 December 1927 to ?
            HMV AW 4004

125. **LEONCAVALLO:** *Pagliacci—Andiam!*
    Metropolitan Opera Chorus & Metropolitan Opera House Orchestra - Giulio Setti.
        matrix: **BVE-41000 -1 -2**
            speed: 78.26 rpm
    78 rpm   **Victor 4028** / released 24 February 1928 to ?

126. **LEONCAVALLO:** *Pagliacci—Son qua!*
    Metropolitan Opera Chorus & Metropolitan Opera House Orchestra - Giulio Setti.
        matrix: **BVE-40666 -3**
    Not released. This had been recorded previously on 26 October 1927 which was not released. It would be recorded again on 17 November 1927, and that performance would be released. (In Dr. Bolig's *Victor Discography Series*, he indicates that take -2 of this title recorded on 26 October 1927 was also released on Victor 4028.)

127. **VERDI:** *Rigoletto—Scorrendo uniti.*
    Metropolitan Opera Chorus & Metropolitan Opera House Orchestra - Giulio Setti. [It sounds as if it may be Setti who sings the part of the Duke during the introductory "Duca, duca" passage. The few notes of the Duke during the chorus proper are omitted.]
        matrix: **BVE-41001 -1 -2**
            speed: 78.26 rpm
    78 rpm   **Victor 4027** / released 27 January 1928 to ?

Session of 17 November 1927, 2:30 to 4:55 P.M.; Liederkranz Hall, NYC.
[Information from Victor archives.]

128. **LEONCAVALLO:** *Pagliacci—No, Pagliaccio non son!*
    Giovanni Martinelli, Grace Anthony, Metropolitan Opera Chorus & Metropolitan Opera House Orchestra – Giulio Setti.
        matrix: **CVE-41045 -1 -2** (both takes were used)

                  speed: 78.26 rpm

78 rpm	**Victor 6754** / released 29 November 1927 to ?
	HMV DB 1139
33⅓ rpm	**Camden CAL-274** / released January 1956 to 1 April 1958
	RCA Victor LM-2710 / released 18 October 1963 to ?
Cassette	**MET 512-C** / released 1991 to ?
CD	**MET 512-CD** / released 1991 to ?
	Nimbus NI 7804

129. VERDI: *Il Trovatore—Di quella pira.*
Giovanni Martinelli, Grace Anthony, Giulio Setti, Metropolitan Opera Chorus & Metropolitan Opera House Orchestra - Giulio Setti. [Setti sings the few words allotted to Ruiz.]

        matrix: **CVE-41046 -1 -2**

           speed: 78.26 rpm

78 rpm	**Victor 8109** / released 29 March 1929 to ?
	HMV DB 1288
33⅓ rpm	**Camden CAL-274** / released January 1956 to 1 April 1958
	RCA Victor LM-2631
	RCA Victor LM-2710 / released 18 October 1963 to ?
	RCA Victrola VIC-1684
	RCA VL 42799 / released 1979 to ?
	Pearl GEMM 181/2

130. MASCAGNI: *Cavalleria Rusticana—Regina Coeli.*
Grace Anthony, Metropolitan Opera Chorus & Metropolitan Opera House Orchestra - Giulio Setti.

        matrix: **CVE-40665 -3 -4**

           speed: 78.26 rpm

This had been recorded previously on 26 October 1927 which performances were not released.

78 rpm	**Victor 9150** / released 30 December 1927 to ?
	HMV AW 4004

131. LEONCAVALLO: *Pagliacci—Son qua!*
Metropolitan Opera Chorus & Metropolitan Opera House Orchestra - Giulio Setti.

        matrix: **BVE-40666 -4 -5**

           speed: 78.26 rpm

This had been recorded previously on 26 October 1927 and 7 November 1927 which performances were not released. (In Dr. Bolig's *Victor Discography Series*, he indicates that take -2 of this title recorded on 26 October 1927 was also released on Victor 4028.)

78 rpm	**Victor 4028** / released 24 February 1928 to ?

Session of 29 November 1927, 10 A.M. to 1 P.M.; Liederkranz Hall, NYC.
[Information from Victor archives.]

132. PONCHIELLI: *La Gioconda—Marinaresca.*
Metropolitan Opera Chorus & Metropolitan Opera House Orchestra - Giulio Setti.

matrix: **CVE-41073 -1 -2**
speed: 79.12 rpm
78 rpm   **Victor 9334** / released 26 July 1929 to ?

133. **PONCHIELLI:** *La Gioconda—Pescator, affonda l'esca.* *("Barcarola")*
Giuseppe De Luca, Metropolitan Opera Chorus & Metropolitan Opera House Orchestra –
Giulio Setti.
matrix: **CVE-41074 -1 -2**
Not released by Victor. This was re-recorded during the session of 26 January 1928, and that performance was released.

134. **VERDI:** *Rigoletto—Povero Rigoletto!* [*Cortigiani,* vil razza dannata, the second part of this scene, was recorded on 5 April 1928.]
Giuseppe De Luca, Grace Anthony, Metropolitan Opera Chorus & Metropolitan Opera House Orchestra –
Giulio Setti. [Setti and perhaps another solo voice are also heard.]
matrix: **CVE-41075 -1 -2**
speed: 79.12 rpm
78 rpm   **Victor 8161** / released 29 November 1929 to ? [In the late 1940s Victor had assigned catalogue numbers EM-32 and 15-1031 for this recording in their vinylite "Heritage Series," but it was not issued.]
HMV DB 1371
33⅓ rpm   **Camden CAL-320** / released 21 September 1956 to 1 October 1958
Camden CDN.1012
RCA TVM1-7209 / released 1976 to ?
CD   **Preiser 89073** / released 1993 to ?
Nimbus NI 7851
Nimbus NI 7815

135. **VERDI:** *Aïda—Temple Scene, Part 2.* *("Nume, custode e vindice")* [Part 1 was recorded 5 January 1928.]
Giovanni Martinelli, Ezio Pinza, Metropolitan Opera Chorus & Metropolitan Opera House Orchestra –
Giulio Setti.
matrix: **CVE-41076 -1 -2**
speed: 79.12 rpm
78 rpm   **Victor 8111** / released 26 April 1929 to ?
HMV DB 1214
45 rpm   **RCA Victor WCT-51**
RCA Victor ERAT 15 / released 24 December 1953 to April 1956
33⅓ rpm   **RCA Victor LCT-1035** / released 1952 to ?
RCA Victor LM-6171 / released September 1966 to 1 March 1967
RCA Gold Seal AGM3-4805 / released 1983 to ?
RCA LMD 60005
Cantilena 6239
Preiser LV 220
MET 105 / released 1978 to ?
Cassette   **RCA Gold Seal CGK2-4805** / released 1983 to ?
MET 105-C / released 1980 to ?

                  MET 503-C

CD   **MET 105-CD** / released 1989 to ?

                  Nimbus NI 7875

                  Pearl GEMM 9306 / released 1988 to ?

Session of 3 December 1927, 10 A.M. to 12:05 P.M.; Liederkranz Hall, NYC.
[Information from Victor archives.]

136. **BELLINI:** *Norma—Non parti?*
    Metropolitan Opera Chorus & Metropolitan Opera House Orchestra - Giulio Setti.
        matrix: **CVE-41095 -1 -2**
           speed: 79.12 rpm

78 rpm   **Victor 9484** / released 29 November 1929-?

               HMV AW 166

137. **VERDI:** *La Forza del Destino—Il santo nome di Dio. ("Maledizione")*
    Ezio Pinza, Metropolitan Opera Chorus & Metropolitan Opera House Orchestra - Giulio Setti.
        matrix: **CVE-41096 -1 -2**
           speed: 79.12 rpm

78 rpm   **Victor 8158** / released 27 September 1929 to ?

               HMV DB 1203

33⅓ rpm   **RCA Victrola VIC-1418** / released April 1969 to ?

               MET 105 / released 1978 to ?

               Pearl GEMM 181/2

Cassette   **MET 105-C** / released 1980 to ?

CD   **MET 105-CD** / released 1989 to ?

138. **BELLINI:** *Norma—Ite sul colle, o Druidi!*
    Ezio Pinza, Metropolitan Opera Chorus & Metropolitan Opera House Orchestra - Giulio Setti.
        matrix: **CVE-41097 -1 -2**
           speed: 79.12 rpm

78 rpm   **Victor 8158** / released 27 September 1929 to ?

               HMV DB 1203

               HMV DB 2396

33⅓ rpm   **RCA Victrola VIC-1418** / released April 1969 to ?

               MET-105 / released 1978 to ?

Cassette   **MET 105-C** / released 1980 to ?

CD   **MET 105-CD** / released 1989 to ?

               Nimbus NI 7875

               Pearl GEM 0090 / released 2001 to ?

               Preiser 89050 / released 1991 to ?

Session of 12 December 1927, from ? to 5:25 P.M.; Liederkranz Hall, NYC.
[Information from Victor archives.]

139. **DONIZETTI:** *Lucia di Lammermoor—Giusto Cielo! rispondete.*
Beniamino Gigli, Ezio Pinza, Metropolitan Opera Chorus & Metropolitan Opera House Orchestra –
Giulio Setti.
    matrix: **CVE-41225 -1 -2 -3** (both takes -1 and -2 were used)
        speed: 78.26 rpm
78 rpm   **Victor 8096** / released 31 August 1928 to ?
        HMV DB 1229
45 rpm   **RCA Victor WCT-57**
33⅓ rpm   **RCA Victor LCT-1037** / released 1952 to ?
Cassette   **MET 521-C** / released 1993 to ?
CD   **RCA Victor Gold Seal 7811-2-RG** / released 1990 to ?
        MET 521-CD / released 1993 to ?
        Nimbus NI 7892/3
        Pearl GEM 0214
        Romophone 82004-2 [includes both takes -1 and -2] / released 1996 to ?
        Naxos 8.110266 [includes both takes -1 and -2]

140. **DONIZETTI:** *Lucia di Lammermoor—Tu che a Dio.*
Beniamino Gigli, Ezio Pinza, Metropolitan Opera Chorus & Metropolitan Opera House Orchestra –
Giulio Setti.
    matrix: **CVE-41226 -1 -2** (In Dr. Bolig's *Victor Discography Series*, he indicates take -2 was
    also used.)
        speed: 78.26 rpm
78 rpm   **Victor 8096** / released 31 August 1928 to ?
        HMV DB 1229
45 rpm   **RCA Victor WCT-57**
33⅓ rpm   **RCA Victor LCT-1057** / released 1952 to ?
        RCA Victor LM-2337 / released 19 February 1960 to ?
Cassette   **MET 521-C** / released 1993 to ?
CD   **RCA Victor Gold Seal 7811-2-RG** / released 1990 to ?
        MET 521-CD / released 1993 to ?
        Nimbus NI 7892/3
        Romophone 82004-2 / released 1996 to ?
        Naxos 8.110266

141. **DONIZETTI:** *Lucia di Lammermoor—Fra poco a me ricovero.*
Beniamino Gigli & Metropolitan Opera House Orchestra - Giulio Setti.
    matrix: **CVE-41227 -1 -2**
        speed: 78.26 rpm
78 rpm   **Victor 6876** / released 28 December 1928 to ?
        HMV DB 1222
        HMV DB 2235
33⅓ rpm   **RCA Victor LM-6705** / released 16 February 1962 to ?
        RCA Victor LM-2624 / released 16 October 1962 to ?

_CD_	**RCA Victor Gold Seal 7811-2-RG** / released 1990 to ?
	Nimbus NI 1763
	Nimbus NI 7817
	Nimbus NI 7892/3
	Romophone 82004-2 [includes both take -1 and unpublished take -2] / released 1996 to ?
	Naxos 8.110266 [includes both take -1 and unpublished take -2]

Session of 16 December 1927, 10:30 A.M. to 4:25 P.M.; Liederkranz Hall, NYC.
[Information from Victor archives.]

142. **DONIZETTI:** _Lucia di Lammermoor—Chi mi frena._ _("Sextet")_
> _Amelita Galli-Curci, Louise Homer, Beniamino Gigli, Angelo Bada, Giuseppe De Luca, Ezio Pinza &_
> _Metropolitan Opera House Orchestra - Giulio Setti._
>> matrix: **CVE-41232** -1 -2 -**3**
>> _speed: 78.26 rpm_

78 rpm	**Victor 10012** / released 10 February 1928 to ?
	HMV DQ 102
45 rpm	**Electrola 7RW 19-539**
33⅓ rpm	**Seraphim 60054**
	Pearl GEMM 165
_CD_	**Nimbus NI 7852** / released 1993 to ?
	EMI Classics CDH 761051-2 / released 1988 to ?
	Romophone 82004-2 / released 1996 to ?
	Naxos 8.110266

143. **VERDI:** _Rigoletto—Bella figlia dell'amore._ _("Quartet")_
> _Amelita Galli-Curci, Louise Homer, Beniamino Gigli, Giuseppe De Luca & Metropolitan Opera House_
> _Orchestra - Giulio Setti._
>> matrix: **CVE-41233** -**1** -2 -**3** (both takes -1 and -3 were used)
>> _speed: 78.26 rpm_

78 rpm	**Victor 10012** / released 10 February 1928 to ?
	HMV DQ 102
45 rpm	**RCA Victor ERAT 8** / released 24 December 1953 to 1 September 1956
	Electrola 7RW 19-539
33⅓ rpm	**Seraphim 60054**
	Pearl GEMM 165
	OASI-599
	La Voix de Son Maître 2910753
Cassette	**MET 518-C** / released 1993 to ?
_CD_	**MET 518-CD** / released 1993 to ?
	Nimbus NI 7852 / released 1993 to ?
	EMI Classics 7243 5 74217 2 0 / released 2000 to ?

Romophone 82004-2 [includes both takes -1 and -3] / released 1996 to ?
Naxos 8.110266 [includes both takes -1 and -3]
Gala GL 308

144. VERDI: *La Traviata—Imponete.*
Amelita Galli-Curci, Giuseppe De Luca & Metropolitan Opera House Orchestra - Giulio Setti.
    matrix: **CVE-41234 -1 -2**
    speed: 78.26 rpm

78 rpm   **Victor 8089** / released 30 March 1928 to ? [For unknown reasons this selection, which is the second half of the duet, is on the A side of Victor 8089, while the next selection, *Dite alla giovine*, which is the first half of the duet, is on the B side of Victor 8089.]
                HMV DB 1165
33⅓ rpm   **RCA Victor LM-6171** / released September 1966 to 1 March 1967
                RCA Gold Seal AGM3-4805 / released 1983 to ?
Cassette   **RCA Gold Seal CGK2-4805** / released 1983 to ?
                MET 505-C / released 1989 to ?
CD   **Preiser 89073** / released 1993 to ?
                MET 505-CD / released 1989 to ?

145. VERDI: *La Traviata—Dite alla giovine.*
Amelita Galli-Curci, Giuseppe De Luca & Metropolitan Opera House Orchestra - Giulio Setti.
    matrix: **CVE-41235 -1 -2 -3**
    speed: 78.26 rpm

78 rpm   **Victor 8089** / released 30 March 1928 to ? [For unknown reasons this selection, which is the first half of the duet, is on the B side of Victor 8089, while the previous selection, *Imponete*, which is the second half of the duet, is on the A side of Victor 8089.]
                HMV DB 1165
33⅓ rpm   **RCA Victor LM-6171** / released September 1966 to 1 March 1967
                RCA Gold Seal AGM3-4805 / released 1983 to ?
Cassette   **RCA Gold Seal CGK2-4805** / released 1983 to ?
                MET 505-C / released 1989 to ?
CD   **Preiser 89073** / released 1993 to ?
                MET 505-CD / released 1989 to ?

146. VERDI: *Rigoletto—Ah! veglia, o donna.*
Amelita Galli-Curci, Giuseppe De Luca & Metropolitan Opera House Orchestra - Giulio Setti.
[It sounds as if it may be Setti who sings the two words "Sua figlia!" allotted to the Duke.]
    matrix: **BVE-41236 -1 -2**
    speed: 78.26 rpm

78 rpm   **Victor 3051** / released 1 March 1929 to 1934
                Victor 1878 [This number was used in Argentina.]
                Victor 1899 [This number *may* have been used in Brazil.]
                HMV DA 1028
33⅓ rpm   **RCA Victrola VIC-1633** / released October 1971 to ?
CD   **Preiser 89073** / released 1993 to ?
                Nimbus NI 7815

147. **VERDI:** *Rigoletto—Piangi, piangi, fanciulla.*
    Amelita Galli-Curci, Giuseppe De Luca & Metropolitan Opera House Orchestra - Giulio Setti.
        matrix: **BVE-41237 -<u>1</u> -2**
          speed: 78.26 rpm

78 rpm	**Victor 3051** / released 1 March 1929 to 1934
	Victor 1878 [This number was used in Argentina.]
	Victor 1899 [This number *may* have been used in Brazil.]
	HMV DA 1028
CD	**Preiser 89073** / released 1993 to ?

Session of 5 January 1928, 2:30 to 4:45 P.M.; Liederkranz Hall, NYC.
[Information from Victor archives.]

148. **MASCAGNI:** *Cavalleria Rusticana—Brindisi.* *("Viva il vino")*
    Beniamino Gigli, Metropolitan Opera Chorus & Metropolitan Opera House Orchestra - Giulio Setti.
        matrix: **CVE-41298 -1 -<u>2</u> -3**
          speed: 78.26 rpm

78 rpm	**Victor 8222** / released 18 December 1931 to ?
	HMV DB 1499
33⅓ rpm	**RCA Victor LM-2624** / released 16 October 1962 to ?
CD	**Romophone 82004-2** / released 1996 to ?
	Naxos 8.110266

149. **MOZART:** *Die Zauberflöte—O Isis und Osiris.* *("Possenti Numi")*
    Ezio Pinza, Metropolitan Opera Chorus & Metropolitan Opera House Orchestra - Giulio Setti.
        matrix: **CVE-41299 -<u>1</u> -2**

78 rpm	***Not released on 78 rpm***
33⅓ rpm	**RCA Victrola VIC-1418** / released April 1969 to ?
CD	**RCA Gold Seal 09026-61245-2** / released 1990 to ?
	Pearl GEMM CD 9958 / released 1992 to ?

150. **VERDI:** *Aïda—Temple Scene, Part 1.* *("Possente, possente Fthà")* [Part 2 was recorded 29 November 1927.]
    Ezio Pinza, Grace Anthony, Metropolitan Opera Chorus & Metropolitan Opera House Orchestra – Giulio Setti.
        matrix: **CVE-41600 -<u>1</u> -2**
          speed: 78.26 rpm

78 rpm	**Victor 8111** / released 26 April 1929 to ?
	HMV DB 1214
45 rpm	**RCA Victor WCT-51**
	RCA Victor ERAT 15 / released 24 December 1953 to April 1956
33⅓ rpm	**RCA Victor LCT-1035** / released 1952 to ?
	RCA Victor LM-6171 / released September 1966 to 1 March 1967

             RCA Gold Seal AGM3-4805 / released 1983 to ?

             MET 105 [This contains only the last quarter of the side, beginning where Pinza sings "Mortal, diletto ai Numi."] / released 1978 to ?

             Cantilena 6239

             Preiser LV 220

Cassette   **RCA Gold Seal CGK2-4805** / released 1983 to ?

             MET 105-C [This contains only the last quarter of the side, beginning where Pinza sings "Mortal, diletto ai Numi."] / released 1980 to ?

             MET 503-C

CD   **MET 105-CD** [This contains only the last quarter of the side, beginning where Pinza sings "Mortal, diletto ai Numi."] / released 1989 to ?

             MET 503-CD / released 1988 to ?

             Nimbus NI 7875

             Pearl GEMM 9306 / released 1988 to ?

Session of 23 January 1928, 2:00 to 5:15 P.M.; Liederkranz Hall, NYC.
[Information from Victor archives.]

151. **VERDI:** *La Forza del Destino—La Vergine degli Angeli.*
    Rosa Ponselle, Ezio Pinza, Metropolitan Opera Chorus & Metropolitan Opera House Orchestra – Giulio Setti.

          matrix: **CVE-41636 -1**

            speed: 79.12 rpm

78 rpm   **Victor 8097** / released 28 September 1928 to ?

             HMV DB 1199

45 rpm   **RCA Victor WCT-4**

             RCA Victor ERAT 20 / released 24 December 1953 to ?

33⅓ rpm   **RCA Victor LCT-1003** / released 29 December 1950 to 1 September 1956

             Camden CBL-100 / released 16 August 1957 to 1 September 1961

             Pearl GEMM 181/2

             MET 105 / released 1978 to ?

             La Voix de Son Maître 2910753

Cassette   **MET 105-C** / released 1980 to ?

CD   **MET 105-CD** / released 1989 to ?

             Nimbus NI 1742

             Nimbus NI 1795

             Nimbus NI 1777

             Nimbus NI 7805 / released 1989 to ?

             EMI Classics 7243 5 74217 2 0 / released 2000 to ?

             Naxos 8.110728

152. **VERDI:** *Il Trovatore—Miserere.*
    Rosa Ponselle, Giovanni Martinelli, Metropolitan Opera Chorus & Metropolitan Opera House Orchestra – Giulio Setti.

matrix: **CVE-41637 -1 -2** (both takes were used)
speed: 79.12 rpm

78 rpm   **Victor 8097** / released 28 September 1928 to ?
               HMV DB 1199

33⅓ rpm   **RCA Victrola VIC-1684**
               RCA VL 42799 / released 1979 to ?
               Pearl GEMM 181/2

CD   **Nimbus NI 7804**
               Naxos 8.110728

Session of 26 January 1928, 3:00 to 5:15 P.M.; Liederkranz Hall, NYC.
[Information from Victor archives.]

153. **BIZET:** *Carmen—Habañera.* *("L'amour est un oiseau rebelle")*
     Maria Jeritza, Metropolitan Opera Chorus & Metropolitan Opera House Orchestra - Giulio Setti.
        matrix: **CVE-41650 -1 -2** (both takes were used)
        speed: 76.59 rpm

78 rpm   **Victor 8091** / released 30 March 1928 to 1946
               HMV DB 1159

33⅓ rpm   **Camden CAL-275** / released March 1956 to 11 July 1957

154. **BIZET:** *Carmen—Chanson bohème.* *("Les tringles des sistres tintaient")*
     Maria Jeritza, Merle Alcock & Metropolitan Opera House Orchestra - Giulio Setti.
        matrix: **CVE-41651 -1 -2 -3** (both takes -1 and -2 were used)
        speed: 76.59 rpm

78 rpm   **Victor 8091** / released 30 March 1928 to 1946
               HMV DB 1159

33⅓ rpm   **Camden CAL-275** / released March 1956 to 11 July 1957

155. **PONCHIELLI:** *La Gioconda—Pescator, affonda l'esca.* *("Barcarola")*
     Giuseppe De Luca, Metropolitan Opera Chorus & Metropolitan Opera House Orchestra - Giulio Setti.
        matrix: **CVE-41074 -3 -4 -5**
        speed: 76.59 rpm
This had been previously recorded during the session of 29 November 1927, but those performances were not
released.

78 rpm   **Victor 8174** / released 30 May 1930 to ?
               HMV DB 1436

Cassette   **MET 524-C** / released 1994 to ?
CD   **MET 524-CD** / released 1994 to ?
               Preiser 89073 / released 1993 to ?
               Nimbus NI 7815

Session of 5 April 1928, 2:00 to 5:05 P.M.; Liederkranz Hall, NYC.
[Information from Victor archives.]

156. **TAYLOR:** *The King's Henchman—Oh Caesar, great wert thou!*
    Lawrence Tibbett, Metropolitan Opera Chorus & Metropolitan Opera House Orchestra - Giulio Setti.
        matrix: **CVE-43613** -1 -2 -3
              speed: 76 rpm

78 rpm	**Victor 8103** / released 26 October 1928 to ?
33⅓ rpm	**New World Records NW 241** / released 1978 to ?

157. **TAYLOR:** *The King's Henchman—Nay, Maccus, lay him down.*
    Lawrence Tibbett, Metropolitan Opera Chorus & Metropolitan Opera House Orchestra - Giulio Setti.
        matrix: **CVE-43614** -1 -2 -3
              speed: 76 rpm

78 rpm	**Victor 8103** / released 26 October 1928 to ?
	Victor M-1015 (11-8932) / released 1 September 1945 to ?
33⅓ rpm	**Camden CAL-171** / released 5 March 1954 to 1 July 1957
	RCA Red Seal CRM8-5177 / released 1984 to ?
Cassette	**RCA Red Seal CRK8-5177** / released 1984 to ?
CD	**RCA Red Seal 09026-61580-2** / released 1993 to ?
	New World Records NW 241 / released 1978 to ?
	MET 219-CD / released 1993 to ?

158. **VERDI:** *Ernani—O sommo Carlo.*
    Giuseppe De Luca, Grace Anthony, Alfio Tedesco, Metropolitan Opera Chorus & Metropolitan Opera House Orchestra - Giulio Setti.
        matrix: **CVE-43615** -1 -2 -3
              speed: 76 rpm

78 rpm	**Victor 8174** / released 30 May 1930 to ?
	HMV DB 1436
33⅓ rpm	**Camden CAL-320** / released 21 September 1956 to 1 October 1958
	Camden CDN.1012
	RCA TVM1-7209 / released 1976 to ?
CD	**Preiser 89073** / released 1993 to ?

159. **VERDI:** *Rigoletto—Cortigiani, vil razza dannata.* [*Povero Rigoletto!,* the first part of this scene, was recorded on 29 November 1927.]
    Giuseppe De Luca, Metropolitan Opera Chorus & Metropolitan Opera House Orchestra - Giulio Setti.
        matrix: **CVE-43616** -1 -2
              speed: 76 rpm

78 rpm	**Victor 8161** / released 29 November 1929 to ? [In the late 1940s Victor had assigned catalogue numbers EM-32 and 15-1031 for this recording in their vinylite "Heritage Series," but it was not issued.]
	HMV DB 1371
33⅓ rpm	**Camden CAL-320** / released 21 September 1956 to 1 October 1958
	Camden CDN.1012
	RCA TVM1-7209 / released 1976 to ?

CD   **Preiser 89073** / released 1993 to ?
                Nimbus NI 7851
                Nimbus NI 7815

Session of 24 December 1928, 11:30 A.M. to 2:30 P.M.; Liederkranz Hall, NYC.
[Information from Victor archives.]

160. **HALÉVY:** *La Juive—Passover Music.*
              Part 1: *("O Dieu, Dieu de nos pères")*
              Part 2: *("Si trahison ou perfidie")*
         Giovanni Martinelli, Metropolitan Opera Chorus & Metropolitan Opera House Orchestra - Giulio Setti.
              matrix: *Side 1* **CVE-49015 -1 -2**
              matrix: *Side 2* **CVE-49016 -1 -2**
                    speed: 77.42 rpm for both sides
    78 rpm   **Victor 8165** / released 25 June 1929 to ?
                    HMV DB 1411
    33⅓ rpm   **Camden CAL-283** / released 23 December 1955 to 1 April 1958

161. **PONCHIELLI:** *La Gioconda—Feste! Pane!*
         Metropolitan Opera Chorus & Metropolitan Opera House Orchestra - Giulio Setti.
              matrix: **CVE-49017 -1 -2**
                    speed: 77.42 rpm
    78 rpm   **Victor 9334** / released 26 July 1929 to ?

162. **VERDI:** *La Traviata—Coro delle Zingarelle.*
         Metropolitan Opera Chorus & Metropolitan Opera House Orchestra - Giulio Setti.
         [Unknown voices sing the few lines of Flora and the Marquis d'Obigny.]
              matrix: **CVE-49018 -1 -2 -3**
                    speed: 77.42 rpm
    78 rpm   **Victor 4103** / released 29 March 1929 to ?

163. **VERDI:** *La Traviata—Coro dei Mattadori.*
         Metropolitan Opera Chorus & Metropolitan Opera House Orchestra - Giulio Setti.
              matrix: **CVE-49019 -1 -2**
                    speed: 77.42 rpm
    78 rpm   **Victor 4103** / released 29 March 1929 to ?

Session of 31 December 1928, 3:00 to 4:45 P.M.; Liederkranz Hall, NYC.
[Information from Victor archives.]

164. **BELLINI:** *Norma—Casta Diva.*
              Part 1: *("Sediziose voci")*
              Part 2: *("Ah! bello a me ritorna")*

Rosa Ponselle, Metropolitan Opera Chorus & Metropolitan Opera House Orchestra - Giulio Setti.
> matrix: *Side 1* **CVE-49031** -1 -2
> matrix: *Side 2* **CVE-49032** -1 -<u>2</u>
> > speed: *78.26 rpm for Side 2*

Although Part 2 was passed for release, Part 1 was rejected and re-recorded during the session of 30 January 1929. Please see that session for release information.

<u>**Session of 30 January 1929, 1:30 to 4:15 P.M.; Liederkranz Hall, NYC.**</u>
[Information from Victor archives.]

165. **BELLINI:** *Norma—Casta Diva.*
> > *Part 1:* ("Sediziose voci")

Rosa Ponselle, Metropolitan Opera Chorus & Metropolitan Opera House Orchestra - Giulio Setti.
> matrix: *Side 1* **CVE-49031** -<u>3</u> -4
> > speed: *78.26 rpm*

Part 2 had been successfully recorded during the session of 31 December 1928. Please see that session also. The takes made of Part 1 during that session were rejected and so Part 1 was re-recorded during this session, and this produced a successful take.

<u>*78 rpm*</u>	**Victor 8125** / released 28 June 1929 to ?
	HMV DB 1280
<u>*45 rpm*</u>	**RCA Victor ERAT 19** / released 24 December 1953 to April 1956
<u>*33⅓ rpm*</u>	**RCA Victor LCT-1138** / released 19 February 1954 to ?
	RCA Victor LM-1909 / released August 1955 to 1 October 1958
	Camden CBL-100 / released 16 August 1957 to 1 September 1961
	RCA Victor LM-6705 / released 16 February 1962 to ?
<u>*CD*</u>	**Nimbus NI 7801**
	Nimbus NI 1795
	Nimbus NI 1777
	Nimbus NI 7805 / released 1989 to ?
	Pearl GEM 0090 / released 2001 to ?

166. **BELLINI:** *Norma—Mira, O Norma!*
> > *Part 1:* ("Mira, O Norma!")
> > *Part 2:* ("Cedi ... deh! cedi!")

Rosa Ponselle, Marion Telva & Metropolitan Opera House Orchestra - Giulio Setti.
> matrix: *Side 1* **CVE-49703** -1 -<u>2</u>
> matrix: *Side 2* **CVE-49704** -<u>1</u> -2
> > speed: *78.26 rpm*

<u>*78 rpm*</u>	**Victor 8110** / released 29 March 1929 to ?
	HMV DB 1276
<u>*45 rpm*</u>	**RCA Victor WCT-6**
	RCA Victor ERAT 19 / released 24 December 1953 to April 1956

33⅓ rpm   **RCA Victor LCT-1004** / released 29 December 1950 to ?
              Camden CBL-100 / released 16 August 1957 to 1 September 1961
              RCA Victor LM-6705 / released 16 February 1962 to ?
              La Voix de Son Maître FJLP 5010
              La Voce del Padrone QJLP 101
CD   **Nimbus NI 1795**
              Nimbus NI 1777
              Nimbus NI 7805 / released 1989 to ?
              ASV Living Era CD AJA 5177 / released 1995 to ?
              Pearl GEM 0090 / released 2001 to ?

Session of 7 February 1929, 2:30 to 5:00 P.M.; Liederkranz Hall, NYC.
[Information from Victor archives.]

167. **SAINT-SAËNS:** *Samson et Dalila—Arrêtez, ô mes frères!*
     Giovanni Martinelli, Metropolitan Opera Chorus & Metropolitan Opera House Orchestra - Giulio Setti.
              matrix: **CVE-49714 -1 -2**
              speed: 77.42 rpm
78 rpm   **Victor 8159** / released 27 September 1929 to ?
              HMV VB 42
33⅓ rpm   **Camden CAL-274** / released 23 December 1955 to 1 April 1958

168. **SAINT-SAËNS:** *Samson et Dalila—L'as-tu donc.*
     Giovanni Martinelli, Metropolitan Opera Chorus & Metropolitan Opera House Orchestra - Giulio Setti.
              matrix: **CVE-49715 -1 -2 -3**
              speed: 77.42 rpm
78 rpm   **Victor 8159** / released 27 September 1929 to ?
              HMV VB 42
33⅓ rpm   **Camden CAL-274** / released 23 December 1955 to 1 April 1958

169. **SAINT-SAËNS:** *Samson et Dalila—L'aube qui blanchit.*
     Metropolitan Opera Chorus & Metropolitan Opera House Orchestra - Giulio Setti.
              matrix: **BVE-49716 -1 -2**
              speed: 77.42 rpm
78 rpm   **Victor 4152** / released 27 September 1929 to ?

170. **GOUNOD:** *Roméo et Juliette—Prologue.*
     Metropolitan Opera Chorus & Metropolitan Opera House Orchestra - Giulio Setti.
              matrix: **BVE-49717 -1 -2**
              speed: 77.42 rpm
78 rpm   **Victor 4152** / released 27 September 1929 to ?

Session of 28 March 1929, 2:00 to 4:05 P.M.; Liederkranz Hall, NYC.
[Information from Victor archives.]

171. **BIZET:** *Carmen—Dans l'air.* *("Chœur des cigarières")*
    Metropolitan Opera Chorus & Metropolitan Opera House Orchestra - Giulio Setti.
        matrix: **BVE-49799 -1 -2**
           speed: 78.26 rpm
    78 rpm   **Victor 4173** / released 28 February 1930 to ?

172. **WEBER:** *Der Freischütz—Was gleicht wohl auf Erden.* *("Jägerchor")*
    Metropolitan Opera Chorus & Metropolitan Opera House Orchestra - Giulio Setti.
        matrix: **BVE-51100 -1 -2**
           speed: 78.26 rpm
    78 rpm   **Victor 4173** / released 28 February 1930 to ?

173. **GIORDANO:** *Andrea Chénier—Coro pastorelle.*
    Metropolitan Opera Chorus & Metropolitan Opera House Orchestra - Giulio Setti.
        matrix: **BVE-51101 -1 -2**
           speed: 78.26 rpm
    78 rpm   **Victor 4199** / released 1932 to ?

174. **VERDI:** *Il Trovatore—Squilli, echeggi la tromba guerriera.* *("Soldiers' Chorus")*
    Metropolitan Opera Chorus & Metropolitan Opera House Orchestra - Giulio Setti.
        matrix: **CVE-51102 -1**
           speed: 78.26 rpm
    78 rpm   **Victor 9484** / released 29 November 1929 to ?
                    HMV AW 166
    Cassette   **MET 509-C**
    33⅓ rpm   **RCA Victrola VIC-1684**
                    RCA VL 42799 / released 1979 to ?
    CD   **MET 509-CD** / released 1990 to ?

Session of 3 April 1929, 2:00 to 4:00 P.M.; Liederkranz Hall, NYC.
[Information from Victor archives.]

175. **PUCCINI:** *Tosca—Te Deum.*
    Lawrence Tibbett, Metropolitan Opera Chorus & Metropolitan Opera House Orchestra - Giulio Setti.
    (Fausto Cleva, assistant and organ)
        matrix: **CVE-51116 -1 -2 -3** (Take -4 from the session of 10 April 1929 was also used after
    take -2 showed signs of wear. Please see also the session of 10 April 1929.)
           speed: 76.59 rpm
    78 rpm   **Victor 8124** / released 31 May 1929 to ?
                    HMV DB 1298
    CD   **RCA Victor 7808-2-RG** / released 1989 to ?

176. BIZET: *Carmen—Chanson du Toréador.* *("Toreador Song")*
   Lawrence Tibbett, L. M. Belleri, F. Cingolani, Metropolitan Opera Chorus & Metropolitan Opera House Orchestra - Giulio Setti. (Fausto Cleva, assistant)
   matrix: **CVE-51117** **-1** **-2** **-3**

Not released. This was re-recorded during the session of 8 April 1929, and that performance was released.

Session of 8 April 1929, 1:45 to 4:30 P.M.; Liederkranz Hall, NYC.
[Information from Victor archives.]

177. GOUNOD: *Faust—Le veau d'or.*
   Ezio Pinza, Metropolitan Opera Chorus & Metropolitan Opera House Orchestra - Giulio Setti. (Fausto Cleva, assistant)
   matrix: **BVE-51133** **-1** **-2** **-3**
   speed: 76.59 rpm

78 rpm	**Victor 3053** / released 31 January 1930 to ?
	Victor 1753
	HMV DA 1108
33⅓ rpm	**Camden CAL-401** / released 22 November 1957 to 1 September 1961
	RCA Victor LM-6705 / released 16 February 1962 to ?
	RCA Victrola VIC-1470 / released October 1969 to ?
	MET 105 / released 1978 to ?
Cassette	**MET 105-C** / released 1980 to ?
CD	**RCA Gold Seal 09026-61245-2** / released 1990 to ?
	MET 105-CD / released 1989 to ?
	Nimbus NI 7875
	Preiser 89050 / released 1991 to ?
	Pearl GEMM 9306 / released 1988 to ?

178. BELLINI: *Norma—Ah! del Tebro.*
   Ezio Pinza, Metropolitan Opera Chorus & Metropolitan Opera House Orchestra - Giulio Setti. (Fausto Cleva, assistant)
   matrix: **BVE-51134** **-1** **-2** **-3**
   speed: 76.59 rpm

78 rpm	**Victor 3053** / released 31 January 1930 to ?
	Victor 1753
	HMV DA 1108
	HMV DA 1412
33⅓ rpm	**Camden CAL-401** / released 22 November 1957 to 1 September 1961
	RCA Victor LM-6705 / released 16 February 1962 to ?
	RCA Victrola VIC-1470 / released October 1969 to ?
	MET 105 / released 1978 to ?
Cassette	**MET 105-C** / released 1980 to ?

CD   **RCA Gold Seal 09026-61245-2** / released 1990 to ?
              MET 105-CD / released 1989 to ?
              Pearl GEM 0090 / released 2001 to ?
              Preiser 89050 / released 1991 to ?

179. **BIZET:** *Carmen—Chanson du Toréador.* *("Toreador Song")*
     Lawrence Tibbett, L. M. Belleri, F. Cingolani, Metropolitan Opera Chorus & Metropolitan Opera House Orchestra - Giulio Setti. (Fausto Cleva, assistant)
     matrix: **CVE-51117 -4 -5** (Both takes were used. Take -4 was used in the RCA Victor CD reissue.)
     speed: 76.59 rpm
This had been recorded previously during the session of 3 April 1929, but those takes were not passed for release. Both takes from this session were issued. After take -5 showed signs of wear, take -4 was used.

78 rpm   **Victor 8124** / released 31 May 1929 to ?
              Victor M-329 (14202)
              HMV DB 1298
33⅓ rpm   **Camden CAL-171** / released 5 March 1954 to 1 July 1957
              RCA Victor LM-6705 / released 16 February 1962 to ?
              RCA Victrola VIC-1340 / released 20 May 1968 to ?
              RCA Victrola VIC-1340(e) (synthetic stereo) / released 20 May 1968 to ?
CD   **RCA Victor 7808-2-RG** / released 1989 to ?
              MET 219-CD / released 1993 to ?
              Nimbus NI 7825
              Nimbus NI 1742

180. **VERDI:** *Il Trovatore—Ah, se l'error.*
     Metropolitan Opera Chorus & string orchestra and organ - Giulio Setti. (Fausto Cleva, assistant)
     [For unknown reasons, the Metropolitan Opera House Orchestra is not credited on the label. An unknown voice sings the lines of the Count di Luna. There is no separate voice for the lines of Ferrando, but this is identical to a chorus part.]
     matrix: **BVE-51135 -1 -2 -3**
     speed: 76.59 rpm
78 rpm   **Victor 4199** / released 1932 to ?
33⅓ rpm   **RCA Victrola VIC-1684**

Session of 10 April 1929, 2:00 to 5:05 P.M.; Liederkranz Hall, NYC.
[Information from Victor archives.]

181. **PONCHIELLI:** *La Gioconda—Assassini!*
     Giacomo Lauri-Volpi, Metropolitan Opera Chorus & Metropolitan Opera House Orchestra - Giulio Setti.
     [All solo voices except that of Enzo Grimaldo, sung by Lauri-Volpi, are omitted.]
     matrix: **BVE-51148 -1 -2**
     speed: 78.26 rpm

78 rpm	**Victor 3052** / released 1 November 1929 to ?
	HMV DA 1081
	Addison Foster AGSA 28
33⅓ rpm	**RCA LM 20117**
Cassette	**MET 524-C** / released 1994 to ?
CD	**MET 524-CD** / released 1994 to ?
	Preiser 89012 / released 1990 to ?

182. **OFFENBACH:** *Les Contes d'Hoffmann—Il était une fois à la cour d'Eisenach.*
    ("Légende de Kleinzach")
       Giacomo Lauri-Volpi, Metropolitan Opera Chorus & Metropolitan Opera House Orchestra - Giulio Setti.
              matrix: **BVE-51149 -1 -2 -3**
                 speed: 78.26 rpm

78 rpm	**Victor 3052** / released 1 November 1929 to ?
	HMV DA 1081
	Addison Foster AGSA 28
33⅓ rpm	**RCA Victrola VIC-1394** / released 24 January 1969 to ?
	RCA LM 20117
CD	**Nimbus NI 7845**
	Preiser 89012 / released 1990 to ?
	Pearl GEMM 0078 / released 2000 to ?

183. **WOLF-FERRARI:** *I Gioielli della Madonna—Aprila, o bella.* *("Serenata Rafaele"*
    "Rafaele's Serenade")
       Giuseppe De Luca, Metropolitan Opera Chorus & Metropolitan Opera House Orchestra - Giulio Setti.
              matrix: **BVE-51150 -1 -2**
    Not released by Victor. This was re-recorded during the session of 24 March 1930, and that performance
    was released.

184. **VERDI:** *La Traviata—Di Provenza il mar.*
       Giuseppe De Luca & Metropolitan Opera House Orchestra - Giulio Setti. (Fausto Cleva, assistant)
              matrix: **CVE-51151 -1 -2**
                 speed: 78.26 rpm

78 rpm	**Victor 7086** / released 30 August 1929 to ?
	HMV DB 1340
33⅓ rpm	**Camden CAL-320** / released 21 September 1956 to 1 October 1958
	Camden CDN.1012
	RCA Red Seal CRM8-5177 / released 1984 to ?
Cassette	**RCA Red Seal CRK8-5177** / released 1984 to ?
CD	**RCA Red Seal 09026-61580-2** / released 1993 to ?
	Preiser 89073 / released 1993 to ?

185. **PUCCINI:** *Tosca—Te Deum.*
       Lawrence Tibbett, Metropolitan Opera Chorus & Metropolitan Opera House Orchestra - Giulio Setti.
       (Fausto Cleva, assistant and organ)

matrix: **CVE-51116 -4** (Take -4 from this session was used after take -2 from the session of 3 April 1929 showed signs of wear. See also the session of 3 April 1929.)

speed: 78.26 rpm

78 rpm   **Victor 8124**

              Victor M-1015 (11-8861) / released 1 September 1945 to ?

33⅓ rpm   **Camden CAL-171** / released 3 March 1954 to 1 July 1957

              RCA Victrola VIC-1340 / released 20 May 1968 to ?

              RCA Victrola VIC-1340(e) (synthetic stereo) / released 20 May 1968 to ?

CD   **Nimbus NI 7825**

              Nimbus NI 1783

              Nimbus NI 7819

Session of 24 March 1930, 2:00 to 4:30 P.M.; Liederkranz Hall, NYC.

[Information from Victor archives.]

186. **BEETHOVEN:** *Fidelio—O welche Lust!* *("Prisoners' Chorus")*
Metropolitan Opera Chorus & Metropolitan Opera House Orchestra - Giulio Setti.
(Fausto Cleva, assistant)
          matrix: **CVE-59722 -1 -2**
              speed: 78.26 rpm
78 rpm   **Victor 11249** / released 1932 to ?

187. **WOLF-FERRARI:** *I Gioielli della Madonna—Aprila, o bella.* *("Serenata Rafaele"*
"Rafaele's Serenade")
Giuseppe De Luca, Metropolitan Opera Chorus & Metropolitan Opera House Orchestra - Giulio Setti.
(Fausto Cleva, assistant and piano; Nickolos Laucella, flute)
          matrix: **BVE-51150 -3 -4 -5**
              speed: 78.26 rpm
This was previously recorded during the session of 10 April 1929, but the takes made on that day were not released.
78 rpm   **Victor 3055** / released 26 December 1930 to 1936
              HMV DA 1169
33⅓ rpm   **Camden CAL-320** / released 21 September 1956 to 1 October 1958
              Camden CDN.1012
CD   **Preiser 89073** / released 1993 to ?
              Nimbus NI 7815
              Preiser 89073 / released 1993 to ?

188. **VERDI:** *Il Trovatore—Per me ora fatale.*
Giuseppe De Luca, Metropolitan Opera Chorus & Metropolitan Opera House Orchestra - Giulio Setti.
(Fausto Cleva, assistant) [An unknown voice sings the few lines of Ferrando.]
          matrix: **BVE-59723 -1 -2**
              speed: 78.26 rpm
78 rpm   **Victor 3055** / released 26 December 1930 to 1936
              HMV DA 1169

33⅓ rpm	**Camden CAL-320** / released 21 September 1956 to 1 October 1958
	Camden CDN.1012
	RCA Victrola VIC-1684
	RCA VL 42799 / released 1979 to ?
	RCA TVM1-7209 / released 1976 to ?
CD	**Preiser 89073** / released 1993 to ?
	Nimbus NI 7815

Session of 9 April 1930, 2:00 to 4:15 P.M.; Liederkranz Hall, NYC.
[Information from Victor archives.]

189. **DONIZETTI:** *La Favorita—Splendon più belle in ciel.*
    Ezio Pinza, Metropolitan Opera Chorus & Metropolitan Opera House Orchestra - Giulio Setti. (Fausto Cleva, organ)

        matrix: **CVE-59745 -1 -2 -3** (Take -1 used for 78 rpm; take -3 for RCA Victrola VIC-1418)
        speed: 79.12 rpm

78 rpm	**Victor 7552** / released 29 July 1932 to ?
	HMV DB 1750
33⅓ rpm	**RCA Victrola VIC-1418** / released April 1969 to ?
CD	**Nimbus NI 7892/3**
	Preiser 89050 / released 1991 to ?

190. **VERDI:** *Il Trovatore—Abbietta zingara.*
    Ezio Pinza, Metropolitan Opera Chorus & Metropolitan Opera House Orchestra - Giulio Setti. (Fausto Cleva, chimes)

        matrix: **CVE-59746 -1 -2**

Although this was once listed in Victor catalogues as being *"in preparation"* for 78 rpm release on record 8231, it was not released by Victor and had to wait for a Camden 33⅓ rpm release. According to recordings authority Lawrence F. Holdridge, the Addison Foster 78 rpm was never actually issued by Foster as a producer and distributor of re-pressed historical recordings, but a few copies *"escaped"* after his death.

78 rpm	**Addison Foster AGSB 103**
33⅓ rpm	**Camden CAL-401** / released 22 November 1957 to 1 September 1961.
	RCA Victrola VIC-1470 / released October 1969 to ?
	RCA Victrola VIC-1684
	RCA VL 42799 / released 1979 to ?
Cassette	**MET 509-C**
CD	**RCA Gold Seal 09026-61245-2** / released 1990 to ?
	MET 509-CD / released 1990 to ?
	Preiser 89050 / released 1991 to ?
	Pearl GEM 0214

Session of 17 April 1930, 2:00 to 4:50 P.M.; Liederkranz Hall, NYC.
[Information from Victor archives.]

191. **WAGNER:** *Lohengrin—Treulich geführt. ("Brautchor" "Bridal Chorus")*
> *Metropolitan Opera Chorus & Metropolitan Opera House Orchestra - Giulio Setti. (Fausto Cleva, assistant and organ)*
>> matrix: **CVE-59754 -1 -2 -3**
>> *speed: 78.26 rpm*
>
> *78 rpm*   **Victor 11249** / released 1932 to ?
> *Cassette*   **MET 510-C** / released 1990 to ?
> *CD*   **MET 510-CD** / released 1990 to ?

192. **GOUNOD:** *Faust—La Kermesse. ("Vin ou bière")*
> *Metropolitan Opera Chorus & Metropolitan Opera House Orchestra - Giulio Setti. (Fausto Cleva, assistant)*
> [An unknown voice sings the few lines of Wagner.]
>> matrix: **CVE-59755 -1 -2**
>> *speed: 78.26 rpm*
>
> *78 rpm*   **Victor 9697** / released 28 November 1930 to ?

193. **GOUNOD:** *Faust—Valse. ("Ainsi que la brise")*
> *Metropolitan Opera Chorus & Metropolitan Opera House Orchestra - Giulio Setti.*
> *(Fausto Cleva, assistant)*   [All solo voices are omitted except for a few lines of Siebel.]
>> matrix: **CVE-59756 -1 -2**
>> *speed: 78.26 rpm*
>
> *78 rpm*   **Victor 9697** / released 28 November 1930 to ?

Session of 19 January 1934, 2:30 to 5:30 P.M.; Studio No. 2, 24th St. Studios, NYC.
[Information from Victor archives.]

194. **HANSON:** *Merry Mount—'Tis an earth defiled.*
> *Lawrence Tibbett & Metropolitan Opera Orchestra - Wilfred Pelletier.*
>> matrix: **CS-81086 -1 -1A -2 -2A** (Take -1 was used for the 78 rpm edition and presumably other reissues with the exception that take -2 was used only for the Delos CD.)
>
> *78 rpm*   **Victor 7959** / released April 1934 to ? [The Metropolitan Opera Orchestra is not credited on the label. This first issues of this recording included a sheet with a synopsis of the opera and a description of this aria.]
>   **Victor M-1015** (11-8932) [The Metropolitan Opera Orchestra is not credited on the label.] / released 1 September 1945 to ?
>   **HMV ED 24**
> *33⅓ rpm*   **Camden CAL-171** / released 5 March 1954 to 1 July 1957
>   **New World Records NW 241** / released 1978 to ?
> *CD*   **RCA Victor 7808-2-RG** / released 1989 to ?
>   **Nimbus NI 7881**
>   **Delos DE 5500** / released 1997 to ?

195. GRUENBERG: *Emperor Jones—Standin' in the need of prayer.*
   Lawrence Tibbett & Metropolitan Opera Orchestra - Wilfred Pelletier.
          matrix: **CS-81087** **-1** **-1A** **-2** **-2A** (Take -2A was used for the 78 rpm edition and presumably other reissues. Take -1 was used for the RCA Victor CD reissue.)

78 rpm	**Victor 7959** / released April 1934 to ? [The Metropolitan Opera Orchestra is not credited on the label. This first issues of this recording included a sheet with a synopsis of the opera and a description of this aria.]
33⅓ rpm	**RCA Victor LM-6705** / released 16 February 1962 to ?
	MET 403 / released 1984 to ?
	New World Records NW 241 / released 1978 to ?
Cassette	**MET 403-C** / released 1984 to ?
CD	**RCA Victor 7808-2-RG** / released 1989 to ?
	Nimbus NI 7881

<u>**Session of 4 October 1934, 2:00 to 4:00 P.M.**</u>
[Information from Columbia archives.]

196. *Ciribiribin* **(Dole, Pestalozza).**
   Grace Moore, Metropolitan Opera House Male Chorus & orchestra - Wilfred Pelletier.
          matrix: **B 16101** **-A** **-B** **-C** (Other takes may also have been used.)

78 rpm	**Brunswick 6994** / released 18 October 1934 to ?
	Columbia 35969 / released 31 January 1941 to ?
	Brunswick 01922
	Brunswick 500.497 [The Metropolitan Opera House Male Chorus is not credited on this French issue label.]
	Rex 8871
	Columbia DB-1801
CD	**Pearl GEMM CD 9116** / released 1994 to ?

197. *One Night of Love* **(Gus Kahn, Victor Schertzinger).**
   Grace Moore, Metropolitan Opera House Male Chorus & orchestra - Wilfred Pelletier.
          matrix: **B 16102** **-A** **-B** **-C** (Other takes may also have been used.)

78 rpm	**Brunswick 6994** / released 18 October 1934 to ?
	Columbia 35969 / released 31 January 1941 to ?
	Brunswick 01922
	Brunswick 500.497 [The Metropolitan Opera House Male Chorus is not credited on this French issue label.]
	Rex 8871
	Columbia DB-1801
33⅓ rpm	**Epic SN-6059**
CD	**Pearl GEMM CD 9116** / released 1994 to ?

Performance of 12 November 1938; NBC Studio 8-H, RCA Building, NYC.

This thrilling performance from a radio broadcast may be the only commercial recording of Arturo Toscanini conducting an ensemble of the Metropolitan Opera for which he conducted 479 performances between 1908 and 1915. None of the issues listed below, even the official Testament recording, gives credit to the Metropolitan Opera Chorus. Although none of these three issues contain the radio announcer's remarks, the participation of the Metropolitan Opera Chorus is clear from Olin Downes' review of the performance in the *New York Times* on the next day, and the Metropolitan Opera Chorus is also listed in Robert Hupka's discography of the recorded repertoire of Arturo Toscanini in Samuel Antek's *This Was Toscanini* (New York: The Vanguard Press, 1963).

198. **MEYERBEER:** *Dinorah—Overture.*
> *Metropolitan Opera Chorus & NBC Symphony Orchestra - Arturo Toscanini.*
>
> <u>CD</u>   **Testament SBT2 1404** / released 2006 to ?
> **Music & Arts CD-898** / released 1995 to ?
> **Dell'Arte CDDA 9021** / released 1990 to ?

Session of 3 May 1939, 1:30 to 5:07 P.M.; Studio No. 2, 24th St. Studios, NYC.

[Information from Victor archives.]

199. *Battle Hymn of the Republic* (Julia Ward Howe, William Steffe). (orchestrated by Bruno Reibold)
> *Lawrence Tibbett & Metropolitan Opera Orchestra - Wilfred Pelletier.*
> matrix: **BS-036848 -1 -1A**
>
> <u>78 rpm</u>   **Victor 4433** / released July 1939 to ? [The Metropolitan Opera Orchestra is not listed on the record labels or in the catalogues.]

200. **VERDI:** *Otello—Inaffia l'ugola! ("Brindisi")*
> *Lawrence Tibbett, Nicholas Massue, Herman Dreeben, Metropolitan Opera Chorus (Fausto Cleva, director) & Metropolitan Opera Orchestra - Wilfred Pelletier.*
> matrix: **CS-036849 -1 -1A**
> For release information please see items #215 and #216.

201. **VERDI:** *Simon Boccanegra—Plebe! Patrizi! ... Piango su voi.*
> *Lawrence Tibbett, Rose Bampton, Giovanni Martinelli, Leonard Warren, Robert Nicholson, Metropolitan Opera Chorus (Fausto Cleva, director) & Metropolitan Opera Orchestra - Wilfred Pelletier.*
> matrix: **CS-036850 -1 -1A**
>
> <u>78 rpm</u>   **Victor 15642** / released November 1939 to ? [A letter from Leonard Warren to Victor in 1946 requested that his name be removed from the record labels for this side. Beginning in 1946 the 78 rpm labels no longer listed his name. This letter is in the Victor archives.]
> **HMV DB 3950**
> **HMV DB 6018**
> <u>33⅓ rpm</u>   **RCA Victor LCT-6701** / released 22 April 1955 to ?
> **RCA Victor LM-6171** / released September 1966 to 1 March 1967
> **RCA Gold Seal AGM3-4805** / released 1983 to ?
> **Time-Life STLM-111** / released 1981 to ?
> <u>CD</u>   **RCA Gold Seal CGK2-4805** / released 1983 to ?
> **MET 219-CD** / released 1993 to ?

Pearl GEMM CD 9914 / released 1991 to ?
Nimbus NI 7825

202. **VERDI:** *Otello—Vieni, l'aula è deserta.*
    Lawrence Tibbett, Giovanni Martinelli, Nicholas Massue & Metropolitan Opera Orchestra –
    Wilfred Pelletier.
        matrix: **CS-036851 -1 -1A -2 -2A**
    For release information please see items #215 and #223.

203. *My Own United States* (Stanislaus Stangé, Julian Edwards). (orchestrated by Bruno Reibold)
    Lawrence Tibbett & Metropolitan Opera Orchestra - Wilfred Pelletier.
        matrix: **BS-036852 -1 -1A -2 -2A**
   78 rpm   **Victor 4433** / released July 1939 to ? [The Metropolitan Opera Orchestra is not listed on
              the record labels or in the catalogues.]

204. **VERDI:** *Simon Boccanegra—Figlia, a tal nome palpito.*
    Rose Bampton, Lawrence Tibbett & Metropolitan Opera Orchestra - Wilfred Pelletier.
        matrix: **CS-036853 -1 -1A**
   78 rpm   **Victor 15642** / released November 1939 to ? [The Metropolitan Opera Orchestra is not
              listed on the record labels or in the catalogues.]
              HMV DB 3950
              HMV DB 6018
   45 rpm   **RCA Victor ERAT-24**
   CD   **RCA Victor 7808-2-RG** / released 1989 to ?
              Pearl GEMM CD 9914 / released 1991 to ?

205. **VERDI:** *Otello—E qual certezza sognate ... Era la notte.*
    Lawrence Tibbett & Metropolitan Opera Orchestra - Wilfred Pelletier.
        matrix: **CS-036854 -1 -1A**
    For release information please see items #215 and #220.

206. **VERDI:** *Otello—Credo in un Dio crudel.*
    Lawrence Tibbett & Metropolitan Opera Orchestra - Wilfred Pelletier.
        matrix: **CS-036855 -1 -1A** (This take was used for the 33⅓ rpm reissues on RCA Victrola
        VIC-1365 and RCA Victrola VIC-1185 and for the 45 rpm reissue on RCA Victor ERAT-24. Take -2
        made on 9 May was used for the 78 rpm issue and the 33⅓ rpm reissues on RCA Victor LCT-1138
        and RCA Victor LM-6705.)
        For release information please see items #215 and #217.

Session of 9 May 1939; Studio No. 2, 24th St. Studios, NYC.
[Information from Victor archives.]

207. **VERDI:** *Otello—Non pensateci più ... Ora e per sempre.*
    Giovanni Martinelli, Lawrence Tibbett & Metropolitan Opera Orchestra - Wilfred Pelletier.

matrix: **CS-036869 -1 -1A -2 -2A** (Take -1 was used for the 78 rpm edition, and take -2 was used for the 33⅓ rpm reissue.)
For release information please see items #215 and #219.

208. VERDI: *Otello—Oh! mostruosa colpa! ... Sì, pel ciel.*
Giovanni Martinelli, Lawrence Tibbett & Metropolitan Opera Orchestra - Wilfred Pelletier.
matrix: **CS-036870 -1 -1A -2 -2A** (Take -1 was used for the 78 rpm edition, and take -2 was used for the 33⅓ rpm reissue.)
For release information please items #215 and #221.

209. VERDI: *Otello—Dio! mi potevi scagliar.*
Giovanni Martinelli, Lawrence Tibbett & Metropolitan Opera Orchestra - Wilfred Pelletier.
matrix: **CS-036871 -1 -1A**
For release information please items #215 and #222.

210. VERDI: *Otello—Canzone del Salce. ("Willow Song" "Mia madre aveva una povera ancella")*
Helen Jepson & Metropolitan Opera Orchestra - Wilfred Pelletier.
matrix: **CS-036872 -1 -1A -2 -2A** (Take -1 was used for the 33⅓ rpm reissue, and take -2 was used for the 78 rpm edition.)
For release information please see item #215.

211. VERDI: *Otello—Niun mi tema.*
Giovanni Martinelli & Metropolitan Opera Orchestra - Wilfred Pelletier.
matrix: **CS-036873 -1 -1A**
For release information please see items #215 and #224.

212. VERDI: *Otello—Ave Maria.*
Helen Jepson & Metropolitan Opera Orchestra - Wilfred Pelletier.
matrix: **CS-036874 -1 -1A**
For release information please see item #215.

213. VERDI: *Otello—Già nella notte densa.*
Part 1: *("Già nella notte densa")*
Part 2: *("Ed io vedea fra le tue tempie oscure")*
Helen Jepson, Giovanni Martinelli & Metropolitan Opera Orchestra - Wilfred Pelletier.
matrix: *Side 1* **CS-036875 -1 -1A**
matrix: *Side 2* **CS-036876 -1 -1A**
For release information please see item #215.

214. VERDI: *Otello—Credo in un Dio crudel.*
Lawrence Tibbett & Metropolitan Opera Orchestra - Wilfred Pelletier.
matrix: **CS-036855 -2 -2A** (This take was used for the 78 rpm edition and for the 33⅓ rpm reissues on RCA Victor LCT-1138 and RCA Victor LM-6705. Take -1 made during the session of 3 May 1939 was used for the for the 33⅓ rpm reissues on RCA Victrola VIC-1365 and RCA Victrola VIC-1185 and for the 45 rpm reissue on RCA Victor ERAT-24.)
For release information please see items #215 and #218.

215. **All of the *Otello* recordings made during the sessions of 3 May 1939 and 9 May 1939 were released as a set with the following cast and side arrangement:**

VERDI: *Otello — Excerpts.*

Otello   **Giovanni Martinelli**
Iago   **Lawrence Tibbett**
Desdemona   **Helen Jepson**
Cassio   **Nicholas Massue**
Roderigo   **Herman Dreeben**

**Metropolitan Opera Chorus
(Fausto Cleva, director)
Metropolitan Opera Orchestra
Wilfred Pelletier**

Side 1	*Inaffia l'ugola! ("Brindisi")* [#200]
Sides 2 & 3	*Già nella notte densa.* [#213]
Side 4	*Credo in un Dio crudel.* [#206 & 214]
Side 5	*Non pensateci più ... Ora e per sempre.* [#207]
Side 6	*E qual certezza sognate ... Era la notte.* [#205]
Side 7	*Oh! mostruosa colpa! ... Sì, pel ciel.* [#208]
Side 8	*Dio! mi potevi scagliar.* [#209]
Side 9	*Vieni, l'aula è deserta.* [#202]
Side 10	*Canzone del Salce. ("Willow Song" "Mia madre aveva una povera ancella")* [#210]
Side 11	*Ave Maria.* [#212]
Side 12	*Niun mi tema.* [#211]

78 rpm	**Victor M-620** (15801/6) *manual sequence* / released January 1940 to ?
	Victor AM-620 (15807/12) *slide automatic sequence* / released January 1940 to ?
	Victor DM-620 (15989/94) *drop automatic sequence*
	HMV DB 5788/93
	HMV DB 5716/21
33⅓ rpm	**RCA Victrola VIC-1365** / released August 1968 to ?
	RCA Victrola VIC-1185
CD	**Pearl GEMM CD 9914** / released 1991 to ?

Selections from this set were also released as follows:

216. **VERDI: *Otello—Inaffia l'ugola! ("Brindisi")* [#200]**

CD	**MET 219-CD** / released 1993 to ?
	Nimbus 7825

217. **VERDI:** *Otello—Credo in un Dio crudel.* (take -1 of 3 May 1939) [#206]
      45 rpm   **RCA Victor ERAT-24**

218. **VERDI:** *Otello—Credo in un Dio crudel.* (take -2 of 9 May 1939) [#214]
      33⅓ rpm   **RCA Victor LCT-1138** / released 19 February 1954 to ?
                        RCA Victor LM-6705 / released 16 February 1962 to ?
      CD   **Nimbus NI 7825**

219. **VERDI:** *Otello—Non pensateci più ... Ora e per sempre.* [#207]
      Cassette   **MET 514-C** / released 1992 to ?
      CD   **MET 514-CD** / released 1992 to ?

220. **VERDI:** *Otello—E qual certezza sognate ... Era la notte.* [#205]
      Cassette   **MET 514-C** / released 1992 to ?
      CD   **MET 514-CD** / released 1992 to ?
                        Nimbus NI 7825

221. **VERDI:** *Otello—Oh! mostruosa colpa! ... Sì, pel ciel.* [#208]
      Cassette   **MET 514-C** / released 1992 to ?
      CD   **MET 514-CD** / released 1992 to ?

222. **VERDI:** *Otello—Dio! mi potevi scagliar.* [#209]
      33⅓ rpm   **Camden CAL-283** / released 23 December 1955 to 1 April 1958
                        RCA Victor LM-2710 / released 18 October 1963 to ?
                        MET 404 / released 1984 to ?
      Cassette   **MET 404-C** / released 1984 to ?

223. **VERDI:** *Otello—Vieni, l'aula è deserta.* [#202]
      Cassette   **MET 514-C** / released 1992 to ?
      CD   **MET 514-CD** / released 1992 to ?

224. **VERDI:** *Otello—Niun mi tema.* [#211]
      33⅓ rpm   **Camden CAL-283** / released 23 December 1955 to 1 April 1958
                        RCA Victor LM-2710 / released 18 October 1963 to ?

Session of 26 May 1940; Location? - Please see note below.

[Information from Victor archives and Rose Bampton.]

There is incomplete documentation in the Victor archives about this session and the following eight sessions through 26 June 1940. The record cards and session sheets in the archives do not list the artists involved except for the sessions of 25 and 26 June 1940 when the artists' names are added. The session sheets, which are headed with "NEWSPAPER SYNDI-CATE RECORDS. PUBLISHERS SERVICE SYMPHONY ORCHESTRA. (PERSONAL RECORDS)," list the sessions of 26 May, 27 May and 17 June as taking place in Philadelphia's Academy of Music and the other six sessions as taking place in New York's Town Hall. Rose Bampton, who sang in the three sessions ascribed to Philadelphia and whose husband, Wilfred Pelletier, also conducted the 17 June session ascribed to Philadelphia, objected to the location being given as Phila-delphia. She wrote to the compiler of this discography, "Regarding the recordings of Tristan, Tannhauser and Lohengrin, I do not recall that they were made in Philadelphia!! Also Aida, Pagliacci, Faust and Carmen!! I think everything was made in Town Hall." Eleanor Steber, who sang in the session of 17 June, also gave the location as Town Hall. Rose Bampton also stated that "Met people" were used throughout these sessions.

The distinctive voices of Rose Bampton, Eleanor Steber, Leonard Warren, Arthur Carron, and Raoul Jobin are easy to identify on these recordings, but, with the absence of hard written proof of the artists involved, all artist listings in these sessions are given in quotation marks followed by a question mark. Since the sessions of 25 and 26 June do have some artists' names listed in the files, those names are given without quotation marks followed by a question mark and are underlined to emphasize that there is written as well as aural proof to identify their participation. Please see the *Introduc-tion* to the discography for more about these sessions. It is important to remember that official documentation for participa-tion by ensembles of the Metropolitan Opera is lacking.

225. **WAGNER:** *Tristan und Isolde—Prelude, Part 1.*
"*Metropolitan Opera Orchestra - William Steinberg*" ?
matrix: **CS-050313** -**1** -1A
For release information please see item #239.

226. **?**
matrix: **CS-050314** **?** (This matrix number is unaccounted for. It may have been a spoiled at-tempt at the second part of the prelude.)

227. **WAGNER:** *Tristan und Isolde—Wohl kenn' ich Irlands Königin.*
"*Arthur Carron, Rose Bampton & Metropolitan Opera Orchestra - William Steinberg*" ?
matrix: **CS-050315** -1 -1A -**1R**
For release information please see items #239 and #240.

228. **WAGNER:** *Tristan und Isolde—Mild und leise.* ("*Liebestod*")
"*Rose Bampton & Metropolitan Opera Orchestra - William Steinberg*" ?
matrix: **CS-050316** -1 -1A -2 -2A -**1R** -2R
This was also recorded during the next session, but that day's take was not issued.
For release information please see items #239 and #247.

229. **WAGNER:** *Tristan und Isolde—Seligste Frau! Heil! König Marke, Heil!*
"*Rose Bampton, Lydia Summers, Arthur Carron, Metropolitan Opera Chorus & Metropolitan Opera Orchestra - William Steinberg*" ?
matrix: **CS-050317** -1 -1A -2 -2A -1R -**2R**
For release information please see items #239 and #241.

230. **WAGNER:** *Tristan und Isolde—O sink' hernieder.*
"*Rose Bampton, Arthur Carron & Metropolitan Opera Orchestra - William Steinberg*" ?
matrix: **CS-050318** -1 -**1A** -1R
For release information please see items #239 and #242.

231. **WAGNER:** *Tristan und Isolde—Einsam wachend.* ("*Brangäne's Warning*")
"*Lydia Summers, Rose Bampton, Arthur Carron & Metropolitan Opera Orchestra - William Steinberg*" ?
matrix: **CS-050319** -**1** -1A
For release information please see items #239 and #243.

232. **WAGNER:** *Tristan und Isolde—Das Schiff? Siehst du's noch nicht?*
   "Arthur Carron & Metropolitan Opera Orchestra - William Steinberg" ?
   matrix: **CS-050320 -1 -1A**
   For release information please see item #239.

233. **WAGNER:** *Tristan und Isolde—Wohin nun Tristan scheidet.*
   "Rose Bampton, Arthur Carron & Metropolitan Opera Orchestra - William Steinberg" ?
   matrix: **CS-050321 -1 -1A**
   For release information please see items #239 and #246.

234. **WAGNER:** *Tristan und Isolde—So stürben wir.*
   "Rose Bampton, Lydia Summers, Arthur Carron & Metropolitan Opera Orchestra – William Steinberg" ?
   matrix: **CS-050322 -1 -1A -1R -2R**
   For release information please see items #239 and #244.

235. **WAGNER:** *Tristan und Isolde—O ew'ge Nacht.*
   "Rose Bampton, Arthur Carron & Metropolitan Opera Orchestra - William Steinberg" ?
   matrix: **CS-050322 -1 -1A -1R -2R**
   For release information please see items #239 and #245.

Session of 27 May 1940; Location?
[Information from Victor archives and Rose Bampton.]
Please see the note under the session of 26 May 1940.

236. **WAGNER:** *Tristan und Isolde—Prelude to Act III.*
   "Metropolitan Opera Orchestra - William Steinberg" ?
   matrix: **CS-050326 -1 -1A**
   For release information please see item #239.

237. **WAGNER:** *Tristan und Isolde—Prelude, Part 2.*
   "Metropolitan Opera Orchestra - William Steinberg" ?
   matrix: **CS-050327 -1 -1A -1R -2R**
   For release information please see item #239.

238. **WAGNER:** *Tristan und Isolde—Mild und leise.* *("Liebestod")*
   "Rose Bampton & Metropolitan Opera Orchestra - William Steinberg" ?
   matrix: **CS-050316 -3 -3A**
   This was recorded successfully during the previous day's session and that take was issued.
   Not released.

239. All of the *Tristan und Isolde* recordings made during the sessions of 26 May 1940 and 27 May 1940 were released as a set with the following cast and side arrangement. Please see the note at the beginning of the 26 May 1940 session.

WAGNER: *Tristan und Isolde — Excerpts.*

Tristan	**Arthur Carron**
Isolde	**Rose Bampton**
Brangäne	**Lydia Summers**

Metropolitan Opera Chorus
Metropolitan Opera Orchestra
William Steinberg

Sides 1 & 2	*Prelude.* [#225 & #237]
Side 3	*Wohl kenn' ich Irlands Königin.* [#227]
Side 4	*Seligste Frau! Heil! König Marke, Heil!* [#229]
Side 5	*O sink' hernieder.* [#230]
Side 6	*Einsam wachend.* [#231]
Side 7	*So stürben wir.* [#234]
Side 8	*O ew'ge Nacht.* [#235]
Side 9	*Wohin nun Tristan scheidet.* [#233]
Side 10	*Prelude to Act III.* [#236]
Side 11	*Das Schiff? Siehst du's noch nicht?* [#232]
Side 12	*Mild und leise.* ("*Liebestod*") [#228]

78 rpm	**World's Greatest Operas SR-76/81**
	Music Appreciation O 211
33⅓ rpm	**Camden CAL-224** / released January 1954 to 30 November 1956
	Parade 1012 [Parade also issued 9039, a 45 rpm disc with *Mild und leise.*]
	Parade OP-111 (2 discs) [with added narration by Milton Cross]
	Music Appreciation Series WWL-20212

Selections from this set were also released as follows:

240. **WAGNER:** *Tristan und Isolde—Wohl kenn' ich Irlands Königin.* [#227]

    CD   **VAI Audio VAIA 1084** / released 1995 to ?

241. **WAGNER:** *Tristan und Isolde—Seligste Frau! Heil! König Marke, Heil!* [#229]

    CD   **VAI Audio VAIA 1084** / released 1995 to ?

242. **WAGNER:** *Tristan und Isolde—O sink' hernieder.* [#230]

    CD   **VAI Audio VAIA 1084** / released 1995 to ?

243. **WAGNER:** *Tristan und Isolde—Einsam wachend. ("Brangäne's Warning")* [#231]
    CD   **VAI Audio VAIA 1084** / released 1995 to ?

244. **WAGNER:** *Tristan und Isolde—So stürben wir.* [#234]
    CD   **VAI Audio VAIA 1084** / released 1995 to ?

245. **WAGNER:** *Tristan und Isolde—O ew'ge Nacht.* [#235]
    CD   **VAI Audio VAIA 1084** / released 1995 to ?

246. **WAGNER:** *Tristan und Isolde—Wohin nun Tristan scheidet.* [#233]
    CD   **VAI Audio VAIA 1084** / released 1995 to ?

247. **WAGNER:** *Tristan und Isolde—Mild und leise. ("Liebestod")* [#228]
    CD   **VAI Audio VAIA 1084** / released 1995 to ?

Session of 27 May 1940; Location? continued.

248. **WAGNER:** *Tannhäuser—Nach Rom gelangt' ich so. ("Romerzählung" "Rome Narrative")*
    "Arthur Carron & Metropolitan Opera Orchestra - William Steinberg" ?
        matrix: **CS-050328 -1 -1A**
    For release information please see item #256.

249. **WAGNER:** *Tannhäuser—Dich, teure Halle.*
    "Rose Bampton & Metropolitan Opera Orchestra - William Steinberg" ?
        matrix: **CS-050329 -1 -1A -1R**
    For release information please see items #256 and #257.

250. **WAGNER:** *Tannhäuser—O du mein holder Abendstern. ("Evening Star")*
    "Mack Harrell & Metropolitan Opera Orchestra - William Steinberg" ?
        matrix: **CS-050330 -1 -1A**
    For release information please see items #256 and #258.

251. **WAGNER:** *Lohengrin—Das süsse Lied verhallt.*
    "Rose Bampton, Arthur Carron & Metropolitan Opera Orchestra - William Steinberg" ?
        matrix: **CS-050331 -1 -1A**
    For release information please see items #263 and #266.

252. **WAGNER:** *Lohengrin—In fernem Land.*
    "Arthur Carron & Metropolitan Opera Orchestra - William Steinberg" ?
        matrix: **CS-050332 -1 -1A**
    For release information please see item #263.

Session of 28 May 1940; Town Hall, NYC.
[Information from Victor archives and Rose Bampton.]
Please see the note under the session of 26 May 1940.

253. **WAGNER:** *Tannhäuser—Einzug der Gäste.* *("Fest-Marsch" "Entrance of the Guests")*
   "Metropolitan Opera Chorus & Metropolitan Opera Orchestra - William Steinberg" ?
      matrix: **CS-050333 -1 -1A**
      For release information please see item #256.

254. **WAGNER:** *Tannhäuser—Elisabeth!*
   *"Arthur Carron, Mack Harrell, Beal Hober, Metropolitan Opera Chorus & Metropolitan Opera Orchestra –
   William Steinberg" ?*
      matrix: **CS-050334 -1 -1A**
      For release information please see item #256.

255. **WAGNER:** *Tannhäuser—Geliebter, komm! Sieh dort die Grotte.*
   *"Beal Hober, Arthur Carron, Metropolitan Opera Chorus & Metropolitan Opera Orchestra –
   William Steinberg" ?*
      matrix: **CS-050335 -1 -1A**
      For release information please see item #256.

256. All of the *Tannhäuser* recordings made during the sessions of 27 May 1940 and 28 May 1940
   were released as a set with the following cast and side arrangement. Please see the note at the
   beginning of the 26 May 1940 session.

WAGNER: *Tannhäuser — Excerpts.*

Tannhäuser	**Arthur Carron**
Elisabeth	**Rose Bampton**
Wolfram	**Mack Harrell**
Venus	**Beal Hober**

Metropolitan Opera Chorus
Metropolitan Opera Orchestra
William Steinberg

Side 1	*Geliebter, komm! Sieh dort die Grotte.* [#255]
Side 2	*Dich, teure Halle.* [#249]
Side 3	*Einzug der Gäste.* *("Fest-Marsch" "Entrance of the Guests")* [#253]
Side 4	*O du mein holder Abendstern.* *("Evening Star")* [#250]
Side 5	*Nach Rom gelant' ich so.* *("Romerzählung" "Rome Narrative")* [#248]
Side 6	*Elisabeth!* [#254]

78 rpm	**World's Greatest Operas SR-64/6** / released September 1940 to ?
	Music Appreciation O 207
33⅓ rpm	**Camden CAL-233** / released January 1955 to 1 July 1957
	Camden CFL-101
	Parade 1011 [Parade also issued 9038, a 45 rpm disc with *O du mein holder Abendstern.*]
	Parade OP-107 [with added narration by Milton Cross]
	Music Appreciation Series WWL-20211

Selections from this set were also released as follows:

257. **WAGNER:** *Tannhäuser—Dich, teure Halle.* [#249]
     CD   **VAI Audio VAIA 1084** / released 1995 to ?

258. **WAGNER:** *Tannhäuser—O du mein holder Abendstern.("Evening Star")* [#250]
     33⅓ rpm   **Camden CAL-249**

Session of 28 May 1940; Town Hall, NYC. continued.

259. **WAGNER:** *Lohengrin—Mein Herr und Gott. ("Königs Gebet")*
     "Norman Cordon, Arthur Carron, Rose Bampton, Lydia Summers, Mack Harrell, Metropolitan Opera Chorus & Metropolitan Opera Orchestra - William Steinberg" ?
     matrix: **CS-050336 -1 -1A -1R**
     For release information please see items #263 and #265.

260. **WAGNER:** *Lohengrin—Durch Gottes Sieg.*
     "Arthur Carron, Rose Bampton, Lydia Summers, Mack Harrell, Norman Cordon, Metropolitan Opera Chorus & Metropolitan Opera Orchestra - William Steinberg" ?
     matrix: **CS-050337 -1 -1A -1R**
     For release information please see item #263.

261. **WAGNER:** *Lohengrin—Prelude to Act III & Treulich geführt. ("Brautchor" "Bridal Chorus")*
     "Metropolitan Opera Chorus & Metropolitan Opera Orchestra - William Steinberg" ?
     matrix: **CS-050338 -1 -1A**
     For release information please see item #263.

262. **WAGNER:** *Lohengrin—Einsam in trüben Tagen. ("Elsas Traum" "Elsa's Dream")*
     "Rose Bampton, Norman Cordon, Metropolitan Opera Chorus & Metropolitan Opera Orchestra – William Steinberg" ?
     matrix: **CS-050339 -1 -1A -1R -2R -3R**
     For release information please see items #263 and #264.

263. All of the *Lohengrin* recordings made during the sessions of 27 May 1940 and 28 May 1940
     were released as a set with the following cast and side arrangement. Please see the note at the
     beginning of the 26 May 1940 session.

WAGNER: *Lohengrin* — *Excerpts.*

Lohengrin	**Arthur Carron**
Elsa	**Rose Bampton**
Ortrud	**Lydia Summers**
Friedrich	**Mack Harrell**
Heinrich	**Norman Cordon**

Metropolitan Opera Chorus
Metropolitan Opera Orchestra
William Steinberg

Side 1	*Einsam in trüben Tagen. ("Elsas Traum" "Elsa's Dream")* [#262]
Side 2	*Mein Herr und Gott. ("Königs Gebet")* [#259]
Side 3	*Durch Gottes Sieg.* [#260]
Side 4	*Prelude to Act III & Treulich geführt. ("Brautchor" "Bridal Chorus")* [#261]
Side 5	*Das süsse Lied verhallt.* [#251]
Side 6	*In fernem Land.* [#252]

78 rpm   **World's Greatest Operas SR-73/5**
            Music Appreciation O 210

33⅓ rpm   **Camden CAL-223** / released January 1955 to 1 July 1957
            Camden CFL-101
            Parade 1006 [Parade also issued 9037, a 45 rpm disc with the *Prelude to Act III & Treulich geführt.*]
            Parade OP-110 [with added narration by Milton Cross]
            Music Appreciation Series WWL-20206

Selections from this set were also released as follows:

264. **WAGNER:** *Lohengrin—Einsam in trüben Tagen. ("Elsas Traum" "Elsa's Dream")*
     [#262]
     CD   **VAI Audio VAIA 1084** / released 1995 to ?

265. **WAGNER:** *Lohengrin—Mein Herr und Gott. ("Königs Gebet")* [#259]
     Cassette **MET 510-C** / released 1990 to ?
     CD   **MET 510-CD** / released 1990 to ?

266. **WAGNER:** *Lohengrin—Das süsse Lied verhallt.* [#251]
     CD   **VAI Audio VAIA 1084** / released 1995 to ?

Session of 28 May 1940; Town Hall, NYC. continued.

267. **VERDI:** *Aïda—Gloria all' Egitto.*
   "Metropolitan Opera Chorus & Metropolitan Opera Orchestra - Wilfred Pelletier" ?
   matrix: **CS-050340** -1 -1A **-1R** -1AR
   For release information please see item #313.

268. **VERDI:** *Aïda—Che veggo! Egli? Mio Padre!*
   "Rose Bampton, Lydia Summers, Arthur Carron, Lorenzo Alvary, Norman Cordon, Leonard Warren, Metropolitan Opera Chorus & Metropolitan Opera Orchestra - Wilfred Pelletier" ?
   matrix: **CS-050341** -1 -1A **-1R** -1AR
   For release information please see items #313 and #316.

Session of 30 May 1940; Town Hall, NYC.
[Information from Victor archives and Rose Bampton.]
Please see the note under the session of 26 May 1940.

269. **GOUNOD:** *Faust—La Kermesse.* *("Vin ou bière")*
   "George Cehanovsky, Metropolitan Opera Chorus & Metropolitan Opera Orchestra - Wilfred Pelletier" ?
   matrix: **CS-050342** -1 -1A **-2** **-2A** (both takes were used)
   For release information please see item #305.

270. **GOUNOD:** *Faust—Chœur des Soldats.* *("Soldiers' Chorus")*
   "Metropolitan Opera Chorus & Metropolitan Opera Orchestra - Wilfred Pelletier" ?
   matrix: **CS-050343** **-1** **-1A** (both takes were used)
   For release information please see item #305.

271. **GOUNOD:** *Faust—Le veau d'or & Choral des épées.*
   "Norman Cordon, George Cehanovsky, Metropolitan Opera Chorus & Metropolitan Opera Orchestra – Wilfred Pelletier" ?
   matrix: **CS-050344** -1 **-1A** -1R
   For release information please see item #305.

272. **VERDI:** *Aïda—La fatal pietra.*
   "Rose Bampton, Arthur Carron, Metropolitan Opera Chorus & Metropolitan Opera Orchestra - Wilfred Pelletier" ?
   matrix: **CS-050345** -1 **-1A** -1R **-1AR** (both takes were used)
   For release information please see items #313 and #319.

273. **VERDI:** *Aïda—O terra, addio.*
   "Rose Bampton, Arthur Carron, Lydia Summers, Metropolitan Opera Chorus & Metropolitan Opera Orchestra - Wilfred Pelletier" ?
   matrix: **CS-050346** -1 **-1A**
   For release information please see items #313 and #320.

274. **LEONCAVALLO:** *Pagliacci—Andiam!*
   "Arthur Carron, Metropolitan Opera Chorus & Metropolitan Opera Orchestra - Wilfred Pelletier" ?

matrix: **CS-050347** -1 -1A -<u>**1R**</u> -2R
For release information please see item #299.

275. **PUCCINI:** *La Bohème—Quando me'n vo' & Act II Finale.*
   "Annamary Dickey, Eleanor Steber, George Cehanovsky & Metropolitan Opera Chorus, Metropolitan Opera Orchestra - Wilfred Pelletier" ?
      matrix: **CS-050348** -1 -<u>**1A**</u>
   For release information please see item #364.

276. **PUCCINI:** *Madama Butterfly—Ier l'altro, il Consolato & Ancora un passo.*
   "Armand Tokatyan, Eleanor Steber, George Cehanovsky, P. Bontempi, Metropolitan Opera Chorus & Metropolitan Opera Orchestra - Wilfred Pelletier" ?
      matrix: **CS-050349** -<u>**1**</u> -1A
   For release information please see items #355 and #356.

Session of 31 May 1940; Town Hall, NYC.
[Information from Victor archives and Rose Bampton.]
Please see the note under the session of 26 May 1940.

277. **LEONCAVALLO:** *Pagliacci—No, Pagliaccio non son! & Finale.*
   "Arthur Carron, George Cehanovsky, (soprano is not Steber), Metropolitan Opera Chorus & Metropolitan Opera Orchestra - Wilfred Pelletier" ?
      matrix: **CS-050350** -<u>**1**</u> -1A
   For release information please see item #299.

278. **BIZET:** *Carmen—Habañera. ("L'amour est un oiseau rebelle") & Séguedille.*
   ("Près des remparts de Séville")
   "Joan Peebles, Metropolitan Opera Chorus & Metropolitan Opera Orchestra - Wilfred Pelletier" ?
      matrix: **CS-050351** -<u>**1**</u> -1A
   For release information please see items #344 and #345.

279. **BIZET:** *Carmen—Chanson du Toréador. ("Toreador Song")*
   "Leonard Warren, Joan Peebles, Metropolitan Opera Chorus & Metropolitan Opera Orchestra - Wilfred Pelletier" ?
      matrix: **CS-050352** -<u>**1**</u> -1A -1R
   For release information please see items #344 and #346.

280. **BIZET:** *Carmen—Carmen, il en temps encore.*
   "Raoul Jobin, Joan Peebles, Metropolitan Opera Chorus & Metropolitan Opera Orchestra – Wilfred Pelletier" ?
      matrix: **CS-050353** -<u>**1**</u> -1A
   For release information please see item #344.

281. **GOUNOD:** *Faust—Valse. ("Ainsi que la brise")*
   "Eleanor Steber, Armand Tokatyan, (unknown mezzo sings the few words of Siebel), Norman Cordon, Metropolitan Opera Chorus & Metropolitan Opera Orchestra - Wilfred Pelletier" ?

matrix: **CS-050354 -1 -1A**
For release information please see items #305 and #306.

282. **VERDI:** *La Traviata—Libiamo, libiamo ne' lieti calici.* *("Brindisi")*
"Eleanor Steber, Armand Tokatyan, Metropolitan Opera Chorus & Metropolitan Opera Orchestra – Wilfred Pelletier" ?
matrix: **CS-050355 -1 -1A**
For release information please see items #325 and #326.

283. **VERDI:** *La Traviata—Di sprezzo degno ... Ah sì! che feci!*
"Leonard Warren, Eleanor Steber, Armand Tokatyan, Metropolitan Opera Chorus & Metropolitan Opera Orchestra - Wilfred Pelletier" ?
matrix: **CS-050356 -1 -1A**
[Record labels incorrectly read *"Finale to Opera."*]
For release information please see items #325 and #330.

284. **VERDI:** *Rigoletto—Questo o quella. & Ah, più di Ceprano.*
"Armand Tokatyan, Norman Cordon, P. Bontempi, Metropolitan Opera Chorus & Metropolitan Opera Orchestra - Wilfred Pelletier" ?
matrix: **CS-050357 -1 -1A**
For release information please see items #336 and #337.

285. **PUCCINI:** *Madama Butterfly—Humming Chorus & Tu, tu piccolo Iddio!*
"Eleanor Steber, Metropolitan Opera Chorus & Metropolitan Opera Orchestra - Wilfred Pelletier" ?
matrix: **CS-050358 -1 -1A**
For release information please see items #355 and #361.

Session of 5 June 1940; Town Hall, NYC.
[Information from Victor archives.]
Please see the note under the session of 26 May 1940.

286. **MOZART:** *Le Nozze di Figaro—Se a caso madama. & Che soave zefiretto.*
"Annamary Dickey, Norman Cordon, Vivian Della Chiesa & Metropolitan Opera Orchestra - William Steinberg" ?
matrix: **CS-050361 -1 -1A -2 -2A**
For release information please see item #292.

287. **MOZART:** *Le Nozze di Figaro—Non più andrai. & Aprite, presto aprite.*
"Norman Cordon, Annamary Dickey, Lucielle Browning & Metropolitan Opera Orchestra – William Steinberg" ?
matrix: **CS-050362 -1 -1A**
For release information please see item #292.

288. **MOZART:** *Le Nozze di Figaro—Voi che sapete. & Aprite un po'.*
"Lucielle Browning, Norman Cordon & Metropolitan Opera Orchestra - William Steinberg" ?
matrix: **CS-050363 -1 -1A**
For release information please see item #292.

289. **MOZART:** *Le Nozze di Figaro—Susanna, or via sortite! & Crudel! perchè finora.*
  "*George Cehanovsky, Vivian Della Chiesa, Annamary Dickey & Metropolitan Opera Orchestra –
  William Steinberg*" ?
  matrix: **CS-050364** -<u>1</u> -1A
  For release information please see item #292.

290. **MOZART:** *Le Nozze di Figaro—Deh vieni, non tardar. & Porgi amor.*
  "*Annamary Dickey, Vivian Della Chiesa & Metropolitan Opera Orchestra – William Steinberg*" ?
  matrix: **CS-050365** -<u>1</u> -1A
  For release information please see item #292.

291. **MOZART:** *Le Nozze di Figaro—Overture.*
  "*Metropolitan Opera Orchestra - William Steinberg*" ?
  matrix: **CS-050366** -1 -1A -<u>2</u> -2A
  For release information please see item #292.

292. All of the *Nozze di Figaro* recordings made during this session of 5 June 1940 were released as a
set with the following cast and side arrangement. Please see the note at the beginning of the
26 May 1940 session.

MOZART: *Le Nozze di Figaro — Excerpts.*

Susanna	**Annamary Dickey**
Cherubino	**Lucielle Browning**
Countess	**Vivian Della Chiesa**
Figaro	**Norman Cordon**
Count Almaviva	**George Cehanovsky**

Metropolitan Opera Orchestra
William Steinberg

Side 1	*Overture.* [#291]
Side 2	*Se a caso madama. & Che soave zefiretto.* [#286]
Side 3	*Non più andrai. & Aprite, presto aprite.* [#287]
Side 4	*Deh vieni, non tardar. & Porgi amor.* [#290]
Side 5	*Susanna, or via sortite! & Crudel! perchè finora.* [#289]
Side 6	*Voi che sapete. & Aprite un po'.* [#288]

<u>78 rpm</u>	**World's Greatest Operas SR-82/4**
	Music Appreciation O 212
<u>33⅓ rpm</u>	**Camden CAL-227** / released January 1955 to 1 July 1957
	Camden CFL-101

Parade 1008 [Parade also issued 9039, a 45 rpm disc with the *Overture* and *Se a caso madama.*]
Parade OP-112 [with added narration by Milton Cross]
Music Appreciation Series WWL-20208

Session of 17 June 1940; Location?
[Information from Victor archives and Rose Bampton.]
Please see the note under the session of 26 May 1940.

293. **BIZET:** *Carmen—Prelude & Entr'acte to Act II.*
   "Metropolitan Opera Orchestra - Wilfred Pelletier" ?
   matrix: **CS-051100** -1 -1A -2 -2A
   For release information please see item #344.

294. **BIZET:** *Carmen—Nous avons en tête une affaire. ("Quintet")*
   "Joan Peebles, Thelma Votipka, Helen Oelheim, George Cehanovsky, P. Bontempi & Metropolitan Opera Orchestra - Wilfred Pelletier" ?
   matrix: **CS-051101** -1 -1A -2 -2A
   For release information please see item #344.

295. **LEONCAVALLO:** *Pagliacci—Prologue.*
   "Leonard Warren & Metropolitan Opera Orchestra - Wilfred Pelletier" ?
   matrix: **CS-051102** -1 -1A -2 -2A
   For release information please see items #299 and #300.

296. **LEONCAVALLO:** *Pagliacci—Vesti la giubba.*
   "Arthur Carron & Metropolitan Opera Orchestra - Wilfred Pelletier" ?
   matrix: **CS-051103** -1 -1A -2 -2A
   For release information please see items #299 and #302.

297. **LEONCAVALLO:** *Pagliacci—Decidi il mio destin.*
   "Eleanor Steber, George Cehanovsky, Leonard Warren & Metropolitan Opera Orchestra – Wilfred Pelletier" ?
   matrix: **CS-051104** -1 -1A -1R -2R
   For release information please see items #299 and #301.

298. **LEONCAVALLO:** *Pagliacci—O Colombina & Arlecchin! Colombina!*
   "P. Bontempi, Eleanor Steber, Leonard Warren, Arthur Carron & Metropolitan Opera Orchestra – Wilfred Pelletier" ?
   matrix: **CS-051105** -1 -1A
   For release information please see item #299.

299. All of the *Pagliacci* recordings made during the sessions of 30 May 1940, 31 May 1940 and 17 June 1940 were released as a set with the following cast and side arrangement. Please see the note at the beginning of the 26 May 1940 session.

LEONCAVALLO: *Pagliacci — Excerpts.*

Canio	**Arthur Carron**
Nedda	**Eleanor Steber**
Tonio	**Leonard Warren**
Beppe	**P. Bontempi**
Silvio	**George Cehanovsky**

Metropolitan Opera Chorus
Metropolitan Opera Orchestra
Wilfred Pelletier

Side 1	*Prologue.*	[#295]
Side 2	*Andiam!*	[#274]
Side 3	*Decidi il mio destin.*	[#297]
Side 4	*Vesti la giubba.*	[#296]
Side 5	*O Colombina & Arlecchin! Colombina!*	[#298]
Side 6	*No, Pagliaccio non son! & Finale.*	[#277]

78 rpm   **World's Greatest Operas SR-70/2**
               Music Appreciation O 209

33⅓ rpm   **Camden CAL-226** / released 2 June 1954 to 1 July 1957
               Camden CFL-101
               Parade 1004 [Parade also issued 9037, a 45 rpm disc with *Vesti la giubba* and *O Colombina.*]
               Parade OP-109 [with added narration by Milton Cross]
               Music Appreciation Series WWL-20209

Selections from this set were also released as follows:

300. **LEONCAVALLO:** *Pagliacci—Prologue.* [#295]
     Cassette   **MET 512-C** / released 1991 to ?
     CD   **MET 512-CD** / released 1991 to ?
                   VAI Audio VAIA 1017 / released 1992 to ?

301. **LEONCAVALLO:** *Pagliacci—Decidi il mio destin.* [#297]
     CD   **VAI Audio VAIA 1072** / released 1994 to ?

302. **LEONCAVALLO:** *Pagliacci—Vesti la giubba.* [#296]
     33⅓ rpm   **Camden CAL-249**

Session of 17 June 1940; Location? continued.

303. **GOUNOD:** *Faust—Il se fait tard.*
   "Eleanor Steber, Armand Tokatyan & Metropolitan Opera Orchestra - Wilfred Pelletier" ?
   matrix: **CS-051106 -1 -1A**
   For release information please see items #305 and #307.

304. **GOUNOD:** *Faust—Marguerite! Ah! c'est la voix du bien-aimé! ... Alerte! alerte!*
   "Eleanor Steber, Armand Tokatyan, Norman Cordon & Metropolitan Opera Orchestra –
   Wilfred Pelletier" ?
   matrix: **CS-051107 -1 -1A**
   For release information please see items #305 and #308.

305. All of the *Faust* recordings made during the sessions of 30 May 1940, 31 May 1940 and 17 June 1940 were released as a set with the following cast and side arrangement. Please see the note at the beginning of the 26 May 1940 session.

GOUNOD: *Faust — Excerpts.*

Faust	**Armand Tokatyan**
Marguerite	**Eleanor Steber**
Méphistophélès	**Norman Cordon**
Valentin	**George Cehanovsky**
Wagner	**George Cehanovsky**

Metropolitan Opera Chorus
Metropolitan Opera Orchestra
Wilfred Pelletier

Side 1	*La Kermesse. ("Vin ou bière")*	[#269]
Side 2	*Le veau d'or & Choral des épées.*	[#271]
Side 3	*Valse. ("Ainsi que la brise")*	[#281]
Side 4	*Il se fait tard.*	[#303]
Side 5	*Chœur des Soldats. ("Soldiers' Chorus")*	[#270]
Side 6	*Marguerite! Ah! c'est la voix du bien-aimé! ... Alerte! alerte!* [#304]	

78 rpm	**World's Greatest Operas SR-48/50** / released 23 September 1940 to ?
	Music Appreciation O 202
33⅓ rpm	**Camden CAL-221** / released 24 May 1954 to 1 April 1958
	Camden CFL-101

Parade 1002 [Parade also issued 9033, a 45 rpm disc with *La Kermesse* and
Le veau d'or.]
Parade OP-102 [with added narration by Milton Cross]
Music Appreciation Series WWL-20203

<u>Selections from this set were also released as follows:</u>

306. **GOUNOD:** *Faust—Valse. ("Ainsi que la brise")* [#281]
    <u>*CD*</u>   **VAI Audio VAIA 1023** / released 1993 to ?

307. **GOUNOD:** *Faust—Il se fait tard.* [#303]
    <u>*CD*</u>   **VAI Audio VAIA 1023** / released 1993 to ?

308. **GOUNOD:** *Faust—Marguerite! Ah! c'est la voix du bien-aimé! ... Alerte! alerte!* [#304]
    <u>*Cassette*</u>   **MET 513-C** / released 1991 to ?
    <u>*CD*</u>   **MET 513-CD** / released 1991 to ?
                VAI Audio VAIA 1023 / released 1993 to ?

Session of 17 June 1940; Location? continued.

309. **VERDI:** *Aïda—Celeste Aïda.*
    "Arthur Carron & Metropolitan Opera Orchestra - Wilfred Pelletier" ?
        matrix: **CS-051108 -<u>1</u> -1A**
    For release information please see items #313 and #314.

310. **VERDI:** *Aïda—Ritorna vincitor!*
    "Rose Bampton & Metropolitan Opera Orchestra - Wilfred Pelletier" ?
        matrix: **CS-051109 -1 -<u>1A</u>**
    For release information please see items #313 and #315.

311. **VERDI:** *Aïda—Rivedrai le foreste imbalsamate.*
    "Rose Bampton, Leonard Warren & Metropolitan Opera Orchestra - Wilfred Pelletier" ?
        matrix: **CS-051110 -1 -<u>1A</u>**
    For release information please see items #313 and #317.

312. **VERDI:** *Aïda—Odimi, Aïda.*
    "Rose Bampton, Arthur Carron & Metropolitan Opera Orchestra - Wilfred Pelletier" ?
        matrix: **CS-051111 -1 -1A -1R -<u>2R</u>**
    For release information please see items #313 and #318.

313. **All of the *Aïda* recordings made during the sessions of 28 May 1940, 30 May 1940 and 17 June 1940 were released as a set with the following cast and side arrangement. Please see the note at the beginning of the 26 May 1940 session.**

VERDI: *Aïda — Excerpts.*

Aïda	**Rose Bampton**
Amneris	**Lydia Summers**
Radamès	**Arthur Carron**
Amonasro	**Leonard Warren**
Ramfis	**Norman Cordon**
King	**Lorenzo Alvary**

Metropolitan Opera Chorus
Metropolitan Opera Orchestra
Wilfred Pelletier

Side 1	*Celeste Aïda.*	[#309]
Side 2	*Ritorna vincitor.*	[#310]
Side 3	*Gloria all' Egitto.*	[#267]
Side 4	*Che veggo! Egli? Mio Padre!*	[#268]
Side 5	*Rivedrai le foreste imbalsamate.*	[#311]
Side 6	*Odimi, Aïda.*	[#312]
Side 7	*La fatal pietra.*	[#272]
Side 8	*O terra, addio.*	[#273]

78 rpm   **World's Greatest Operas SR-51/4** / released 21 August 1940 to ?
                 Music Appreciation O 203
33⅓ rpm   **Camden CAL-225** / released 25 May 1954 to 1 July 1957
                 Camden CFL-101
                 Parade 1003 [Parade also issued 9032, a 45 rpm disc with *O terra, addio.*]
                 Parade OP-103 [with added narration by Milton Cross]
                 Music Appreciation Series WWL-20201

Selections from this set were also released as follows:

314. **VERDI: *Aïda—Celeste Aïda.*** [#309]
    33⅓ rpm   **Camden CAL-249**

315. **VERDI: *Aïda—Ritorna vincitor!*** [#310]
    33⅓ rpm   **Camden CAL-249**
    CD   **VAI Audio VAIA 1084** / released 1995 to ?

316. **VERDI: *Aïda—Che veggo! Egli? Mio Padre!*** [#268]
    CD   **VAI Audio VAIA 1017** / released 1992 to ?

317. **VERDI:** *Aïda—Rivedrai le foreste imbalsamate.* [#311]
     CD   **VAI Audio VAIA 1017** / released 1992 to ?
                       VAI Audio VAIA 1084 / released 1995 to ?

318. **VERDI:** *Aïda—Odimi, Aïda.* [#312]
     CD   **VAI Audio VAIA 1084** / released 1995 to ?

319. **VERDI:** *Aïda—La fatal pietra.* [#272]
     CD   **VAI Audio VAIA 1084** / released 1995 to ?

320. **VERDI:** *Aïda—O terra, addio.* [#273]
     CD   **VAI Audio VAIA 1084** / released 1995 to ?

Session of 25 June 1940; Town Hall, NYC.
[Information from Victor archives and Rose Bampton.]
Please see the note under the session of 26 May 1940.

321. **VERDI:** *La Traviata—Ah! fors' è lui ... Sempre libera.*
     Eleanor Steber & *"Metropolitan Opera Orchestra" ? - Wilfred Pelletier*
                 matrix: **CS-051112 -1 -1A**
     For release information please see items #325 and #327.

322. **VERDI:** *La Traviata—Pura siccome un angelo.*
     Leonard Warren, Eleanor Steber & *"Metropolitan Opera Orchestra" ? - Wilfred Pelletier*
                 matrix: **CS-051113 -1 -1A -2 -2A**
     For release information please see items #325 and #328.

323. **VERDI:** *La Traviata—Così alla misera ... Morrò! morrò! la mia memoria.*
     Eleanor Steber, Leonard Warren & *"Metropolitan Opera Orchestra" ? - Wilfred Pelletier*
                 matrix: **CS-051114 -1 -1A**
     For release information please see item #325.

324. **VERDI:** *La Traviata—Parigi, o cara.*
     Eleanor Steber, Armand Tokatyan & *"Metropolitan Opera Orchestra" ? - Wilfred Pelletier*
                 matrix: **CS-051115 -1 -1A**
     For release information please see items #325 and #329.

325. All of the *Traviata* recordings made during the sessions of **31 May 1940** and **25 June 1940** were released as a set with the following cast and side arrangement. Please see the note at the beginning of the **26 May 1940** session.

VERDI: *La Traviata — Excerpts.*

Violetta	**Eleanor Steber**
Alfredo	**Armand Tokatyan**
Germont	**Leonard Warren**
D'Obigny	Lorenzo Alvary

Metropolitan Opera Chorus
Metropolitan Opera Orchestra
Wilfred Pelletier

Side 1	*Libiamo, libiamo ne'lieti calici. ("Brindisi")* [#282]
Side 2	*Ah! fors' è lui ... Sempre libera.* [#321]
Side 3	*Pura siccome un angelo.* [#322]
Side 4	*Così alla misera ... Morrò! morrò! la mia memoria.* [#323]
Side 5	*Parigi, o cara.* [#324]
Side 6	*Di sprezzo degno ... Ah sì! che feci!* [#283]

78 rpm **World's Greatest Operas SR-67/9** / released 1940 to ?
Music Appreciation O 208

33⅓ rpm **Camden CAL-227** / released January 1955 to 1 July 1957
Camden CFL-101
Parade 1009 [Parade also issued 9032, a 45 rpm disc with *Così alla misera* although it is incorrectly labeled as *Ah! fors' è lui.*]
Parade OP-108 [with added narration by Milton Cross]
Music Appreciation Series WWL-20205

Selections from this set were also released as follows:

326. **VERDI:** *La Traviata—Libiamo, libiamo ne' lieti calici. ("Brindisi")* [#282]
CD **VAI Audio VAIA 1072** / released 1994 to ?

327. **VERDI:** *La Traviata—Ah! fors' è lui ... Sempre libera.* [#321]
CD **VAI Audio VAIA 1072** / released 1994 to ?

328. **VERDI:** *La Traviata—Pura siccome un angelo.* [#322]
CD **VAI Audio VAIA 1017** / released 1992 to ?

329. **VERDI:** *La Traviata—Parigi, o cara.* [#324]
CD **VAI Audio VAIA 1072** / released 1994 to ?

330. **VERDI:** *La Traviata—Di sprezzo degno ... Ah sì! che feci!* [#283]
Cassette **MET 505-C** / released 1989 to ?
CD **MET 505-CD** / released 1989 to ?
VAI Audio VAIA 1017 / released 1992 to ?

Session of 25 June 1940; Town Hall, NYC continued.

331. **VERDI:** *Rigoletto—Caro nome.*
     Jean Dickenson & "Metropolitan Opera Orchestra" ? - Wilfred Pelletier
     matrix: **CS-051116 -1 -1A**
     For release information please see items #336 and #338.

332. **VERDI:** *Rigoletto—Cortigiani, vil razza dannata.*
     Leonard Warren & "Metropolitan Opera Orchestra" ? - Wilfred Pelletier
     matrix: **CS-051117 -1 -1A**
     For release information please see items #336 and #339.

333. **VERDI:** *Rigoletto—La donna è mobile. & Bella figlia dell'amore. ("Quartet")*
     Armand Tokatyan, Jean Dickenson, Lucielle Browning, Leonard Warren & "Metropolitan Opera Orchestra" ? - Wilfred Pelletier
     matrix: **CS-051118 -1 -2 -2A**
     For release information please see items #336 and #342.

334. **VERDI:** *Rigoletto—Tutte le feste ... Piangi, piangi, fanciulla.*
     Jean Dickenson, Leonard Warren & "Metropolitan Opera Orchestra" ? - Wilfred Pelletier
     matrix: **CS-051119 -1 -1A**
     For release information please see items #336 and #340.

335. **VERDI:** *Rigoletto—Compiuto pur quanto ... Sì, vendetta.*
     Jean Dickenson, Leonard Warren, Lorenzo Alvary (as both Monterone & Usciere) & "Metropolitan Opera Orchestra" ? - Wilfred Pelletier
     matrix: **CS-051120 -1 -1A**
     For release information please see items #336 and #341.

336. All of the *Rigoletto* recordings made during the sessions of 31 May 1940 and 25 June 1940 were released as a set with the following cast and side arrangement. Please see the note at the beginning of the 26 May 1940 session.

VERDI: *Rigoletto — Excerpts.*

Rigoletto	**Leonard Warren** (Sides 3, 4, 5, 6)
Rigoletto	**Norman Cordon** (Side 1)
Gilda	**Jean Dickenson**
Duke	**Armand Tokatyan**
Maddalena	**Lucielle Browning**
Monterone	**Lorenzo Alvary**
Borsa	**P. Bontempi**
Usciere	**Lorenzo Alvary**

Metropolitan Opera Chorus
Metropolitan Opera Orchestra
Wilfred Pelletier

Side 1	*Questo o quella. & Ah, più di Ceprano.* [#284]
Side 2	*Caro nome.* [#331]
Side 3	*Cortigiani, vil razza dannata.* [#332]
Side 4	*Tutte le feste ... Piangi, piangi, fanciulla.* [#334]
Side 5	*Compiuto pur quanto ... Sì, vendetta.* [#335]
Side 6	*La donna è mobile. & Bella figlia dell'amore. (Quartet)* [#333]

78 rpm **World's Greatest Operas SR-58/60** / released September 1940 to ?
     Music Appreciation O 205
33⅓ rpm **Camden CAL-226** / released 2 June 1954 to 1 July 1957
     Camden CFL-101
     Parade 1007 [Parade also issued 9038, a 45 rpm disc with *Caro nome.*]
     Parade OP-105 [with added narration by Milton Cross]
     Music Appreciation Series WWL-20210

<u>Selections from this set were also released as follows:</u>

337. **VERDI:** *Rigoletto—Ah, più di Ceprano.* [#284]
  CD   **VAI Audio VAIA 1017** / released 1992 to ?

338. **VERDI:** *Rigoletto—Caro nome.* [#331]
  33⅓ rpm **Camden CAL-249**

339. **VERDI:** *Rigoletto—Cortigiani, vil razza dannata.* [#332]
  CD   **VAI Audio VAIA 1017** / released 1992 to ?

340. **VERDI:** *Rigoletto—Tutte le feste ... Piangi, piangi, fanciulla.* [#334]
  CD   **VAI Audio VAIA 1017** / released 1992 to ?

341. **VERDI:** *Rigoletto—Compiuto pur quanto ... Sì, vendetta.* [#335]
  CD   **VAI Audio VAIA 1017** / released 1992 to ?

342. **VERDI:** *Rigoletto—Bella figlia dell'amore. (Quartet)* [#333]
  CD   **VAI Audio VAIA 1017** / released 1992 to ?

Session of 25 June 1940; Town Hall, NYC continued.

343. **BIZET:** *Carmen—Air de fleur. ("La fleur que tu m'avais jetée")*
  Raoul Jobin & "Metropolitan Opera Orchestra" ? - *Wilfred Pelletier*
   matrix: **CS-051121 -1 -1A -<u>2</u> -2A**
  For release information please see items #344 and #347.

344. All of the *Carmen* recordings made during the sessions of **31 May 1940, 17 June 1940** and **25 June 1940** were released as a set with the following cast and side arrangement. Please see the note at the beginning of the 26 May 1940 session.

BIZET: *Carmen — Excerpts.*

Carmen	**Joan Peebles**
Don José	**Raoul Jobin**
Escamillo	**Leonard Warren**
Frasquita	**Thelma Votipka**
Mercédès	**Helen Oelheim**
Dancairo	**George Cehanovsky**
Remendado	**P. Bontempi**

Metropolitan Opera Chorus
Metropolitan Opera Orchestra
Wilfred Pelletier

Side 1	*Prelude. & Entr'acte to Act II.* [#293]
Side 2	*Habañera ("L'amour est un oiseau rebelle") &* *Séguedille ("Près des remparts de Séville")* [#278]
Side 3	*Chanson du Toréador. ("Toreador Song")* [#279]
Side 4	*Nous avons en tête une affaire. ("Quintet")* [#294]
Side 5	*Air de fleur. ("La fleur que tu m'avais jetée")* [#343]
Side 6	*Carmen, il en temps encore.* [#280]

78 rpm	**World's Greatest Operas SR-45/7** / released 23 September 1940 to ?
	Music Appreciation O 201
33⅓ rpm	**Camden CAL-221** / released 24 May 1954 to 1 April 1958
	Camden CFL-101
	Parade 1001 [Parade also issued 9033, a 45 rpm disc with the *Prelude & Entr'acte to Act II.*]
	Parade OP-101 [with added narration by Milton Cross]
	Music Appreciation Series WWL-20202

Selections from this set were also released as follows:

345. **BIZET:** *Carmen—Habañera ("L'amour est un oiseau rebelle")* **& Séguedille** *("Près des remparts de Séville")* [#278]
     33⅓ rpm   **Camden CAL-249**

346. **BIZET:** *Carmen—Chanson du Toréador. ("Toreador Song")* [#279]
     33⅓ rpm   **Camden CAL-249**
     CD   **VAI Audio VAIA 1017** / released 1992 to ?

347. **BIZET:** *Carmen—Air de fleur. ("La fleur que tu m'avais jetée")* [#343]
     33⅓ rpm   **Camden CAL-249**

**Session of 25 June 1940; Town Hall, NYC continued.**

348. **PUCCINI:** *La Bohème—Addio dolce svegliare.* *("Quartet")*
     Eleanor Steber, Annamary Dickey, Armand Tokatyan, George Cehanovsky & "_Metropolitan Opera_
     Orchestra" ? - _Wilfred Pelletier_
           matrix: **CS-051122** -<u>1</u> -1A
     For release information please see items #364 and #367.

349. **PUCCINI:** *La Bohème—O Mimì, tu più non torni & Sono andati?*
     Armand Tokatyan, George Cehanovsky, Eleanor Steber & "_Metropolitan Opera Orchestra_" ? -
     Wilfred Pelletier
           matrix: **CS-051123** -<u>1</u> -1A
     For release information please see items #364 and #368.

350. **PUCCINI:** *La Bohème—Torno al nido la rondine (Finale).*
     Eleanor Steber, Annamary Dickey, Armand Tokatyan, George Cehanovsky, Lorenzo Alvary,
     "_Arthur Kent & Metropolitan Opera Orchestra_" ? - _Wilfred Pelletier_
           matrix: **CS-051124** -<u>1</u>
     For release information please see items #364 and #369.

**Session of 26 June 1940; Town Hall, NYC.**
[Information from Victor archives and Rose Bampton.]
Please see the note under the session of 26 May 1940.

351. **PUCCINI:** *Madama Butterfly—Bimba dagli occhi.*
     Eleanor Steber, Armand Tokatyan & "_Metropolitan Opera Orchestra_" ? - _Wilfred Pelletier_
           matrix: **CS-051125** -<u>1</u> -1A -<u>2</u> -2A
     For release information please see items #355 and #357.

352. **PUCCINI:** *Madama Butterfly—Dicon ch'oltre mare.*
     Eleanor Steber, Armand Tokatyan & "_Metropolitan Opera Orchestra_" ? - _Wilfred Pelletier_
           matrix: **CS-051126** -<u>1</u> -1A -<u>2</u> -2A
     For release information please see items #355 and #358.

353. **PUCCINI:** *Madama Butterfly—Un bel dì, vedremo.*
     Eleanor Steber & "_Metropolitan Opera Orchestra_" ? - _Wilfred Pelletier_
           matrix: **CS-051127** -<u>1</u> -1A
     For release information please see items #355 and #359.

354. **PUCCINI:** *Madama Butterfly—Scuoti quella fronda di ciliegio.* *("Flower Duet")*
     Eleanor Steber, Lucielle Browning & "_Metropolitan Opera Orchestra_" ? - _Wilfred Pelletier_
           matrix: **CS-051128** -<u>1</u> -1A
     For release information please see items #355 and #360.

355. All of the *Madama Butterfly* recordings made during the sessions of 30 May 1940, 31 May 1940 and 26 June 1940 were released as a set with the following cast and side arrangement. Please see the note at the beginning of the 26 May 1940 session.

PUCCINI: *Madama Butterfly — Excerpts.*

Cio-cio-san	**Eleanor Steber**
Pinkerton	**Armand Tokatyan**
Suzuki	**Lucielle Browning**
Sharpless	**George Cehanovsky**
Goro	**P. Bontempi**

Metropolitan Opera Chorus
Metropolitan Opera Orchestra
Wilfred Pelletier

Side 1	*Ier l'altro, il Consolato. & Ancora un passo.* [#276]
Side 2	*Bimba dagli occhi.* [#351]
Side 3	*Dicon ch'oltre mare.* [#352]
Side 4	*Un bel dì, vedremo.* [#353]
Side 5	*Scuoti quella fronda di ciliegio. ("Flower Duet")* [#354]
Side 6	*Humming Chorus & Tu, tu piccolo Iddio!* [#285]

78 rpm	**World's Greatest Operas SR-55/7** / released September 1940 to ?
	Music Appreciation O 204
33⅓ rpm	**Camden CAL-222** / released January 1955 to 1 October 1958
	Camden CFL-101
	Parade 1010 [Parade also issued 9031, a 45 rpm disc with *Un bel dì.*]
	Parade OP-104 [with added narration by Milton Cross]
	Music Appreciation Series WWL-20207

Selections from this set were also released as follows:

356. **PUCCINI:** *Madama Butterfly—Ier l'altro, il Consolato & Ancora un passo.* [#276]
   CD   **VAI Audio VAIA 1023** / released 1993 to ?

357. **PUCCINI:** *Madama Butterfly—Bimba dagli occhi.* [#351]
   CD   **VAI Audio VAIA 1023** / released 1993 to ?

358. **PUCCINI:** *Madama Butterfly—Dicon ch'oltre mare.* [#352]
   CD   **VAI Audio VAIA 1023** / released 1993 to ?

359. **PUCCINI:** *Madama Butterfly—Un bel dì, vedremo.* [#353]
   33⅓ rpm   **Camden CAL-249**
   CD   **VAI Audio VAIA 1023** / released 1993 to ?

360. **PUCCINI:** *Madama Butterfly—Scuoti quella fronda di ciliegio.* *("Flower Duet")* [#354]
  <u>*CD*</u>   **VAI Audio VAIA 1023** / released 1993 to ?

361. **PUCCINI:** *Madama Butterfly—Tu, tu piccolo Iddio!* [#285]
  <u>*CD*</u>   **VAI Audio VAIA 1023** / released 1993 to ?

<u>**Session of 26 June 1940; Town Hall, NYC continued.**</u>

362. **PUCCINI:** *La Bohème—Che gelida manina.*
  <u>Armand Tokatyan</u> & "Metropolitan Opera Orchestra" ? - <u>Wilfred Pelletier</u>
    matrix: **CS-051129 -1 -1A <u>-2</u> -2A**
  For release information please see items #364 and #365.

363. **PUCCINI:** *La Bohème—O soave fanciulla.*
  <u>Eleanor Steber</u>, <u>Armand Tokatyan</u> & "Metropolitan Opera Orchestra" ? - <u>Wilfred Pelletier</u>
    matrix: **CS-051130 -1 -1A -2 -2A <u>-3</u> -3A**
  For release information please see items #364 and #366.

364. All of the *La Bohème* recordings made during the sessions of 30 May 1940, 25 June 1940 and 26 June 1940 were released as a set with the following cast and side arrangement. Please see the note at the beginning of the 26 May 1940 session.

PUCCINI: *La Bohème — Excerpts.*

Mimì	**<u>Eleanor Steber</u>**
Rodolfo	**<u>Armand Tokatyan</u>**
Musetta	**<u>Annamary Dickey</u>**
Marcello	**<u>George Cehanovsky</u>**
Schaunard	**Arthur Kent**
Colline	**<u>Lorenzo Alvary</u>**

Metropolitan Opera Chorus
Metropolitan Opera Orchestra
<u>Wilfred Pelletier</u>

Side 1	*Che gelida manina.* [#362]
Side 2	*O soave fanciulla.* [#363]
Side 3	*Quando me'n vo' & Act II Finale.* [#275]
Side 4	*Addio dolce svegliare.* [#348]
Side 5	*O Mimì, tu più non torni & Sono andati?* [#349]
Side 6	*Torno al nido la rondine (Finale).* [#350]

78 rpm   **World's Greatest Operas SR-61/3** / released September 1940 to ?
                  Music Appreciation O 206
33⅓ rpm   **Camden CAL-222** / released January 1955 to 1 October 1958
                  Camden CFL-101
                  Parade 1005 [Parade also issued 9031, a 45 rpm disc with *Che gelida manina* and a
                      portion of *O soave fanciulla.*]
                  Parade OP-106 [with added narration by Milton Cross]
                  Music Appreciation Series WWL-20204

                  Selections from this set were also released as follows:

365. **PUCCINI:** *La Bohème—Che gelida manina.* [#362]
      33⅓ rpm   **Camden CAL-249**

366. **PUCCINI:** *La Bohème—O soave fanciulla.* [#363]
      33⅓ rpm   **Camden CAL-249**
      CD   **VAI Audio VAIA 1023** / released 1993 to ?

367. **PUCCINI:** *La Bohème—Addio dolce svegliare.* *("Quartet")* [#348]
      CD   **VAI Audio VAIA 1023** / released 1993 to ?

368. **PUCCINI:** *La Bohème—Sono andati?* [#349]
      CD   **VAI Audio VAIA 1023** / released 1993 to ?

369. **PUCCINI:** *La Bohème—Torno al nido la rondine (Finale).* [#350]
      CD   **VAI Audio VAIA 1023** / released 1993 to ?

Session of 14 July 1941, 2:00 to 5:30 P.M.
[Information from Columbia archives.]

370. **DONIZETTI:** *La Fille du Régiment—Chacun le sait.*
      Lily Pons & Metropolitan Opera Orchestra - Pietro Cimara
            matrix: **XCO 30934**
      For release information please see items #374 and #375.

371. **DONIZETTI:** *La Fille du Régiment—Il faut partir.*
      Lily Pons & Metropolitan Opera Orchestra - Pietro Cimara
            matrix: **XCO 30935**
      For release information please see items #374 and #376.

372. **DONIZETTI:** *La Fille du Régiment—Et mon cœur va changer.*
      Lily Pons & Metropolitan Opera Orchestra - Pietro Cimara
            matrix: **XCO 30936**
      For release information please see item #374.

373. DONIZETTI: *La Fille du Régiment—Salût à la France.*
Lily Pons & Metropolitan Opera Orchestra - Pietro Cimara
matrix: **XCO 30937**
For release information please see item #374.

374. All of the *Fille du Régiment* recordings were released as a set with the following side arrangement.

DONIZETTI: *La Fille du Régiment — Excerpts.*

Marie   **Lily Pons**

Metropolitan Opera Orchestra
Pietro Cimara

Side 1	*Chacun le sait.* [#370]
Side 2	*Il faut partir.* [#371]
Side 3	*Et mon cœur va changer.* [#372]
Side 4	*Salût à la France.* [#373]

78 rpm   **Columbia X-206** (71248/9-D) *manual sequence*
              Columbia MX-206 (72119/20-D) *automatic sequence*
              Columbia 264692/3
33⅓ rpm   **Odyssey Y 31152** [This edition incorrectly credits the Columbia Concert Orchestra instead of the Metropolitan Opera Orchestra.]
CD   **Sony Classical MH2K 60655** / released 1998 to ?

Selections from this set were also released as follows:

375. DONIZETTI: *La Fille du Régiment—Chacun le sait.* [#370]
78 rpm   **Columbia LOX 574**

376. DONIZETTI: *La Fille du Régiment—Il faut partir.* [#371]
78 rpm   **Columbia LOX 574**
33⅓ rpm   **Columbia D3M 34294** [This edition is a different incomplete take which concludes with a few words from the artist and another voice.]

Session of 22 December 1944, 8:00 to 11:00 P.M.

[Information from Columbia archives.]

The excerpts from *Boris Godunov* recorded during this session and the next one were recorded with the Metropolitan Opera Chorus but not with the Metropolitan Opera Orchestra. However, all of the selections in this set are included here for completeness.

377. **MUSSORGSKY:** *Boris Godunov—Monologue.* (in Italian as *"Ho il poter supremo!"*)
   ("I have attained the highest power")
   Ezio Pinza & Orchestra - Emil Cooper
       matrix: **XCO 34036**
       For release information please see items #385 and #386.

378. **MUSSORGSKY:** *Boris Godunov—Clock Scene.* (in Italian as *"Oh, soffocai!"*)
   Ezio Pinza & Orchestra - Emil Cooper
       matrix: **XCO 34037**
       For release information please see items #385 and #387.

379. **MUSSORGSKY:** *Boris Godunov—Pimen's Tale.* (in Italian as *"Un umil frate"*)
   Ezio Pinza & Orchestra - Emil Cooper
       matrix: **XCO 34039**
       For release information please see items #385 and #388.

380. **MUSSORGSKY:** *Boris Godunov—Farewell of Boris.* (in Italian as *"Addio, mio figlio, io muoio"*)
   Ezio Pinza & Orchestra - Emil Cooper
       matrix: **XCO 34040**
       For release information please see items #385 and #389.

Session of 23 December 1944, 3:00 to 6:30 P.M.

[Information from Columbia archives.]

The excerpts from *Boris Godunov* recorded during this session and the previous one were recorded with the Metropolitan Opera Chorus but not with the Metropolitan Opera Orchestra. However, all of the selections in this set are included here for the sake of completeness.

381. **MUSSORGSKY:** *Boris Godunov—Prologue.* (in Italian)
       Part 1: *("Ebbene! Siete voi di Stucco?")*
       Part 2: *("Ma perchè tu ci abbandoni?")*
   Metropolitan Opera Chorus (Giacomo Spadoni, chorus master) & Orchestra - Emil Cooper.
       matrix: *Side 1* **XCO 34032**
       matrix: *Side 2* **XCO 34033**
       For release information please see item #385.

382. **MUSSORGSKY:** *Boris Godunov—Coronation Scene.* (in Italian)
       Part 1: *("Salute ed ogni ben al nostro Zar!")*
       Part 2: *("O trist' è il cor!")*

*Ezio Pinza (in Part 2), Metropolitan Opera Chorus (Giacomo Spadoni, chorus master) & Orchestra –
Emil Cooper.*
      matrix: *Side 1* **XCO 34034**
      matrix: *Side 2* **XCO 34035**
For release information please see item #385.

383. **MUSSORGSKY:** *Boris Godunov—Polonaise.* (in Italian as *"Il vostro amor mi lascia
indifferente"*)
    Metropolitan Opera Chorus (Giacomo Spadoni, chorus master) & orchestra - Emil Cooper.
      matrix: **XCO 34038**
For release information please see item #385.

384. **MUSSORGSKY:** *Boris Godunov—Death of Boris.* (in Italian as *"Dio! è il suon funebre!"*)
    Ezio Pinza, Metropolitan Opera Chorus (Giacomo Spadoni, chorus master) & Orchestra - Emil Cooper.
      matrix: **XCO 34041**
For release information please see items #385 and #390.

385. All of the *Boris Godunov* recordings made during the sessions of 22 and 23 December 1944
were released as a set with the following side arrangement.

MUSSORGSKY: *Boris Godunov — Excerpts.*
(sung in Italian)

Boris   **Ezio Pinza**

**Metropolitan Opera Chorus
(Giacomo Spadoni, chorus master)
Orchestra**
Emil Cooper

Sides 1 & 2	*Prologue.* [#381]	
Sides 3 & 4	*Coronation Scene.* [#382]	
Side 5	*Monologue.* [#377]	
Side 6	*Clock Scene.* [#378]	
Side 7	*Polonaise.* [#383]	
Side 8	*Pimen's Tale.* [#379]	
Side 9	*Farewell of Boris.* [#380]	
Side 10	*Death of Boris.* [#384]	

78 rpm   **Columbia M-563** (71646/50-D) *manual sequence* / released July 1945 to ?
                Columbia MM-563 (71651/5-D) *automatic sequence* / released July 1945 to ?
                Columbia 15840/4

33⅓ rpm   **Columbia ML 4115**
                Odyssey Y 33129 / released 22 November 1974 to ?
                Columbia WL 5004
                Philips ABL3235

<u>Selections from this set were also released as follows:</u>

386. **MUSSORGSKY:** *Boris Godunov—Monologue.* (*"I have attained the highest power"*)
      [#377]
    33⅓ rpm   **Columbia ML 5239** / released 3 March 1958 to ?
    45 rpm   **Philips ABE10063**
    CD   **CBS MPK 45693** / released 1989 to ?

387. **MUSSORGSKY:** *Boris Godunov—Clock Scene.* [#378]
    33⅓ rpm   **MET 105** / released 1978 to ?
    Cassette   **MET 105-C** / released 1980 to ?
    CD   **MET 105-CD** / released 1989 to ?

388. **MUSSORGSKY:** *Boris Godunov—Pimen's Tale.* [#379]
    33⅓ rpm   **Odyssey Y 31148**
    CD   **Preiser 89132** / released 1996 to ?

389. **MUSSORGSKY:** *Boris Godunov—Farewell of Boris.* [#380]
    33⅓ rpm   **Odyssey Y 31148**
    CD   **Preiser 89132** / released 1996 to ?

390. **MUSSORGSKY:** *Boris Godunov—Death of Boris.* [#384]
    33⅓ rpm   **Odyssey Y 31148**
    CD   **Preiser 89132** / released 1996 to ?

Session of 18 January 1945, 2:00 to 5:30 P.M.
[Information from Columbia archives.]

391. **BERLIOZ:** *La Damnation de Faust—Voici des roses.*
      Martial Singher & Metropolitan Opera Orchestra - Paul Breisach.
        matrix: **XCO 34130** (part of side)
    78 rpm   **Columbia M-578** (71679-D) *manual sequence* / released 15 June 1945 to ?
                Columbia MM-578 (72086-D) *automatic sequence*
    33⅓ rpm   **Columbia ML 4152** / released 4 April 1949 to ?
    CD   **Preiser 89635**

392. **BERLIOZ:** *La Damnation de Faust—Sérénade de Méphisto.*
     Martial Singher & Metropolitan Opera Orchestra - Paul Breisach.
              matrix: **XCO 34130** (part of side)
     78 rpm   **Columbia M-578** (71679-D) *manual sequence* / released 15 June 1945 to ?
                       Columbia MM-578 (72086-D) *automatic sequence*
     33⅓ rpm   **Columbia ML 4152** / released 4 April 1949 to ?
     _CD_   **Preiser 89635**

393. **GRÉTRY:** *Richard Cœur-de-Lion—Ô Richard, ô mon Roi!*
     Martial Singher & Metropolitan Opera Orchestra - Paul Breisach.
              matrix: **XCO 34131**
     78 rpm   **Columbia M-578** (71678-D) *manual sequence* / released 15 June 1945 to ?
                       Columbia MM-578 (72085-D) *automatic sequence*
     _CD_   **Preiser 89635**

394. **MASSENET:** *Hérodiade—Vision fugitive.*
     Martial Singher & Metropolitan Opera Orchestra - Paul Breisach.
              matrix: **XCO 34132**
     78 rpm   **Columbia M-578** (71680-D) *manual sequence* / released 15 June 1945 to ?
                       Columbia MM-578 (72087-D) *automatic sequence*
     33⅓ rpm   **Columbia ML 4152** / released 4 April 1949 to ?
     Cassette   **MET 207-C** / released 1987 to ?
     _CD_   **MET 207-CD** / released 1987 to ?
                       Preiser 89635

395. **BIZET:** *Carmen—Chanson du Toréador.* *("Toreador Song")*
     Martial Singher & Metropolitan Opera Orchestra - Paul Breisach.
              matrix: **XCO 34133**
     78 rpm   **Columbia M-578** (71681-D) *manual sequence* / released 15 June 1945 to ?
                       Columbia MM-578 (72088-D) *automatic sequence*
     33⅓ rpm   **Columbia ML 4152** / released 4 April 1949 to ?
     _CD_   **Preiser 89635**

Session of 4 February 1945, 6:30 to 10:00 P.M.
[Information from Columbia archives.]

396. **LULLY:** *Amadis de Gaule—Bois épais.*
     Martial Singher & Metropolitan Opera Orchestra - Paul Breisach.
              matrix: **XCO 34221**
     78 rpm   **Columbia M-578** (71678-D) *manual sequence* / released 15 June 1945 to ?
                       Columbia MM-578 (72085-D) *automatic sequence*
     _CD_   **Preiser 89635**

397. BERLIOZ: *La Damnation de Faust—Chanson de la puce.*
Martial Singher & Metropolitan Opera Orchestra - Paul Breisach.
matrix: **XCO 34222** (part of side)

78 rpm	**Columbia M-578** (71679-D) *manual sequence* / released 15 June 1945 to ?
	Columbia MM-578 (72086-D) *automatic sequence*
33⅓ rpm	**Columbia ML 4152** / released 4 April 1949 to ?
CD	**Preiser 89635**

398. GOUNOD: *Roméo et Juliette—Ballade de la Reine Mab.*
Martial Singher & Metropolitan Opera Orchestra - Paul Breisach.
matrix: **XCO 34222** (part of side)

78 rpm	**Columbia M-578** (71679-D) *manual sequence* / released 15 June 1945 to ?
	Columbia MM-578 (72086-D) *automatic sequence*
33⅓ rpm	**Columbia ML 4152** / released 4 April 1949 to ?
	Odyssey 32 16 0304
	MET 404 / released 1984 to ?
Cassette	**MET 404-C** / released 1984 to ?
CD	**Preiser 89635**

399. OFFENBACH: *Les Contes d'Hoffmann—Scintille diamant.*
Martial Singher & Metropolitan Opera Orchestra - Paul Breisach.
matrix: **XCO 34223**

78 rpm	**Columbia M-578** (71681-D) *manual sequence* / released 15 June 1945 to ?
	Columbia MM-578 (72088-D) *automatic sequence*
33⅓ rpm	**Columbia ML 4152** / released 4 April 1949 to ?
CD	**Preiser 89635**

400. THOMAS: *Hamlet—O vin dissipe la tristesse.* (*"Chanson Bachique"*)
Martial Singher & Metropolitan Opera Orchestra - Paul Breisach.
matrix: **XCO 34224**

78 rpm	**Columbia M-578** (71680-D) *manual sequence* / released 15 June 1945 to ?
	Columbia MM-578 (72087-D) *automatic sequence*
33⅓ rpm	**Columbia ML 4152** / released 4 April 1949 to ?
CD	**Preiser 89635**

Session of 14 May 1945, 1:00 to 4:30 P.M.
[Information from Columbia archives.]

401. BELLINI: *Norma—Casta Diva.*
Stella Roman, Metropolitan Opera Chorus & Metropolitan Opera Orchestra - Fausto Cleva.
matrix: **XCO 34725**
matrix: **XCO 34726**

Not released commercially by Columbia. This was released, however, on the unauthorized transfer listed below.

33⅓ rpm   **EJS-426** / released February 1968 to ? (an unauthorized release)

402. **BELLINI:** *Norma—Deh! proteggimi, o dio! ("Preghiera")*
    Jennie Tourel & Metropolitan Opera Orchestra - Fausto Cleva.
        matrix: **XCO 34727**
    Not released on 78 rpm.
    33⅓ rpm   **Odyssey Y2 32880**
            EJS-426 / released February 1968 to ? (an unauthorized release)

403. **BELLINI:** *Norma—Oh! rimembranza!* [continued with item #416]
    Stella Roman, Jennie Tourel & Metropolitan Opera Orchestra - Fausto Cleva.
        matrix: **XCO 34728**
    Not released commercially by Columbia. This was released, however, on the unauthorized transfer listed below.
    33⅓ rpm   **EJS-426** / released February 1968 to ? (an unauthorized release)

Session of 29 May 1945, 10:30 A.M. to 2:00 P.M.; Carnegie Hall, NYC.
[Information from Columbia archives.]

404. **WAGNER:** *Tannhäuser—Elisabeths Gebet. ("Allmächt'ge Jungfrau")*
    Helen Traubel & Metropolitan Opera Orchestra - Ernst Knoch.
        matrix: **XCO 34865**
        matrix: **XCO 34866**
    Not released by Columbia.

405. **WAGNER:** *Der Ring des Nibelungen - Die Walküre—Du bist der Lenz.*
    Helen Traubel & Metropolitan Opera Orchestra - Ernst Knoch.
        matrix: **XCO 34867**
    Not released on 78 rpm.
    33⅓ rpm   **Odyssey Y 31725** / released 1972 to ?
    CD   **Preiser 89984** / released 1997 to ?
            Preiser 89120 / released 1996 to ?

406. **WAGNER:** *Der Ring des Nibelungen - Die Walküre—Fort denn eile.*
    Helen Traubel & Metropolitan Opera Orchestra - Ernst Knoch.
        matrix: **XCO 34868**
    Not released on 78 rpm.
    33⅓ rpm   **Odyssey Y 31725** / released 1972 to ?
    CD   **Preiser 89120** / released 1996 to ?
            Preiser 89984 / released 1997 to ?

407. **WAGNER:** *Lohengrin—Euch Lüften, die mein Klagen.*
     Helen Traubel & Metropolitan Opera Orchestra - Ernst Knoch.
                   matrix: **XCO 34869**
     Not released on 78 rpm.
     <u>CD</u>   **Sony Classical MH2K 60896** / released 1999 to ?

408. **RICHARD STRAUSS:** *Zueignung, Op. 10, No. 1.*
     Helen Traubel & Metropolitan Opera Orchestra - Ernst Knoch.
                   matrix: **XCO 34870**
     Not released on 78 rpm.
     <u>33⅓ rpm</u>   **Odyssey Y 31725** / released 1972 to ?
     <u>CD</u>   **Preiser 89120** / released 1996 to ?

409. **RICHARD STRAUSS:** *Cäcilie, Op. 27, No. 2.*
     Helen Traubel & Metropolitan Opera Orchestra - Ernst Knoch.
                   matrix: **XCO 34871**
     Not released by Columbia.

410. **WAGNER:** *Der Ring des Nibelungen - Die Walküre—Ho-jo-to-ho!*
     Helen Traubel & Metropolitan Opera Orchestra - Ernst Knoch.
                   matrix: **XCO 34872**
     Not released on 78 rpm.
     <u>33⅓ rpm</u>   **Odyssey Y 31725** / released 1972 to ?
     <u>CD</u>   **Preiser 89120** / released 1996 to ?

411. **BEETHOVEN:** *Egmont—Die Trommel geruhret.* (in English)
     Helen Traubel & Metropolitan Opera Orchestra - Ernst Knoch.
                   matrix: **XCO 34873**
     Not released by Columbia.

412. **BEETHOVEN:** *Egmont—Freudvoll und Leidvoll.* (in English)
     Helen Traubel & Metropolitan Opera Orchestra - Ernst Knoch.
                   matrix: **XCO 34874**
     Not released by Columbia.

<u>Session of 31 May 1945, 4:00 to 6:30 P.M.</u>
[Information from Columbia archives.]

413. **WAGNER:** *Tannhäuser—O du mein holder Abendstern.*
     Herbert Janssen & Metropolitan Opera Orchestra - Paul Breisach.
                   matrix: **XCO 34875**
     <u>78 rpm</u>   **Columbia 71697-D** / released 15 September 1945 to ?
     <u>33⅓ rpm</u>   **MET 404** / released 1984 to ?
     <u>Cassette</u>   **MET 404-C** / released 1984 to ?

414. WAGNER: *Die Meistersinger von Nürnberg—Fliedermonolog.*
       Part 1: ("Wie düftet doch der Flieder")
       Part 2: ("Kein' Regel wollte da passen")
     Herbert Janssen & Metropolitan Opera Orchestra - Paul Breisach.
        matrix: *Side 1* **XCO 34876**
        matrix: *Side 2* **XCO 34877**
   78 rpm   **Columbia X-269** (71819-D) *manual sequence* / released 14 October 1946 to ?
           Columbia MX-269 (71822/3-D) *automatic sequence* / released 14 October 1946 to ?

415. WAGNER: *Die Meistersinger von Nürnberg—Wahnmonolog.*
       Part 1: ("Wahn! Wahn! Überall Wahn!")
       Part 2: ("Doch eines Abends spät!")
     Herbert Janssen & Metropolitan Opera Orchestra - Paul Breisach.
        matrix: *Side 1* **XCO 34878**
        matrix: *Side 2* **XCO 34879**
   78 rpm   **Columbia X-269** (71820-D) *manual sequence* / released 14 October 1946 to ?
           Columbia MX-269 (71823/2-D) *automatic sequence* / released 14 October 1946 to ?
           Columbia LX 947
   Cassette   **MET 523-C** / released 1994 to ?
   CD   **MET 523-CD** / released 1994 to ?

Session of 4 June 1945, 3:00 to 6:00 P.M.

[Information from Columbia archives.]

416. BELLINI: *Norma—Dolci qual arpa armonica.* [continued from item #403]
     Stella Roman, Jennie Tourel & Metropolitan Opera Orchestra - Fausto Cleva.
        matrix: **XCO 34880**
   Not released commercially. This was released, however, on the unauthorized transfer listed below.
   33⅓ rpm   **EJS-426** / released February 1968 to ? (an unauthorized release)

417. BELLINI: *Norma—Deh! con te, con te li prendi ... Mira, o Norma! ... Sì, fino all'ore estreme.*
     Stella Roman, Jennie Tourel & Metropolitan Opera Orchestra - Fausto Cleva.
        matrix: **XCO 34881**
        matrix: **XCO 34882**
        matrix: **XCO 34883**
   Not released commercially. This was released, however, on the unauthorized transfer listed below.
   33⅓ rpm   **EJS-426** / released February 1968 to ? (an unauthorized release)

Session of 7 June 1945, 3:00 to ? P.M.
[Information from Columbia archives.]

418. GOUNOD: *Faust—Il était un roi de Thulé. ("Ballade de Thulé")*
  Bidú Sayão & Metropolitan Opera Orchestra - Fausto Cleva.
        matrix: **XCO 34911**

78 rpm	**Columbia M-612** (71770-D) *manual sequence* / released 15 June 1946 to ?
	Columbia MM-612 (72095-D) *automatic sequence*
33⅓ rpm	**Columbia ML 4056**
	Odyssey Y 31151
CD	**Sony Classical MHK 62355** / released 1996 to ?

419. GOUNOD: *Faust—Air des bijoux. ("Jewel Song")*
  Bidú Sayão & Metropolitan Opera Orchestra - Fausto Cleva.
        matrix: **XCO 34912**

78 rpm	**Columbia M-612** (71770-D) *manual sequence* / released 15 June 1946 to ?
	Columbia MM-612 (72095-D) *automatic sequence*
33⅓ rpm	**Columbia ML 4056**
	Odyssey Y 31151
CD	**Sony Classical MHK 62355** / released 1996 to ?

420. MASSENET: *Manon—Je suis encore tout étourdie. ("Manon's Entrance")*
  Bidú Sayão & Metropolitan Opera Orchestra - Fausto Cleva.
        matrix: **XCO 34913**

78 rpm	**Columbia M-612** (71769-D) *manual sequence* / released 15 June 1946 to ?
	Columbia MM-612 (72094-D) *automatic sequence*
33⅓ rpm	**Columbia ML 4056**
	Odyssey 32 16 0377
CD	**Sony Classical MHK 62355** / released 1996 to ?

421. MASSENET: *Manon—Adieu, notre petite table.*
  Bidú Sayão & Metropolitan Opera Orchestra - Fausto Cleva.
        matrix: **XCO 34914**

78 rpm	**Columbia M-612** (71769-D) *manual sequence* / released 15 June 1946 to ?
	Columbia MM-612 (72094-D) *automatic sequence*
33⅓ rpm	**Columbia ML 4056**
	Odyssey 32 16 0304
	Odyssey 32 16 0377
	MET 404 / released 1984 to ?
Cassette	**MET 404-C** / released 1984 to ?
CD	**Sony Classical MHK 62355** / released 1996 to ?

Session of 31 December 1945, 2:00 to 5:00 P.M.
[Information from Columbia archives.]

422. **BIZET:** *Carmen—Prelude.*
　　　Metropolitan Opera Orchestra - Georges Sébastian.
　　　　matrix: **XCO 35565**
　　　For release information please see item #434.

423. **BIZET:** *Carmen—Chanson bohème. ("Les tringles des sistres tintaient")*
　　　Risë Stevens & Metropolitan Opera Orchestra - Georges Sébastian.
　　　　matrix: **XCO 35566**
　　　For release information please see items #434 and #437.

424. **BIZET:** *Carmen—Air des cartes. ("En vain pour éviter")*
　　　Risë Stevens & Metropolitan Opera Orchestra - Georges Sébastian.
　　　　matrix: **XCO 35567**
　　　For release information please see items #434 and #440.

Session of 4 January 1946, 2:30 to 6:00 P.M.
[Information from Columbia archives.]

425. **BELLINI:** *Norma—Ite sul colle, o Druidi!*
　　　　　Part 1: *("Ite sul colle, o Druidi!")*
　　　　　Part 2: *("Dell' aura tua profetica")*
　　　Ezio Pinza, Metropolitan Opera Chorus & Metropolitan Opera Orchestra - Fausto Cleva.
　　　　matrix: *Side 1* **XCO 35590**
　　　　matrix: *Side 2* **XCO 35591**

78 rpm	**Columbia 72826-D** / released 4 July 1949 to ?
45 rpm	**Philips ABE10083**
33⅓ rpm	**Columbia 3-229**
	Columbia ML 2060 / released 1 August 1949 to ?
	Odyssey Y 31148
	Philips GBL5577
CD	**Preiser 89132** / released 1996 to ?

426. **VERDI:** *Simon Boccanegra—Il lacerato spirito.*
　　　Ezio Pinza, Metropolitan Opera Chorus & Metropolitan Opera Orchestra - Fausto Cleva.
　　　　matrix: **XCO 35592**

78 rpm	**Columbia M-676** (71975-D) *manual sequence* / released 7 April 1947 to ?
	Columbia MM-676 (71977-D) *automatic sequence* / released 7 April 1947 to ?
33⅓ rpm	**Columbia ML 2060** / released 1 August 1949 to ?
	Columbia ML 2113 / released 22 May 1950 to ?

Columbia ML 5239 / released 3 March 1958 to ?

Odyssey Y 31148

MET 105 / released 1978 to ?

Cassette   **MET 105-C** / released 1980 to ?

CD   **CBS MPK 45693** / released 1989 to ?

MET 105-CD / released 1989 to ?

Preiser 89132 / released 1996 to ?

427. **HALÉVY:** *La Juive—Si la rigueur et la vengeance.*
   Ezio Pinza, Metropolitan Opera Chorus & Metropolitan Opera Orchestra - Fausto Cleva.
   matrix: **XCO 35593**

Not released on 78 rpm.

33⅓ rpm   **Columbia ML 2060** / released 1 August 1949 to ?

Columbia ML 5239 / released 3 March 1958 to ?

Odyssey Y 31148

CD   **CBS MPK 45693** / released 1989 to ?

Preiser 89132 / released 1996 to ?

Session of 14 January 1946, 2:00 to 5:30 P.M.
[Information from Columbia archives.]

428. **BIZET:** *Carmen—Habañera. ("L'amour est un oiseau rebelle")*
   Risë Stevens, Metropolitan Opera Chorus & Metropolitan Opera Orchestra – Georges Sébastian.
   matrix: **XCO 35627**
   For release information please see items #434 and #435.

429. **BIZET:** *Carmen—C'est toi? C'est moi! ... Mais moi, Carmen, je t'aime encore.*
      Part 1: ("C'est toi!")
      Part 2: ("Mais moi, Carmen")
   Risë Steven, Raoul Jobin, Metropolitan Opera Chorus & Metropolitan Opera Orchestra –
   Georges Sébastian.
   matrix: *Side 1* **XCO 35628**
   matrix: *Side 2* **XCO 35629**
   For release information please see items #434 and #441.

Session of 15 January 1946, 2:00 to 5:00 P.M.
[Information from Columbia archives.]

430. **BIZET:** *Carmen—Séguedille. ("Près des remparts de Séville")*
   Risë Steven, Raoul Jobin & Metropolitan Opera Orchestra - Georges Sébastian.
   matrix: **XCO 35630**
   For release information please see items #434 and #436.

431. **BIZET:** *Carmen—Chanson du Toréador. ("Toreador Song")*
   Robert Weede, Metropolitan Opera Chorus & Metropolitan Opera Orchestra – Georges Sébastian.
   matrix: **XCO 35631**
   For release information please see items #434 and #438.

432. **BIZET:** *Carmen—Air de fleur. ("La fleur que tu m'avais jetée")*
   Raoul Jobin & Metropolitan Opera Orchestra - Georges Sébastian.
   matrix: **XCO 35632**
   For release information please see items #434 and #439.

433. **BIZET:** *Carmen—Air de Micaëla. ("Je dis que rien ne m'épouvante")*
   Nadine Conner & Metropolitan Opera Orchestra - Georges Sébastian.
   matrix: **XCO 35633**
   For release information please see item #434.

434. **All of the *Carmen* recordings made during the sessions of 31 December 1945, 14 and 15 January 1946 were released as a set with the following side arrangement.**

BIZET: *Carmen — Excerpts.*

Carmen	**Risë Stevens**
Don José	**Raoul Jobin**
Micaëla	**Nadine Conner**
Escamillo	**Robert Weede**

Metropolitan Opera Chorus
Metropolitan Opera Orchestra
Georges Sébastian

Side 1	*Prelude.* [#422]	
Side 2	*Habañera. ("L'amour est un oiseau rebelle")* [#428]	
Side 3	*Séguedille. ("Près des remparts de Séville")* [#430]	
Side 4	*Chanson bohème. ("Les tringles des sistres tintaient")* [#423]	
Side 5	*Chanson du Toréador. ("Toreador Song")* [#431]	
Side 6	*Air de fleur. ("La fleur que tu m'avais jetée")* [#432]	
Side 7	*Air des cartes. ("En vain pour éviter")* [#424]	
Side 8	*Air de Micaëla. ("Je dis que rien ne m'épouvante")* [#433]	
Sides 9 & 10	*C'est toi? C'est moi! ... Mais moi, Carmen, je t'aime encore.* [#429]	

78 rpm   **Columbia M-607** (71739/43-D) *manual sequence* / released 18 March 1946 to ?
   Columbia MM-607 (71744/8-D) *automatic sequence* / released 18 March 1946 to ?
   Columbia D 152 (15923/7)

45 rpm	**Columbia A 607** / released 18 May 1954 to ?
33⅓ rpm	**Columbia ML 4013** / released 22 May 1950 to ?
	Odyssey Y 32102 / released 27 April 1973 to ?
	Philips GBL5641
Cassette	**Odyssey YT 32102**

<u>Selections from this set were also released as follows:</u>

435. **BIZET:** *Carmen—Habañera. ("L'amour est un oiseau rebelle")* [#428]

Cassette	**Sony Classical MLT 64594** / released 1995 to ?
	Sony Classical MLT 66707
45 rpm	**Philips CFE15002**
	Fontana EFF519
CD	**Sony Classical MLK 64594** / released 1995 to ?
	Sony Classical MLK 66707
	Sony Classical SM2K 89370 / released 2000 to ?
	Preiser 89556 / released 2002 to ?

436. **BIZET:** *Carmen—Séguedille. ("Près des remparts de Séville")* [#430]

78 rpm	**Columbia M-676** (71974-D) *manual sequence* / released 7 April 1947 to ?
	Columbia MM-676 (71978-D) *automatic sequence* / released 7 April 1947 to ?
45 rpm	**Philips CFE15002**
	Fontana EFF519
33⅓ rpm	**Columbia ML 2113** / released 22 May 1950 to ?
	MET 404 / released 1984 to ?
Cassette	**MET 404-C** / released 1984 to ?
CD	**Preiser 89556** / released 2002 to ?

437. **BIZET:** *Carmen—Chanson bohème. ("Les tringles des sistres tintaient")* [#423]

CD	**Preiser 89556** / released 2002 to ?
45 rpm	**Philips CFE15002**

438. **BIZET:** *Carmen—Chanson du Toréador. ("Toreador Song")* [#431]

45 rpm	**Philips CFE15003**
33⅓ rpm	**Odyssey 32 16 0304**

439. **BIZET:** *Carmen—Air de fleur. ("La fleur que tu m'avais jetée")* [#432]

45 rpm	**Philips CFE15003**
CD	**Preiser 89517** / released 2000 to ?

440. **BIZET:** *Carmen—Air des cartes. ("En vain pour éviter")* [#424]

45 rpm	**Philips CFE15002**
CD	**Preiser 89556** / released 2002 to ?

441. **BIZET:** *Carmen—C'est toi? C'est moi! ... Mais moi, Carmen, je t'aime encore.* [#429]
     45 rpm   **Philips CFE15003**
     Cassette   **MET 502-C** / released 1988 to ?
     CD   **MET 502-CD** / released 1988 to ?
                    Preiser 89556 / released 2002 to ?
                    Preiser 89517 / released 2000 to ?

Session of 21 February 1946, 3:00 to 6:00 P.M.
[Information from Columbia archives.]

442. **MOZART:** *Mentre ti lascio, o figlia, K. 513.*
    Ezio Pinza & Metropolitan Opera Orchestra - Bruno Walter.
        matrix: *Side 1* **XCO 35874**
        matrix: *Side 2* **XCO 35875**
     78 rpm   **Columbia M-643** (71844-D) *manual sequence* / released 9 December 1946 to ?
                    Columbia MM-643 (71848/9-D) *automatic sequence* / released 9 December 1946 to ?
     45 rpm   **Philips ABE10018**
     33⅓ rpm   **Columbia ML 4036**
                    Columbia ML 5239 / released 3 March 1958 to ?
                    Harmony HL 7272 / released 5 September 1960 to ?
                    Odyssey 32 16 0335 / released 19 May 1969 to ?
                    Columbia Club DS 511
                    CBS 61 558 / released 1976 to ?
     CD   **CBS MPK 45693** / released 1989 to ?
                    Sony Classical SM3K 47211 / released 1991 to ?
                    Opera CD 54519 / released 1998 to ?
                    Preiser 89132 / released 1996 to ?

443. **MOZART:** *Don Giovanni—Madamina, il catalogo.*
    Ezio Pinza & Metropolitan Opera Orchestra - Bruno Walter.
        matrix: *Side 1* **XCO 35876**
        matrix: *Side 2* **XCO 35877**
     78 rpm   **Columbia M-643** (71842-D) *manual sequence* / released 9 December 1946 to ?
                    Columbia MM-643 (71846/7-D) *automatic sequence* / released 9 December 1946 to ?
     45 rpm   **Philips ABE10015**
     33⅓ rpm   **Columbia ML 4036**
                    Columbia ML 5239 / released 3 March 1958 to ?
                    Harmony HL 7272 / released 5 September 1960 to ?
                    Odyssey 32 16 0335 / released 19 May 1969 to ?
                    Philips GBL5577

CD   **CBS 61 558** / released 1976 to ?
               CBS MPK 45693 / released 1989 to ?
               Sony Classical SM3K 47211 / released 1991 to ?
               Opera CD 54519 / released 1998 to ?
               Preiser 89132 / released 1996 to ?

Session of 22 March 1946, 2:00 to 5:30 P.M.
[Information from Columbia archives.]

444. ROSSINI: *Il Barbiere di Siviglia—La calunnia.*
       Ezio Pinza & Metropolitan Opera Orchestra - Fausto Cleva.
          matrix: **XCO 36005**

Not released by Columbia. This was re-recorded during the session of 31 March 1946, and that performance was released.

445. PUCCINI: *La Bohème—Vecchia zimarra.*
       Ezio Pinza & Metropolitan Opera Orchestra - Fausto Cleva.
          matrix: **XCO 36006**

78 rpm   **Columbia 72528-D** / released 31 May 1948 to ?
45 rpm   **Philips SBF227**
33⅓ rpm   **Columbia ML 2060** / released 1 August 1949 to ?
               Columbia ML 2142 / released 9 October 1950 to ?
               Columbia ML 5239 / released 3 March 1958 to ?
               Odyssey Y 31148
               Philips GBL5532
CD   **CBS MPK 45693** / released 1989 to ?
               Preiser 89132 / released 1996 to ?

446. VERDI: *Don Carlos—Ella giammai m'amò ... Domirò sol nel manto mio regal.*
       Ezio Pinza & Metropolitan Opera Orchestra - Fausto Cleva.
          matrix: *Side 1* **XCO 36007**
          matrix: *Side 2* **XCO 36008**

78 rpm   **Columbia 72802-D**
45 rpm   **Philips ABE10083**
33⅓ rpm   **Columbia 3-148**
               Columbia ML 2060 / released 1 August 1949 to ?
               Odyssey Y 31148
               Philips GBL5577
CD   **Preiser 89132** / released 1996 to ?

Session of 28 March 1946, 1:00 to 4:30 P.M.
[Information from Columbia archives.]

447. **WAGNER:** *Parsifal—Nur eine Waffe taugt.*
    Torsten Ralf & Metropolitan Opera Orchestra - Fritz Busch.
        matrix: **XCO 36028**

78 rpm	**Columbia M-634** (71824-D) *manual sequence* / released 30 June 1947 to ?
	Columbia MM-634 (71829-D) *automatic sequence* / released 30 June 1947 to ?
_CD_	**Preiser 89152** / released 1997 to ?

448. **WAGNER:** *Lohengrin—In fernem Land.*
    Torsten Ralf & Metropolitan Opera Orchestra - Fritz Busch.
        matrix: **XCO 36029**

78 rpm	**Columbia M-634** (71826-D) *manual sequence* / released 30 June 1947 to ?
	Columbia MM-634 (71829-D) *automatic sequence* / released 30 June 1947 to ?
Cassette	**MET 510-C** / released 1990 to ?
_CD_	**MET 510-CD** / released 1990 to ?
	Preiser 89152 / released 1997 to ?

449. **WAGNER:** *Lohengrin—Mein lieber Schwan!*
    Torsten Ralf & Metropolitan Opera Orchestra - Fritz Busch.
        matrix: **XCO 36030**

78 rpm	**Columbia M-634** (71826-D) *manual sequence* / released 30 June 1947 to ?
	Columbia MM-634 (71830-D) *automatic sequence* / released 30 June 1947 to ?
_CD_	**Preiser 89152** / released 1997 to ?

450. **WAGNER:** *Die Meistersinger von Nürnberg—Fanget an!* *("Probelied" "Trial Song")*
    Torsten Ralf & Metropolitan Opera Orchestra - Fritz Busch.
        matrix: **XCO 36031**

78 rpm	**Columbia M-634** (71825-D) *manual sequence* / released 30 June 1947 to ?
	Columbia MM-634 (71827-D) *automatic sequence* / released 30 June 1947 to ?
Cassette	**MET 523-C** / released 1994 to ?
_CD_	**MET 523-CD** / released 1994 to ?
	Preiser 89152 / released 1997 to ?

Session of 31 March 1946, 4:00 to 7:30 P.M.; New Studio, Liederkranz Hall, NYC.
[Information from Columbia archives.]

451. **ROSSINI:** *Il Barbiere di Siviglia—La calunnia.*
    Ezio Pinza & Metropolitan Opera Orchestra - Fausto Cleva.
        matrix: **XCO 36005**

This is a remake of the work which was first recorded during the session of 22 March 1946 but was not passed for release. This performance was released instead of the earlier one.

78 rpm	**Columbia 72528-D** / released 31 May 1948 to ?

45 rpm	**Philips ABE10063**
33⅓ rpm	**Columbia ML 2060** / released 1 August 1949 to ?
	Columbia ML 2142 / released 9 October 1950 to ?
	Columbia ML 5239 / released 3 March 1958 to ?
	Harmony HL 7272 / released 5 September 1960 to ?
	Odyssey Y 31148
	Philips GBL5577
	MET 105 / released 1978 to ?
Cassette	**MET 105-C** / released 1980 to ?
	MET 508-C / released 1990 to ?
CD	**CBS MPK 45693** / released 1989 to ?
	MET 105-CD / released 1989 to ?
	MET 508-CD / released 1990 to ?
	Opera CD 54519 / released 1998 to ?
	Preiser 89132 / released 1996 to ?

452. **WAGNER:** *Die Meistersinger von Nürnberg—Morgenlich leuchtend. ("Preislied" "Prize Song")*
    Torsten Ralf & Metropolitan Opera Orchestra - Fritz Busch.
        matrix: **XCO 36033**

78 rpm	**Columbia M-634** (71825-D) *manual sequence* / released 30 June 1947 to ?
	Columbia MM-634 (71828-D) *automatic sequence* / released 30 June 1947 to ?
33⅓ rpm	**Odyssey 32 16 0304**
CD	**Preiser 89152** / released 1997 to ?

453. **WAGNER:** *Die Meistersinger von Nürnberg—Am stillen Herd.*
    Torsten Ralf & Metropolitan Opera Orchestra - Fritz Busch.
        matrix: **XCO 36034**

78 rpm	**Columbia M-634** (71824-D) *manual sequence* / released 30 June 1947 to ?
	Columbia MM-634 (71830-D) *automatic sequence* / released 30 June 1947 to ?
CD	**Preiser 89152** / released 1997 to ?

454. **WAGNER:** *Tannhäuser—Inbrunst im Herzen. ("Romerzählung" "Rome Narrative")*
        Part 1: ("Inbrunst im Herzen")
        Part 2: ("Da sah' ich ihn")
    Torsten Ralf & Metropolitan Opera Orchestra - Fritz Busch.
        matrix: *Side 1* **XCO 36035**
        matrix: *Side 2* **XCO 36036**

78 rpm	**Columbia M-634** (71823-D) *manual sequence* / released 30 June 1947 to ?
	Columbia MM-634 (71827/8-D) *automatic sequence* / released 30 June 1947 to ?
CD	**Preiser 89152** / released 1997 to ?

Session of 17 April 1946, 10:00 A.M. to 1:30 P.M.
[Information from Columbia archives.]

455. **MOZART:** *Die Zauberflöte—In diesen heil'gen Hallen.* (in Italian as *"Qui sdegno non s'accende"*)
> *Ezio Pinza & Metropolitan Opera Orchestra - Bruno Walter.*
> matrix: **XCO 36119**

78 rpm	**Columbia M-643** (71843-D) *manual sequence* / released 9 December 1946 to ?
	Columbia MM-643 (71849-D) *automatic sequence* / released 9 December 1946 to ?
45 rpm	**Philips ABE10018**
	Philips SBF204
33⅓ rpm	**Columbia ML 4036**
	Odyssey 32 16 0335 / released 19 May 1969 to ?
	CBS 61 558 / released 1976 to ?
Cassette	**MET 517-C** / released 1992 to ?
CD	**CBS MPK 45693** / released 1989 to ?
	Sony Classical SM3K 47211 / released 1991 to ?
	Opera CD 54519 / released 1998 to ?
	MET 517-CD / released 1992 to ?
	Preiser 89132 / released 1996 to ?

456. **MOZART:** *Die Entführung aus dem Serail—Ha! wie will ich triumphieren.* (in Italian as *"Ah! che voglio trionfare!"*)
> *Ezio Pinza & Metropolitan Opera Orchestra - Bruno Walter.*
> matrix: **XCO 36120**

78 rpm	**Columbia M-643** (71843-D) *manual sequence* / released 9 December 1946 to ?
	Columbia MM-643 (71848-D) *automatic sequence* / released 9 December 1946 to ?
45 rpm	**Philips ABE10018**
33⅓ rpm	**Columbia ML 4036**
	Odyssey 32 16 0335 / released 19 May 1969 to ?
	Philips GBL5577
	CBS 61 558 / released 1976 to ?
CD	**CBS MPK 45693** / released 1989 to ?
	Sony Classical SM3K 47211 / released 1991 to ?
	Opera CD 54519 / released 1998 to ?
	Preiser 89132 / released 1996 to ?

457. **MOZART:** *Le Nozze di Figaro—Se vuol ballare.*
> *Ezio Pinza & Metropolitan Opera Orchestra - Bruno Walter.*
> matrix: **XCO 36121**

78 rpm	**Columbia M-643** (71845-D) *manual sequence* / released 9 December 1946 to ?
	Columbia MM-643 (71847-D) *automatic sequence* / released 9 December 1946 to ?

45 rpm	**Philips ABE10015**
	Philips SBF204
33⅓ rpm	**Columbia ML 4036**
	Columbia ML 5239 / released 3 March 1958 to ?
	Harmony HL 7272 / released 5 September 1960 to ?
	Odyssey 32 16 0304
	Odyssey 32 16 0335 / released 19 May 1969 to ?
	Columbia Club DS 511
	Philips GBL5577
Cassette	**Sony Classical MGT 46579** / released 1990 to ?
	MET 504-C / released 1989 to ?
CD	**CBS MPK 45693** / released 1989 to ?
	Sony Classical SM3K 47211 / released 1991 to ?
	Sony Classical MDK 46579 / released 1990 to ?
	Opera CD 54519 / released 1998 to ?
	Preiser 89132 / released 1996 to ?
	MET 504-CD / released 1989 to ?

458. MOZART: *Le Nozze di Figaro—Aprite un po'.*
  Ezio Pinza & Metropolitan Opera Orchestra - Bruno Walter.
      matrix: **XCO 36122**

78 rpm	**Columbia M-643** (71845-D) *manual sequence* / released 9 December 1946 to ?
	Columbia MM-643 (71846-D) *automatic sequence* / released 9 December 1946 to ?
45 rpm	**Philips ABE10015**
33⅓ rpm	**Columbia ML 4036**
	Columbia ML 5239 / released 3 March 1958 to ?
	Odyssey 32 16 0335 / released 19 May 1969 to ?
	Philips GBL5577
	MET 404 / released 1984 to ?
	Time-Life STLM-111 / released 1981 to ?
Cassette	**Sony Classical MGT 46579** / released 1990 to ?
	MET 404-C / released 1984 to ?
CD	**CBS MPK 45693** / released 1989 to ?
	Sony Classical SM3K 47211 / released 1991 to ?
	Sony Classical MDK 46579 / released 1990 to ?
	Opera CD 54519 / released 1998 to ?
	Preiser 89132 / released 1996 to ?

Session of 31 May 1946, 2:00 to 5:00 P.M.
[Information from Columbia archives.]

459. MASSENET: *Manon—Ah! fuyez, douce image.*
  Raoul Jobin & Metropolitan Opera Orchestra - Wilfred Pelletier.

matrix: **XCO 36373**

78 rpm   **Columbia M-696** (72137-D) *manual sequence* / released 11 August 1947 to ?
                  Columbia MM-696 (72140-D) *automatic sequence* / released 11 August 1947 to ?

CD   **Preiser 89517** / released 2000 to ?

460. **MASSENET:** *Werther—Pourquoi me réveiller?* *("Lied d'Ossian")*
     Raoul Jobin & Metropolitan Opera Orchestra - Wilfred Pelletier.
          matrix: **XCO 36374**
78 rpm   **Columbia M-696** (72136-D) *manual sequence* / released 11 August 1947 to ?
                  Columbia MM-696 (72139-D) *automatic sequence* / released 11 August 1947 to ?

CD   **Preiser 89517** / released 2000 to ?

461. **GOUNOD:** *Roméo et Juliette—Ah! lève-toi, soleil!*
     Raoul Jobin & Metropolitan Opera Orchestra - Wilfred Pelletier.
          matrix: **XCO 36375**
78 rpm   **Columbia M-696** (72137-D) *manual sequence* / released 11 August 1947 to ?
                  Columbia MM-696 (72140-D) *automatic sequence* / released 11 August 1947 to ?

CD   **Preiser 89517** / released 2000 to ?

Session of 6 June 1946, 12:00 to ? P.M.
[Information from Columbia archives.]

462. **BERLIOZ:** *La Damnation de Faust—Nature immense.* *("Invocation à la nature")*
     Raoul Jobin & Metropolitan Opera Orchestra - Wilfred Pelletier.
          matrix: **XCO 36394**
78 rpm   **Columbia M-696** (72135-D) *manual sequence* / released 11 August 1947 to ?
                  Columbia MM-696 (72138-D) *automatic sequence* / released 11 August 1947 to ?

CD   **Preiser 89517** / released 2000 to ?

463. **MEYERBEER:** *L'Africaine—O paradis.*
     Raoul Jobin & Metropolitan Opera Orchestra - Wilfred Pelletier.
          matrix: **XCO 36395**
78 rpm   **Columbia M-696** (72135-D) *manual sequence* / released 11 August 1947 to ?
                  Columbia MM-696 (72138-D) *automatic sequence* / released 11 August 1947 to ?

CD   **Preiser 89517** / released 2000 to ?

464. **MASSENET:** *Hérodiade—Adieu donc, vains objets.* *("Air de Jean")*
     Raoul Jobin & Metropolitan Opera Orchestra - Wilfred Pelletier.
          matrix: **XCO 36396**

78 rpm	**Columbia M-696** (72136-D) *manual sequence* / released 11 August 1947 to ?
	Columbia MM-696 (72139-D) *automatic sequence* / released 11 August 1947 to ?
CD	**Preiser 89517** / released 2000 to ?

Session of 12 July 1946, 2:00 to 5:00 P.M.
[Information from Columbia archives.]

465. **ROSSINI:** *La Cenerentola—Non più mesta.*
      Part 1: *("Nacqui all'affano e al pianto")*
      Part 2: *("Non più mesta")*
   Jennie Tourel & Metropolitan Opera Orchestra - Pietro Cimara.
      matrix: *Side 1* **XCO 36643**
      matrix: *Side 2* **XCO 36644**

78 rpm	**Columbia M-691** (72129-D) *manual sequence* / released 28 July 1947 to ?
	Columbia MM-691 (72132/3-D) *automatic sequence* / released 28 July 1947 to ?
	Columbia LX 1003
33⅓ rpm	**Odyssey Y2 32880**

466. **ROSSINI:** *Il Barbiere di Siviglia—Una voce poca fa.*
      Part 1: *("Una voce poca fa")*
   Jennie Tourel & Metropolitan Opera Orchestra - Pietro Cimara.
      matrix: *Side 1* **XCO 36645**

Only the first part of Rosina's cavatina was recorded during this session. For release information please see the next session when the second half was recorded.

Session of 17 July 1946, 2:00 to 5:00 P.M.
[Information from Columbia archives.]

467. **ROSSINI:** *Il Barbiere di Siviglia—Una voce poca fa.*
      Part 2: *("Io sono docile")*
   Jennie Tourel & Metropolitan Opera Orchestra - Pietro Cimara.
      matrix: *Side 2* **XCO 36655**

The first part of Rosina's cavatina was recorded during the previous session.

78 rpm	**Columbia M-691** (72131-D) *manual sequence* / released 28 July 1947 to ?
	Columbia MM-691 (72133/2-D) *automatic sequence* / released 28 July 1947 to ?
	Columbia LX 1075
33⅓ rpm	**Columbia ML 2024** / released 20 September 1948 to ?
	Odyssey Y2 32880
	Odyssey 32 16 0304

Cassette   **MET 508-C** / released 1990 to ?
CD   **MET 508-CD** / released 1990 to ?
    Naxos 8.110735 / released 2003 to ?

468. **ROSSINI:** *L'Italiana in Algeri—Cruda sorte, amor tiranno.*
    Jennie Tourel & Metropolitan Opera Orchestra - Pietro Cimara.
        matrix: **XCO 36656**
    78 rpm   **Columbia M-691** (72130-D) *manual sequence* / released 28 July 1947 to ?
        Columbia MM-691 (72134-D) *automatic sequence* / released 28 July 1947 to ?
        Columbia LX 1054
    33⅓ rpm   **Columbia ML 2024** / released 20 September 1948 to ?
        Odyssey Y2 32880

469. **ROSSINI:** *Semiramide—Bel raggio lusinghier.*
    Jennie Tourel & Metropolitan Opera Orchestra - Pietro Cimara.
        matrix: **XCO 36657**
    78 rpm   **Columbia M-691** (72130-D) *manual sequence* / released 28 July 1947 to ?
        Columbia MM-691 (72134-D) *automatic sequence* / released 28 July 1947 to ?
        Columbia LX 1054
    33⅓ rpm   **Odyssey Y2 32880**
    CD   **Naxos 8.110735** / released 2003 to ?

Session of 7 February 1947, 1:55 to 5:25 P.M.
[Information from Columbia archives.]

470. **SAINT-SAËNS:** *Samson et Dalila—Mon cœur s'ouvre à ta voix.* *("My heart at thy sweet voice")*
    Risë Stevens & Metropolitan Opera Orchestra - Fausto Cleva.
        matrix: **XCO 37361**
    78 rpm   **Columbia M-676** (71974-D) *manual sequence* / released 7 April 1947 to ?
        Columbia MM-676 (71978-D) *automatic sequence* / released 7 April 1947 to ?
    33⅓ rpm   **Columbia ML 2113** / released 22 May 1950 to ?

471. **MOZART:** *Don Giovanni—Deh, vieni alla finestra.*
    Ezio Pinza & Metropolitan Opera Orchestra - Fausto Cleva.
        matrix: **XCO 37362**
    78 rpm   **Columbia M-676** (71975-D) *manual sequence* / released 7 April 1947 to ?
        Columbia MM-676 (71976-D) *automatic sequence* / released 7 April 1947 to ?
    45 rpm   **Philips SBF227**
    33⅓ rpm   **Columbia ML 2113** / released 22 May 1950 to ?
        Columbia ML 5239 / released 3 March 1958 to ?
        Odyssey Y 31148 [Incorrect recording date given on this release.]
        Philips GBL5577

Philips GBL5532

Cassette   **MET 511-C** / released 1991 to ?
CD   **CBS MPK 45693** / released 1989 to ?
                  MET 511-CD / released 1991 to ?

472. **PONCHIELLI:** *La Gioconda—Bella così, madonna.*
    Risë Stevens, Ezio Pinza & Metropolitan Opera Orchestra - Fausto Cleva.
        matrix: **XCO 37363**

78 rpm   **Columbia 72371-D** / released 1 December 1947 to ?
33⅓ rpm   **Odyssey Y 31148**
Cassette   **MET 524-C** / released 1994 to ?
CD   **MET 524-CD** / released 1994 to ?

473. **THOMAS:** *Mignon—Légères hirondelles.* *("Swallow Duet")*
    Risë Stevens, Ezio Pinza & Metropolitan Opera Orchestra - Fausto Cleva.
        matrix: **XCO 37364**

78 rpm   **Columbia 72371-D** / released 1 December 1947 to ?
33⅓ rpm   **Odyssey Y 31148**
                  MET 114 / released 1982 to ?
CD   **MET 114-CD** / released 1989 to ?

Session of 16 March 1947, 1:30 to 5:30 P.M.; Metropolitan Opera House, NYC.
[Information from Columbia archives.]

474. **WAGNER:** *Tristan und Isolde—O sink' hernieder, Nacht der Liebe.*
    ("Liebesnacht" "Love Duet")
        Part 1: *("O sink' hernieder, Nacht der Liebe")*
        Part 2: *("Einsam wachend in der Nacht")*
        Part 3: *("Doch unsre Liebe")*
        Part 4: *("Soll ich lauschen?")*
  Helen Traubel, Torsten Ralf, Herta Glaz & Metropolitan Opera Orchestra - Fritz Busch.
        matrix: *Side 1* **XCO 37480**
        matrix: *Side 2* **XCO 37481**
        matrix: *Side 3* **XCO 37482** (Both cut, 3 minutes and 45 seconds [take -1] and uncut, 4 minutes and 39 seconds [take -2] versions were made of Side 3. All 78 and 33⅓ rpm releases used the cut version. The uncut take did not appear until the Sony CD was released in 1999.)
        matrix: *Side 4* **XCO 37483**

78 rpm   **Columbia X-286** (72246/7-D) *manual sequence*
                  Columbia X-286 (72248/9-D) *automatic sequence*
                  Columbia LK 1243/4
                  Columbia LHX 8067/8
33⅓ rpm   **Columbia ML 4055**

<u>CD</u>   **Sony Classical MH2K 60896** [Only release employing the uncut take of Side 3.] /
released 1999 to ?
Preiser 89152 / released 1997 to ?

Session of 5 June 1947; Metropolitan Opera House, NYC.
[Information from Columbia archives.]

475. **HUMPERDINCK:** *Hänsel und Gretel.* (in an English translation by Constance Bache)
During this session and the next one a complete recording of *Hänsel und Gretel* was made.
For release information please see item #477.

Session of 6 June 1947; Metropolitan Opera House, NYC.
[Information from Columbia archives.]

476. **HUMPERDINCK:** *Hänsel und Gretel.* (in an English translation by Constance Bache)
During this session and the previous one a complete recording of *Hänsel und Gretel* was made.
For release information please see item #477.

477. The recording sessions of 5 and 6 June 1947 were devoted to the first complete opera recording made in the United States. The recordings were released as a two volume 78 rpm set with the following cast and side arrangement. Following each side is the date of the issued take. Max Rudolf told the compiler of this discography that the recording was hastily arranged. He had studied the score for a tour performance in New Orleans that was cancelled. For the recording there was no rehearsing. The orchestra was in the pit, the singers in chairs in front of the curtain, and the recording equipment was in the boxes and a hallway.

HUMPERDINCK: *Hänsel und Gretel.*
(Translated and adapted into English by Constance Bache)

Hänsel	**Risë Stevens**
Gretel	**Nadine Conner**
Witch & Sandman	**Thelma Votipka**
Peter (Father)	**John Brownlee**
Gertrude (Mother)	**Claramae Turner**
Dew Fairy	**Lillian Raymondi**

Chorus of the Metropolitan Opera Association
Orchestra of the Metropolitan Opera Association
Max Rudolf

Side 1	matrix: **XCO 37849**	*Prelude, part 1*	6 June 1947
Side 2	matrix: **XCO 37850**	*Prelude, part 2*	5 June 1947
Side 3	matrix: **XCO 37851**	*Susy, little Susy*	5 June 1947
Side 4	matrix: **XCO 37852**	*What, Hansel, tasting?*	5 June 1947
Side 5	matrix: **XCO 37853**	*Hallo, here's Mother!*	6 June 1947
Side 6	matrix: **XCO 37854**	*Tra la la la*	6 June 1947
Side 7	matrix: **XCO 37855**	*Most simple is the bill of fare*	6 June 1947
Side 8	matrix: **XCO 37856**	*But where do you think?*	6 June 1947
Side 9	matrix: **XCO 37857**	*Prelude (Act II) "The Witches' Ride"*	6 June 1947
Side 10	matrix: **XCO 37858**	*There stands a little man*	5 June 1947
Side 11	matrix: **XCO 37859**	*Hansel, what have you done?*	6 June 1947
Side 12	matrix: **XCO 37860**	*Did you hear?; I shut the children's peepers*	6 June 1947
Side 13	matrix: **XCO 37861**	*When at night I go to sleep "Prayer"*	5 June 1947
Side 14	matrix: **XCO 37862**	*"Pantomime"*	6 June 1947
Side 15	matrix: **XCO 37863**	*Prelude (Act III); I'm up with early dawning*	6 June 1947
Side 16	matrix: **XCO 37864**	*Where am I?*	6 June 1947
Side 17	matrix: **XCO 37865**	*Stand still!*	5 June 1947
Side 18	matrix: **XCO 37866**	*Nibble, nibble, mousie*	5 June 1947
Side 19	matrix: **XCO 37867**	*Go, get you right out of my sight!*	5 June 1947
Side 20	matrix: **XCO 37868**	*Now, Gretel, be a good little girl*	5 June 1947
Side 21	matrix: **XCO 37869**	*Yes, Gretel mine*	5 June 1947
Side 22	matrix: **XCO 37870**	*Sister dear, O beware!*	5 June 1947
Side 23	matrix: **XCO 37871**	*We're saved*	6 June 1947
Side 24	matrix: **XCO 37872**	*Father, Mother "Finale"*	6 June 1947

> *78 rpm*   **Columbia MOP-26** (712646/57-D) *automatic sequence* / released 15 September 1947 to ?
>
> *33⅓ rpm*   **Columbia SL 2** (ML 4078/9) *manual sequence* / released 11 October 1948 to ?
> **Columbia SL 102** (ML 4165/6) *automatic sequence*
> **Odyssey Y2 32546** (Y 32547/8) / released 9 November 1973 to ?

<u>A selection from this set was also released as follows:</u>

478. HUMPERDINCK: *Hänsel und Gretel—Abends, will ich schlafen geh'n.*
(in English as *"When at night I go to sleep"*) (*"Abendsegen"* *"Evening Prayer"*)

> *33⅓ rpm*   **MET 50** / released 1985 to ?
> **Metropolitan Opera MO-2**
> *Cassette*   **MET 50-C** / released 1985 to ?

Session of 9 June 1947.

[Information from a discography by Charles L. Morgan in *The Record Collector*, vol. 20, nos. 11, 12, p. 243 (December 1972).]

479. *The Whiffenpoof Song* (Meade Minnigerode, George S. Pomeroy, Tod B. Galloway; revision by Rudy Vallée).
Charles Kullman, male chorus & Metropolitan Opera Orchestra - Julius Burger.
matrix: **CO 37890**

78 rpm	**Columbia 4500-M**
45 rpm	**Philips SBF 286**

480. *The Sweetheart of Sigma Chi* (Byron D. Stokes, F. Dudleigh Vernor).
Charles Kullman, male chorus & Metropolitan Opera Orchestra - Julius Burger.
matrix: **CO 37891**

78 rpm	**Columbia 4500-M**
45 rpm	**Philips SBF 286**

481. TOSELLI: *Serenata.*
Charles Kullman & Metropolitan Opera Orchestra - Julius Burger.
matrix: **CO 37892**
Not released by Columbia.

482. CADMAN: *At Dawning, Op. 29, No. 1* (Words by Nelle Richmond Eberhart) (Arranged by Julius Burger).
Charles Kullman & Metropolitan Opera Orchestra - Julius Burger.
matrix: **CO 37893**

78 rpm	**Columbia 4529-M** [The Metropolitan Opera Orchestra is not listed on the record labels.]

Session of 17 June 1947, 1:30 to 4:30 P.M.; Metropolitan Opera House, NYC.
[Information from Columbia archives.]

483. LEONCAVALLO: *Pagliacci—Qual fiamma avea nel guardo.* *("Ballatella")*
Bidú Sayão & Metropolitan Opera Orchestra - Pietro Cimara.
matrix: **XCO 37915**

78 rpm	**Columbia 72899-D** / released 2 January 1950 to ?
33⅓ rpm	**Columbia 3-403**
	Odyssey Y 31151
CD	**Sony Classical MHK 63221** / released 1997 to ?

484. MASSENET: *Manon—Voyons, Manon, plus de chimères.*
Bidú Sayão & Metropolitan Opera Orchestra - Pietro Cimara.
matrix: **XCO 37916**

78 rpm	**Columbia 72899-D** / released 2 January 1950 to ?
33⅓ rpm	**Columbia 3-403**
	Columbia ML 2152 / released 30 October 1950 to ?
	Odyssey 32 46 0377
CD	**Sony Classical MHK 62355** / released 1996 to ?

485. **PUCCINI:** *Gianni Schicchi—O mio babbino caro.*
     Bidú Sayão & Metropolitan Opera Orchestra - Pietro Cimara.
     matrix: **XCO 37917**

78 rpm	**Columbia 17515-D** / released 2 February 1948 to ?
45 rpm	**Philips ABE10095**
	Philips SBF199
33⅓ rpm	**Columbia ML 5231** / released 27 January 1958 to ?
	Odyssey Y 31151
	Philips GBL5532
CD	**Sony Classical MHK 63221** / released 1997 to ?

486. **PUCCINI:** *La Bohème—Quando me'n vo'.* *("Musetta's Waltz Song")*
     Bidú Sayão & Metropolitan Opera Orchestra - Pietro Cimara.
     matrix: **XCO 37918**

78 rpm	**Columbia 17515-D** / released 2 February 1948 to ?
33⅓ rpm	**Columbia ML 5231** / released 27 January 1958 to ?
	Odyssey Y 31151
CD	**Sony Classical MHK 63221** / released 1997 to ?

Session of 18 June 1947, 12:30 to 4:00 P.M.; Metropolitan Opera House, NYC.
[Information from Columbia archives.]

487. **JOHANN STRAUSS, II:** *Der Zigeunerbaron—Ja, das Alles auf Ehr'.*
     ("Barinkay's Entrance Song")
     Mario Berini & Metropolitan Opera Orchestra - Emil Cooper.
     matrix: **XCO 37924**

78 rpm	**Columbia 72459-D** / released 11 April 1949 to ?
33⅓ rpm	**Columbia 3-124**

488. **JOHANN STRAUSS, II:** *"Walzerlied."* (based on "G'schichten aus dem Wiener Wald,"
     Op. 325, arranged by Erich Wolfgang Korngold)
     Mario Berini & Metropolitan Opera Orchestra - Emil Cooper.
     matrix: **XCO 37925**

78 rpm	**Columbia 72459-D** / released 11 April 1949 to ?
33⅓ rpm	**Columbia 3-124**

489. **MEYERBEER:** *L'Africaine—O paradis.* (in Italian as *"O paradiso"*)
     Richard Tucker & Metropolitan Opera Orchestra - Emil Cooper.
     matrix: **XCO 37926**

78 rpm	**Columbia 72399-D** / released 29 December 1947 to ?
	Columbia LX 1329
45 rpm	**Philips ABE10131**

33⅓ rpm	**Columbia ML 4750** / released 19 October 1953 to ?
_CD_	**Preiser 89952** / released 1998 to ?
	Preiser 89552 / released 2001 to ?

490. **PONCHIELLI:** _La Gioconda—Cielo e mar._
    Richard Tucker & Metropolitan Opera Orchestra - Emil Cooper.
      matrix: **XCO 37927**

78 rpm	**Columbia 72399-D** / released 29 December 1947 to ?
	Columbia LX 1329
45 rpm	**Philips ABE10131**
33⅓ rpm	**Columbia ML 4750** / released 19 October 1953 to ?
	Columbia M 30118 / released 19 October 1970 to ?
	Columbia D3M 33448 [an incorrect recording date of 1953 is given]
Cassette	**MET 524-C** / released 1994 to ?
_CD_	**MET 524-CD** / released 1994 to ?
	Preiser 89952 / released 1998 to ?
	Preiser 89552 / released 2001 to ?

Session of 5 November 1947, 7:00 to 11:00 P.M.; Metropolitan Opera House, NYC.
[Information from Columbia archives.]

491. **VERDI:** _Otello—Già nella notte densa._
        Part 1: _("Già nella notte densa")_
        Part 2: _("Ed io vedea fra le tue tempie oscure")_
  Daniza Ilitsch, Richard Tucker & Orchestra of the Metropolitan Opera Association - Max Rudolf.
      matrix: _Side 1_ **XCO 39273**
      matrix: _Side 2_ **XCO 39274**

78 rpm	**Columbia M-798** (72745-D) _manual sequence_ / released 13 December 1948 to ?
	Columbia MM-798 (72723/2-D) _automatic sequence_
	Columbia D233 (C16208/7)
	Columbia LX 1144
33⅓ rpm	**Columbia ML 4230**
_CD_	**Preiser 89552** / released 2001 to ?

492. **VERDI:** _Aïda—Pur ti reveggo._
        Part 1: _("Pur ti reveggo")_
        Part 2: _("Sovra una terra estrania teco fuggir dovrei!")_
  Daniza Ilitsch, Kurt Baum & Orchestra of the Metropolitan Opera Association - Max Rudolf.
      matrix: _Side 1_ **XCO 39275**
      matrix: _Side 2_ **XCO 39276**

78 rpm	**Columbia M-798** (72719-D) _manual sequence_ / released 13 December 1948 to ?
	Columbia MM-798 (72722/3-D) _automatic sequence_
	Columbia D233 (C16207/8)

33⅓ rpm   **Columbia ML 4230**
CD   **Preiser 90429** / released 2000 to ?

493. **WAGNER:** *Die Meistersinger von Nürnberg—Mein Kind.*
     Herbert Janssen & Metropolitan Opera Orchestra - Max Rudolf.
          matrix: **XCO 39277**
     Not released by Columbia. This was re-recorded during the session of 7 December 1947, and that
     performance was released.

Session of 16 November 1947, 1:00 to 4:20 P.M.; Metropolitan Opera House, NYC.
This session was continued in the evening.
[Information from Columbia archives.]

494. **BENATZKY:** *Ich muss wieder einmal in Grinzing sein.*
     Mario Berini & Metropolitan Opera Orchestra - Max Rudolf.
          matrix: **XCO 39350**
     78 rpm   **Columbia 72847-D** / released 12 September 1949 to ?
     33⅓ rpm   **Columbia 3-294**

495. **SIECZYNSKI:** *Wien, du Stadt meiner Träume.*
     Mario Berini & Metropolitan Opera Orchestra - Max Rudolf.
          matrix: **XCO 39351**
     78 rpm   **Columbia 72847-D** / released 12 September 1949 to ?
     33⅓ rpm   **Columbia 3-294**

496. **VERDI:** *Il Trovatore—Miserere.*
     *Daniza Ilitsch, Kurt Baum, Chorus (Kurt Adler, director) & Orchestra of the Metropolitan Opera
     Association - Max Rudolf.*
          matrix: **XCO 39352**
     78 rpm   **Columbia M-798** (72720-D) *manual sequence* / released 13 December 1948 to ?
                       Columbia MM-798 (72746-D) *automatic sequence*
                       Columbia D233 (C16210)
     33⅓ rpm   **Columbia ML 4230**

497. **VERDI:** *Aïda—O terra, addio.*
     *Daniza Ilitsch, Kurt Baum, Chorus (Kurt Adler, director) & Orchestra of the Metropolitan Opera
     Association - Max Rudolf.*
          matrix: **XCO 39353**
     78 rpm   **Columbia M-798** (72720-D) *manual sequence* / released 13 December 1948 to ?
                       Columbia MM-798 (72724-D) *automatic sequence*
                       Columbia D233 (C16209)
     33⅓ rpm   **Columbia ML 4230**

Session of 16 November 1947, 6:00 to 9:30 P.M.; Metropolitan Opera House, NYC.
This session was a continuation of the afternoon session.
[Information from Columbia archives.]

498. **VERDI:** *Un Ballo in Maschera—Teco io sto.*
>> **Part 1:** *("Teco io sto")*
>> **Part 2:** *("M'ami, m'ami")*
>> *Daniza Ilitsch, Richard Tucker & Orchestra of the Metropolitan Opera Association - Max Rudolf.*
>> matrix: *Side 1* **XCO 39354**
>> matrix: *Side 2* **XCO 39355**
>> _78 rpm_   **Columbia M-798** (72721-D) *manual sequence* / released 13 December 1948 to ?
>>   **Columbia MM-798** (72746/72724-D) *automatic sequence*
>>   **Columbia D233** (C16210/9)
>> _33⅓ rpm_   **Columbia ML 4230**
>> _CD_   **MET 525-CD**
>>   **Preiser 90429** / released 2000 to ?
>>   **Preiser 89552** / released 2001 to ?

499. **KORNGOLD:** *Die Tote Stadt—Glück, das mir verblieb.* *("Marietta's Lied"   "Marietta's Lute Song")*
>> *Polyna Stoska & Metropolitan Opera Orchestra - Max Rudolf.*
>> matrix: **XCO 39356**
>> _78 rpm_   **Columbia X-294** (72512-D) *manual sequence* / released 29 March 1948 to ?
>>   **Columbia MX-294** (72515-D) *automatic sequence* / released 29 March 1948 to ?

500. **RICHARD STRAUSS:** *Ariadne auf Naxos—Sei'n wir wieder gut.* *("Aria of the Composer")*
>> *Polyna Stoska & Metropolitan Opera Orchestra - Max Rudolf.*
>> matrix: **XCO 39357**
>> _78 rpm_   **Columbia X-294** (72512-D) *manual sequence* / released 29 March 1948 to ?
>>   **Columbia MX-294** (72514-D) *automatic sequence* / released 29 March 1948 to ?

Session of 23 November 1947, 2:00 to 5:30 P.M.; Metropolitan Opera House, NYC.
[Information from Columbia archives.]

501. **CHARPENTIER:** *Louise—Depuis le jour.*
>> *Nadine Conner & Metropolitan Opera Orchestra - Max Rudolf.*
>> matrix: **XCO 39413**
>> _78 rpm_   **Columbia 72540-D** / released 28 June 1948 to ?

502. **OFFENBACH:** *Les Contes d'Hoffmann—Elle a fui, la tourterelle.*
>> *Nadine Conner & Metropolitan Opera Orchestra - Max Rudolf.*
>> matrix: **XCO 39414**
>> _78 rpm_   **Columbia 72540-D** / released 28 June 1948 to ?

503. MOZART: *Don Giovanni—Vedrai, carino.*
    Nadine Conner & Orchestra of the Metropolitan Opera Association of New York City – Max Rudolf.
        matrix: **XCO 39415**

78 rpm	**Columbia 73072-D** / released 18 September 1950 to ?
33⅓ rpm	**Columbia 3-749**
Cassette	**MET 511-C** / released 1991 to ?
CD	**MET 511-CD** / released 1991 to ?

504. VERDI: *La Traviata—Addio del passato.*
    Nadine Conner & Orchestra of the Metropolitan Opera Association of New York City – Max Rudolf.
        matrix: **XCO 39416**

78 rpm	**Columbia 73072-D** / released 18 September 1950 to ?
33⅓ rpm	**Columbia 3-749**

Session of 7 December 1947, 12:00 to 3:30 P.M.; Metropolitan Opera House, NYC.
This session was continued later in the same afternoon and evening.
[Information from Columbia archives.]

505. WAGNER: *Die Meistersinger von Nürnberg—Mein Kind.*
    Herbert Janssen & Metropolitan Opera Orchestra - Max Rudolf.
        matrix: **XCO 39277**
This is a remake of the work which was first recorded during the session of 5 November 1947 but was not passed for release. This performance was released instead of the earlier one.

78 rpm	**Columbia 72518-D** / released 10 May 1948 to ?
Cassette	**MET 523-C** / released 1994 to ?
CD	**MET 523-CD** / released 1994 to ?

506. WAGNER: *Die Meistersinger von Nürnberg—Selig, wie die Sonne.* *("Quintet")*
    Polyna Stoska, Herbert Janssen, Torsten Ralf, Herta Glaz, John Garris & Metropolitan Opera Orchestra –
    Max Rudolf.
        matrix: **XCO 39551**

78 rpm	**Columbia 72518-D** / released 10 May 1948 to ?
Cassette	**MET 523-C** / released 1994 to ?
CD	**MET 523-CD** / released 1994 to ?

507. WEBER: *Der Freischütz—Leise, leise, fromme Weise.* *("Agathe's Prayer")*
        Part 1: *("Wie nahte mir der Schlummer")*
        Part 2: *("Doch wie! Täuscht mich nicht mein Ohr?")*
    Polyna Stoska & Metropolitan Opera Orchestra - Max Rudolf.
        matrix: *Side 1* **XCO 39552**
        matrix: *Side 2* **XCO 39553**

78 rpm	**Columbia X-294** (72513-D) *manual sequence* / released 29 March 1948 to ?
	Columbia MX-294 (72515/4-D) *automatic sequence* / released 29 March 1948 to ?

Session of 7 December 1947, 4:15 to 8:30 P.M.; Metropolitan Opera House, NYC.
This session was a continuation of the afternoon session.
[Information from Columbia archives.]

508. PUCCINI: *La Bohème.*

During this session and the next two sessions, a complete recording of *La Bohème* was made. For release information please see item #511 which indicates which portions of the opera were recorded on this date.

Session of 14 December 1947, 12:00 to 5:00 P.M.; Metropolitan Opera House, NYC.
[Information from Columbia archives.]

509. PUCCINI: *La Bohème.*

During this session, the preceding session, and the next session, a complete recording of *La Bohème* was made. For release information please see item #511 which indicates which portions of the opera were recorded on this date.

Session of 21 December 1947, 12:00 to 4:20 P.M.; Metropolitan Opera House, NYC.
[Information from Columbia archives.]

510. PUCCINI: *La Bohème.*

During this session and the preceding two sessions, a complete recording of *La Bohème* was made. For release information please see item #511 which indicates which portions of the opera were recorded on this date.

511. The recording sessions of 7, 14 and 21 December 1947 were devoted to the complete recording of *La Bohème*. The recordings were released as a two volume 78 rpm set with the following cast and side arrangement. Following each side is the date of the issued take. Max Rudolf, who was present, remembered that these sessions went badly. Antonicelli spoke no English, and much time was wasted. Rudolf was later involved with the choice of which take to issue—a process made difficult with the results Antonicelli had obtained. For the technically excellent Sony Classical Masterworks Heritage compact disc release in 1997, it may have been possible to combine the best parts of separate takes and thus produce a better result than the earlier technology of the 78 rpm era would have permitted.

PUCCINI: *La Bohème.*

Rodolfo	**Richard Tucker**
Mimì	**Bidú Sayão**
Musetta	**Mimi Benzell**

Marcello	**Francesco Valentino**
Colline	**Nicola Moscona**
Schaunard	**George Cehanovsky**
Benoit & Alcindoro	**Salvatore Baccaloni**
Parpignol	**Ludovico Oliviero**
Sergeant	**Lawrence Davidson**

Chorus of the Metropolitan Opera Association
Orchestra of the Metropolitan Opera Association
Giuseppe Antonicelli

Side 1	matrix: XCO 39557	*Questo Mar Rosso mi ammollisce e assidera*	7 Dec 1947
Side 2	matrix: XCO 39558	*Pensier profondo!*	14 Dec 1947
Side 3	matrix: XCO 39559	*Quando un olezzo di frittelle*	14 Dec 1947
Side 4	matrix: XCO 39560	*Quest'uoma ha moglie*	7 Dec 1947
Side 5	matrix: XCO 39561	*Chi è là?*	7 Dec 1947
Side 6	matrix: XCO 39640	*Che gelida manina*	14 Dec 1947
Side 7	matrix: XCO 39638	*Sì! Mi chiamano Mimì*	14 Dec 1947
Side 8	matrix: XCO 39562	*Eh! Rodolfo*	7 Dec 1947
Side 9	matrix: XCO 39691	*Aranci, datteri!*	21 Dec 1947
Side 10	matrix: XCO 39692	*Chi guardi?*	21 Dec 1947
Side 11	matrix: XCO 39693	*Salame ... Parpignol! Parpignol!*	21 Dec 1947
Side 12	matrix: XCO 39694	*Oh! Essa! Musetta!*	21 Dec 1947
Side 13	matrix: XCO 39695	*Quando m'en vo' soletta per la via*	21 Dec 1947
Side 14	matrix: XCO 39696	*Marcello! Sirena!*	21 Dec 1947
Side 15	matrix: XCO 39697	*Ohè, là, le guardie*	21 Dec 1947
Side 16	matrix: XCO 39563	*O buona donna, mi fate il favore*	7 Dec 1947
Side 17	matrix: XCO 39564	*Da ieri ho l'ossa rotte*	7 Dec 1947
Side 18	matrix: XCO 39565	*Mimì è tanto malata!*	7 Dec 1947
Side 19	matrix: XCO 39639	*Donde lieta uscì*	14 Dec 1947
Side 20	matrix: XCO 39566	*Che facevi? Che dicevi?*	7 Dec 1947
Side 21	matrix: XCO 39567	*In un coupè?*	7 Dec 1947
Side 22	matrix: XCO 39568	*Che ora sia?*	7 Dec 1947
Side 23	matrix: XCO 39641	*C'è Mimì*	14 Dec 1947
Side 24	matrix: XCO 39569	*Ascolta! Forse è l'ultima volta*	7 Dec 1947
Side 25	matrix: XCO 39642	*Sono andati?*	14 Dec 1947
Side 26	matrix: XCO 39643	*Oh Dio! Mimì*	14 Dec 1947

78 rpm — **Columbia OP-27** (12810/22-D) *manual sequence* / released 26 April 1948 to ?
Columbia MOP-27 (12823/35-D) *automatic sequence* / released 26 April 1948 to ?

33⅓ rpm — **Columbia SL 1** (ML 4076/7) *manual sequence* / released 20 September 1948 to ?
Columbia SL 101 (ML 4163/4) *automatic sequence* / released 20 September 1948 to ? [When this set was first released, it, and its manual sequence companion listed directly above, contained the following justifiably proud words by Columbia, "This album, which is coincidental with the advent of Columbia's new LP Long Playing Microgroove Records,

marks a radical departure in the history of recorded opera. For in it, you will find Puccini's *La Bohême* [sic], superbly recorded in its brilliant entirety by distinguished artists of the Metropolitan Opera, on *two* records instead of the conventional thirteen which a work of this size ordinarily demands for its reproduction. With this epochal set, therefore, is realized a long-cherished dream of music-lovers. Through Columbia's LP Records, you may now hear your favorite opera, performed with magnificent fidelity by celebrated artists—complete acts—scenes in their colorful entirety—unmarred by the annoyance of excessive record changing." When a slightly revised edition of this recording with new cover art was released in 1951 under the same number, the paragraph quoted above was omitted.

                 Odyssey Y2 32364 (Y 32365/6) / released 7 September 1973 to ?

CD   **Sony Classical MH2K 62762** / released 1997 to ?

<u>Selections from this set were also released as follows:</u>

512. **PUCCINI:** *La Bohème—O soave fanciulla.*
     Cassette   **CBS MGT 46705** / released 1991 to ?
     CD   **CBS Records MDK 46705** / released 1991 to ?
                  Sony Classical MLK 64597 / released 1995 to ?
                  Sony Classical SB2K 63278 / released 1997 to ?

513. **PUCCINI:** *La Bohème—Quando me'n vo' & Act II Finale.*
     Cassette   **MET 501-C** / released 1988 to ?
     CD   **MET 501-CD** / released 1988 to ?

514. **PUCCINI:** *La Bohème—Donde lieta uscì & Addio dolce svegliare.*
     Cassette   **MET 501-C** / released 1988 to ?
     CD   **MET 501-CD** / released 1988 to ?

515. **PUCCINI:** *La Bohème—O Mimì, tu più non torni.*
     CD   **Sony Classical MLK 64597** / released 1995 to ?
                  Sony Classical SB2K 63278 / released 1997 to ?

Session of 29 December 1947, 7:00 to 10:00 P.M.; Liederkranz Hall, NYC.
[Information from Columbia archives.]

516. **VERDI:** *Rigoletto—Questa o quella & La donna è mobile.*
     Richard Tucker & Metropolitan Opera Orchestra – Emil Cooper.
          matrix: **XCO 39834**
Although the "Metropolitan Opera Orchestra" did not appear on the record labels, the recording sheets in the Columbia archives indicate that the Metropolitan Opera Orchestra was used.
     78 rpm   **Columbia 72828-D** / released 8 August 1949 to ?
     45 rpm   **Columbia A1762**
     33⅓ rpm   **Columbia 3-259**
                  Columbia ML 4248 / released 5 December 1949 to ?

Cassette	**Sony Classical MLT 66707** [This contained only *La donna è mobile*]
	MET 518-C [This contained only *La donna è mobile*] / released 1993 to ?
CD	**Sony Classical J4K 65819** [This contained only *La donna è mobile*] / released 1999 to ?
	Sony Classical MLK 66707 [This contained only *La donna è mobile*]
	MET 518-CD [This contained only *La donna è mobile*] / released 1993 to ?
	Preiser 89552 / released 2001 to ?

517. FLOTOW: *Martha—Ach, so fromm.* (in Italian as *"M'apparì tutt' amor"*)
Richard Tucker & Metropolitan Opera Orchestra – Emil Cooper.
     matrix: **XCO 39835**

Although the "Metropolitan Opera Orchestra" did not appear on the record labels, the recording sheets in the Columbia archives indicate that the Metropolitan Opera Orchestra was used.

78 rpm	**Columbia 72828-D** / released 8 August 1949 to ?
33⅓ rpm	**Columbia 3-259**
	Columbia ML 4248 / released 5 December 1949 to ?
Cassette	**Sony Classical MLT 66707**
CD	**Sony Classical SM2K 89370** / released 2000 to ?
	Sony Classical MLK 66707
	Preiser 89552 / released 2001 to ?

518. BIZET: *Les Pêcheurs de Perles—Je crois entendre encore.*
Richard Tucker & Orchestra of the Metropolitan Opera Association – Emil Cooper.
     matrix: **XCO 39836**

78 rpm	**Columbia 72577-D** / released 12 July 1948 to ?
33⅓ rpm	**Columbia ML 4248** / released 5 December 1949 to ?
CD	**Preiser 89552** / released 2001 to ?

Session of 14 March 1949, 3:15 to 6:45 P.M.; Columbia Studios, 207 E. 30ᵗʰ St. NYC.
[Information from Columbia archives.]

519. RICHARD STRAUSS: *Salome—Ah! Du wolltest mich nicht deinem Mund küssen lassen.*
("Final Scene") [Herod's words are omitted.]
       Part 1: (*"Ah! Du wolltest mich nicht deinem Mund küssen lassen"*)
       Part 2: (*"Öffne doch die Augen"*)
       Part 3: (*"Oh! Warum hast du mich nicht angesehn"*)
       Part 4: (*"Ah! Ich habe ihn geküsst, deinen Mund"*)
Ljuba Welitsch & Metropolitan Opera Orchestra - Fritz Reiner. [A note in the Columbia Archives states that the singer's name is to be changed from the spelling "Welitsch," used in the first run of labels, to "Welitch."]
       matrix: *Side 1* **XCO 41067**
       matrix: *Side 2* **XCO 41068**
       matrix: *Side 3* **XCO 41069**
       matrix: *Side 4* **XCO 41070**

78 rpm	**Columbia MX-316** (72818/9-D) *automatic sequence* / released 2 or 10 May 1949 to ?
	Columbia LK 1241/2
45 rpm	**Philips ABE10025**
33⅓ rpm	**Columbia ML 2048**
	Columbia ML 4795 / released 1 February 1954 to ?
	Odyssey 32 16 0077 / released 24 April 1967 to ?
	Columbia 33C 1011
	CBS 61088 / released November 1969 to ?
CD	**Sony Classical MH2K 62866** / released 1997 to ?
	Preiser 90476 / released 2002 to ?

Session of 26 May 1949, 3:00 to 7:30 P.M.; Columbia Studios, 207 E. 30ᵗʰ St. NYC.
[Information from Columbia archives.]

520. PUCCINI: *Madama Butterfly.*
During this session and the next two sessions, a complete recording of *Madama Butterfly* was made. For release information please see item #523.

Session of 27 May 1949, 3:00 to 6:00 P.M.; Columbia Studios, 207 E. 30ᵗʰ St. NYC.
[Information from Columbia archives.]

521. PUCCINI: *Madama Butterfly.*
During this session, the preceding session, and the next session, a complete recording of *Madama Butterfly* was made. For release information please see item #523.

Session of 28 May 1949, 1:00 to 5:00 P.M.; Columbia Studios, 207 E. 30ᵗʰ St. NYC.
[Information from Columbia archives.]

522. PUCCINI: *Madama Butterfly.*
During this session and the preceding two sessions, a complete recording of *Madama Butterfly* was made. For release information please see item #523.

523. The recording sessions of 26, 27 and 28 May 1949 were devoted to the complete recording of *Madama Butterfly*. The recordings were first released as a thirteen disc 78 rpm set and as a three disc 33⅓ set. It is not known which parts were recorded during each session. Max Rudolf remembered that Columbia insisted on having him conduct and not Antonicelli, who had been conducting *Madama Butterfly* at the Metropolitan Opera in the season just concluded. This was because of Antonicelli's problems during the *La Bohème* recording sessions. Columbia chose *Madama Butterfly* to use Richard Tucker. Max Ruldolf also remembered that Steber had done a concert performance of *Madama Butterfly* at the Lewisohn Stadium which Rudolf heard. He recalled she was given only one day of piano rehearsal for her recording.

PUCCINI: *Madama Butterfly*.

Madama Butterfly	**Eleanor Steber**
Lt. B. F. Pinkerton	**Richard Tucker**
Sharpless	**Giuseppe Valdengo**
Suzuki	**Jean Madeira**
Goro	**Alessio de Paolis**
Prince Yamadori	**George Cehanovsky**
The Bonze	**Melchiorre Luise**
Kate Pinkerton	**Thelma Votipka**
Imperial Commissioner	**John Baker**

Chorus of the Metropolitan Opera Association
(Kurt Adler, chorus master)
Orchestra of the Metropolitan Opera Association
Max Rudolf

matrices: **XCO 41307 through XCO 41338**

78 rpm	**Columbia MOP-30** (13011/26-D) *automatic sequence* / released 3 October 1949 to ?
33⅓ rpm	**Columbia SL 4** *manual sequence* / released 3 October 1949 to ?
	Columbia SL 104 (ML 4225/7) *automatic sequence* / released 3 October 1949 to ?
	Odyssey Y3 32107 (Y 32108/10) / released 27 April 1973 to ?
	Philips A 01119/21 L
	CBS 78246 / released August 1974 to ?
CD	**Sony Classical MH2K 62765** / released 1998 to ?
	Preiser 20050

A selection from this set was also released as follows:

524. **PUCCINI:** *Madama Butterfly—Io so che alle sue pene.*

Cassette	**MET 507-C** / released 1989 to ?
CD	**MET 507-CD** / released 1989 to ?

Session of 9 June 1949, 2:00 to 5:00 P.M.; Columbia Studios, 207 E. 30th St. NYC.
[Information from Columbia archives.]

525. **MASCAGNI:** *Cavalleria Rusticana—Mamma, quell vino è generosa.*
     Richard Tucker & Metropolitan Opera Orchestra – Fausto Cleva.
          matrix: **XCO 41363**

78 rpm	**Columbia MM-870** (72879-D) / released 16 January 1950 to ?
	Columbia LX 1508
45 rpm	**Columbia A-1646**
33⅓ rpm	**Columbia ML 4248** / released 5 December 1949 to ?
CD	**Preiser 89552** / released 2001 to ?

526. **VERDI:** *Aïda—Celeste Aïda.*
     Richard Tucker & Metropolitan Opera Orchestra – Fausto Cleva.
          matrix: **XCO 41364**

78 rpm	**Columbia MM-870** (72879-D) / released 16 January 1950 to ?
	Columbia LX 1508
45 rpm	**Columbia A-1762**
33⅓ rpm	**Columbia ML 4248** / released 5 December 1949 to ?
CD	**Preiser 89552** / released 2001 to ?

527. **LEONCAVALLO:** *Pagliacci—Vesti la giubba.*
     Richard Tucker & Metropolitan Opera Orchestra – Fausto Cleva.
          matrix: **XCO 41365**

78 rpm	**Columbia MM-870** (72880-D) / released 16 January 1950 to ?
	Columbia LX 1545
45 rpm	**Columbia A-1646**
33⅓ rpm	**Columbia ML 4248** / released 5 December 1949 to ?
	Columbia M 30118 / released 19 October 1970 to ?
CD	**Preiser 89552** / released 2001 to ?

Session of 13 June 1949, 2:00 to 5:00 P.M.; Columbia Studios, 207 E. 30th St. NYC.
[Information from Columbia archives.]

528. **VERDI:** *Rigoletto—Parmi veder le lagrime.*
     Richard Tucker & Metropolitan Opera Orchestra – Fausto Cleva.
          matrix: **XCO 41366**

78 rpm	**Columbia MM-870** (72881-D) / released 16 January 1950 to ?
	Columbia LX 1545
45 rpm	**Columbia A-1762**
33⅓ rpm	**Columbia ML 4248** / released 5 December 1949 to ?
	Columbia D3M 33448 [Max Rudolf is incorrectly listed as conductor.]
	MET 404 [Max Rudolf is incorrectly listed as conductor.] / released 1984 to ?

Cassette	**MET 404-C** [Max Rudolf is incorrectly listed as conductor.] / released 1984 to ?
CD	**Preiser 89552** / released 2001 to ?

529. VERDI: *La Forza del Destino—La vita è inferno … O tu che in seno agli angeli.*
Richard Tucker & Metropolitan Opera Orchestra – Fausto Cleva.
        matrix: **XCO 41367**
        matrix: **XCO 41368**

78 rpm	**Columbia MM-870** (72880/1-D) / released 16 January 1950 to ?
33⅓ rpm	**Columbia ML 4248** / released 5 December 1949 to ?
CD	**Preiser 89552** / released 2001 to ?

Session of 10 February 1950, 2:00 to 5:00 P.M.; Columbia Studios, 207 E. 30ᵗʰ St. NYC.
[Information from Columbia archives.]

530. MOZART: *Don Giovanni—Don Ottavio, son morta … Or sai chi l'onore.*
        Part 1: *("Recit: Don Ottavio, son morta!")*
        Part 2: *("Aria: Or sai chi l'onore")*
Ljuba Welitsch, Alessio De Paolis & Orchestra of the Metropolitan Opera Association, New York – Fritz Reiner.
        matrix: *Side 1* **CO 42325**
        matrix: *Side 2* **CO 42326**

78 rpm	**Columbia MX-340** (17611/2-D) / released 29 May 1950 to ?
	Columbia LB 124
	Columbia LW 61
45 rpm	**Philips ABE10074**
33⅓ rpm	**Columbia ML 2118** / released 27 March 1950 to ?
	Odyssey 32 16 0077 / released 24 April 1967 to ?
	Philips SBR6255 / released March 1959 to ?
	CBS 61088 / released November 1969 to ?
Cassette	**MET 511-C** / released 1991 to ?
CD	**Sony Classical MH2K 62866** / released 1997 to ?
	MET 511-CD / released 1991 to ?
	Preiser 90476 / released 2002 to ?

531. MOZART: *Don Giovanni—Crudele? Ah no, mio bene … Non mi dir, bell'idol mio.*
        Part 1: *("Recit: Crudele? Ah no, mio bene!; Aria: Non mi dir, bell'idol mio [beginning]")*
        Part 2: *("Aria: Non mi dir, bell'idol mio [conclusion]")*
Ljuba Welitsch & Orchestra of the Metropolitan Opera Association, New York – Fritz Reiner.
        matrix: *Side 1* **CO 42327**
        matrix: *Side 2* **CO 42328**

78 rpm	**Columbia MX-340** (17612/1-D) / released 29 May 1950 to ?
	Columbia LO-89

	Columbia LB 121
45 rpm	**Philips ABE10074**
33⅓ rpm	**Columbia ML 2118** / released 27 March 1950 to ?
	Odyssey 32 16 0077 / released 24 April 1967 to ?
	Philips SBR6255 / released March 1959 to ?
	CBS 61088 / released November 1969 to ?
CD	**Sony Classical MH2K 62866** / released 1997 to ?
	Preiser 90476 / released 2002 to ?

532. **JOHANN STRAUSS, II:** *Die Fledermaus—Klänge der Heimat.* *("Czardas")*
    Ljuba Welitsch & Orchestra of the Metropolitan Opera Association of New York City – Max Rudolf.
        matrix: **XCO 42329**

78 rpm	**Columbia 73005-D** / released 18 September 1950 to ?
45 rpm	**Philips SBF149**
33⅓ rpm	**Columbia ML 2139**
	Columbia ML 4795 / released 1 February 1954 to ?
	Odyssey 32 16 0077 / released 24 April 1967 to ?
	Philips SBR6255 / released March 1959 to ?
	CBS 61088 / released November 1969 to ?
CD	**Sony Classical MH2K 62866** / released 1997 to ?
	Preiser 90476 / released 2002 to ?

533. **JOHANN STRAUSS, II:** *Der Zigeunerbaron—O habet Acht.* *("Zigeunerlied")*
    Ljuba Welitsch & Orchestra of the Metropolitan Opera Association of New York City – Max Rudolf.
        matrix: **XCO 42330**

78 rpm	**Columbia 73005-D** / released 18 September 1950 to ?
45 rpm	**Philips SBF149**
33⅓ rpm	**Columbia ML 2139**
	Columbia ML 4795 / released 1 February 1954 to ?
	Odyssey 32 16 0077 / released 24 April 1967 to ?
	Philips SBR6255 / released March 1959 to ?
	CBS 61088 / released November 1969 to ?
CD	**Sony Classical MH2K 62866** / released 1997 to ?
	Preiser 90476 / released 2002 to ?

Session of 17 February 1950, 2:00 to 5:00 P.M.; Columbia Studios, 207 E. 30th St. NYC.
[Information from Columbia archives.]

534. **VERDI:** *Falstaff—È sogno? o realtà?* *("Ford's Monologue")*
    Frank Guarrera & Orchestra of the Metropolitan Opera Association of New York City – Fausto Cleva.
        matrix: **XCO 42372**

78 rpm	**Columbia MM-914** (73008-D) / released 27 March 1950 to ?

33⅓ rpm   **Columbia ML 2114** / released 27 March 1950 to ?
CD   **Preiser 90500**

535. **VERDI:** *Otello—Credo in un Dio crudel.*
     Frank Guarrera & Orchestra of the Metropolitan Opera Association of New York City – Fausto Cleva.
        matrix: **XCO 42373**
    78 rpm   **Columbia MM-914 (73009-D)** / released 27 March 1950 to ?
    33⅓ rpm   **Columbia ML 2114** / released 27 March 1950 to ?
                Columbia ML 4499 / released 24 March 1952 to ? [This album, entitled "Great Scenes from Verdi's *Otello*," combined separate recordings made during the sessions of 16 August 1950, 18 June 1951, 31 December 1951 and this date.]
                Philips ABL 3005
                Philips N 02102 L
    CD   **Preiser 90500**

Session of 20 February 1950, 2:00 to 5:00 P.M.; Columbia Studios, 207 E. 30th St. NYC.
[Information from Columbia archives.]

536. **VERDI:** *Un Ballo in Maschera—Eri tu.*
     Frank Guarrera & Orchestra of the Metropolitan Opera Association of New York City – Fausto Cleva.
        matrix: **XCO 42374**
    78 rpm   **Columbia MM-914 (73010-D)** / released 27 March 1950 to ?
    33⅓ rpm   **Columbia ML 2114** / released 27 March 1950 to ?
    CD   **Preiser 90500**

537. **LEONCAVALLO:** *Pagliacci—Prologue.*
     Frank Guarrera & Orchestra of the Metropolitan Opera Association of New York City – Fausto Cleva.
        matrix: **XCO 42375**
    78 rpm   **Columbia MM-914 (73010-D)** / released 27 March 1950 to ?
    45 rpm   **Columbia A-1646** / released 6 April 1953 to ?
    33⅓ rpm   **Columbia ML 2114** / released 27 March 1950 to ?
    CD   **Preiser 90500**

538. **GIORDANO:** *Andrea Chénier—Nemico della patria.*
     Frank Guarrera & Orchestra of the Metropolitan Opera Association of New York City – Fausto Cleva.
        matrix: **XCO 42376**
    78 rpm   **Columbia MM-914 (73009-D)** / released 27 March 1950 to ?
    33⅓ rpm   **Columbia ML 2114** / released 27 March 1950 to ?
    CD   **Preiser 90500**

539. **ROSSINI:** *Il Barbiere di Siviglia—Largo al factotum.*
     Frank Guarrera & Orchestra of the Metropolitan Opera Association of New York City – Fausto Cleva.
        matrix: **XCO 42377**

78 rpm   **Columbia MM-914** (73008-D) / released 27 March 1950 to ?
33⅓ rpm   **Columbia ML 2114** / released 27 March 1950 to ?
CD   **Preiser 90500**

Session of 23 March 1950, 2:00 to 4:30 P.M.; Columbia Studios, 207 E. 30ᵗʰ St. NYC.
[Information from Columbia archives.]

540. **PUCCINI:** *Tosca—Perchè chiuso? ("Love Duet")*
     Ljuba Welitsch, Richard Tucker & Orchestra of the Metropolitan Opera Association of New York City – Max Rudolf.
          matrix: *Side 1* **XCO 43316**
          matrix: *Side 2* **XCO 43317**
          matrix: *Side 3* **XCO 43318**
     78 rpm   **Columbia MX-346** (73070/1-D) / released 18 September 1950 to ?
     33⅓ rpm   **Columbia ML 2139**
                     Columbia ML 4795 / released 1 February 1954 to ?
                     Odyssey 32 16 0077 / released 24 April 1954 to ?
                     Philips SBR6255 / released March 1959 to ?
                     CBS 61088 / released November 1969 to ?
     Cassette   **CBS MGT 46705** / released 1991 to ?
                     MET 516-C / released 1992 to ?
     CD   **CBS MDK 46705** / released 1991 to ?
                     Sony Classical MH2K 62866 / released 1997 to ?
                     Sony Classical SB2K 63278 / released 1997 to ?
                     Sony Classical MLK 64597 / released 1995 to ?
                     MET 516-CD / released 1992 to ?
                     Preiser 90476 / released 2002 to ?

541. **PUCCINI:** *Tosca—Vissi d'arte.*
     Ljuba Welitsch & Orchestra of the Metropolitan Opera Association of New York City – Max Rudolf.
          matrix: **XCO 43319**
     78 rpm   **Columbia MX-346** (73070-D) / released 18 September 1950 to ?
     33⅓ rpm   **Columbia ML 2139**
                     Columbia ML 4795 / released 1 February 1954 to ?
                     Odyssey 32 16 0077 / released 24 April 1954 to ?
                     Philips SBR6255 / released March 1959 to ?
                     Philips GBL5532
                     CBS 61088 / released November 1969 to ?
     CD   **Sony Classical MH2K 62866** / released 1997 to ?
                     Preiser 90476 / released 2002 to ?

Session of 16 August 1950, 2:00 to 5:00 P.M.; Columbia Studios, 207 E. 30th St. NYC.
[Information from Columbia archives.]

542. **VERDI:** *Otello—Canzone del Salce. ("Willow Song" "Mia madre aveva una povera ancella")*
>   *Eleanor Steber & Orchestra of the Metropolitan Opera Association of New York – Fausto Cleva.*
>   matrix: **XCO 43522**

78 rpm	**Columbia MX-351** (73150-D) / released 13 November 1950 to ?
33⅓ rpm	**Columbia ML 2157**
	Columbia ML 4499 / released 24 March 1952 to ? [This album, entitled "Great Scenes from Verdi's *Otello*," combined separate recordings made during the sessions of 17 February 1950, 18 June 1951, 31 December 1951 and this date.]
	Odyssey Y 31149 / released 8 March 1972 to ?
	Philips ABL 3005
	Philips N 02102 L
	Philips N 02609 R
CD	**Preiser 90500**

543. **VERDI:** *Otello—Ave Maria.*
>   *Eleanor Steber & Orchestra of the Metropolitan Opera Association of New York – Fausto Cleva.*
>   matrix: **XCO 43523**

78 rpm	**Columbia MX-351** (73150-D) / released 13 November 1950 to ?
33⅓ rpm	**Columbia ML 2157**
	Columbia ML 4499 / released 24 March 1952 to ? [This album, entitled "Great Scenes from Verdi's *Otello*," combined separate recordings made during the sessions of 17 February 1950, 18 June 1951, 31 December 1951 and this date.]
	Odyssey Y 31149 / released 8 March 1972 to ?
	Philips ABL 3005
	Philips N 02102 L
	Philips N 02609 R
CD	**Preiser 90500**
	Preiser 89636

544. **VERDI:** *Don Carlos—Tu che le vanità.*
>   *Eleanor Steber & Orchestra of the Metropolitan Opera Association of New York – Fausto Cleva.*
>   matrix: **XCO 43524**

78 rpm	**Columbia MX-351** (73149-D) / released 13 November 1950 to ?
33⅓ rpm	**Columbia ML 2157**
	Odyssey Y 31149 / released 8 March 1972 to ?
	Philips NBR 6037
	Philips N 02609 R
CD	**Preiser 89636**

Session of 17 August 1950, 2:00 to 5:00 P.M.; Columbia Studios, 207 E. 30th St. NYC.
[Information from Columbia archives.]

545. **VERDI:** *La Forza del Destino—Pace, pace, mio Dio!*
Eleanor Steber & Orchestra of the Metropolitan Opera Association of New York – Fausto Cleva.
      matrix: **XCO 43525**

78 rpm   **Columbia MX-351** (73149-D) / released 13 November 1950 to ?
33⅓ rpm   **Columbia ML 2157**
                 Odyssey Y 31149 / released 8 March 1972 to ?
                 Philips NBR 6037
                 Philips N 02609 R

546. **VERDI:** *La Traviata—Ah! fors' è lui.*
Eleanor Steber & Orchestra of the Metropolitan Opera Association of New York – Fausto Cleva.
      matrix: **CO 43526**

78 rpm   **Columbia 17622-D** / released 13 November 1950 to ?
33⅓ rpm   **Columbia ML 2157**
                 Odyssey Y 31149 / released 8 March 1972 to ?
                 Philips NBR 6037
                 Philips N 02609 R
CD   **Preiser 89636**

547. **VERDI:** *La Traviata—Sempre libera.*
Eleanor Steber & Orchestra of the Metropolitan Opera Association of New York – Fausto Cleva.
      matrix: **CO 43527**

78 rpm   **Columbia 17622-D** / released 13 November 1950 to ?
33⅓ rpm   **Columbia ML 2157**
                 Odyssey Y 31149 / released 8 March 1972 to ?
                 Philips NBR 6037
                 Philips N 02609 R
CD   **Preiser 89636**

548. **VERDI:** *Ernani—Ernani, involami.*
Eleanor Steber & Orchestra of the Metropolitan Opera Association of New York – Fausto Cleva.
      matrix: **CO 43528**
      matrix: **CO 43529**

         speed: 72.73 rpm [Through a processing error at least some, if not all, 78 rpm issues were not made at the correct speed of 78.26 rpm]
78 rpm   **Columbia 17623-D** / released 13 November 1950 to ?
33⅓ rpm   **Columbia ML 2157**
                 Odyssey Y 31149 / released 8 March 1972 to ?
                 Philips NBR 6037
                 Philips N 02609 R
CD   **Preiser 89636**

Session of 6 December 1950, 2:00 to 5:30 P.M.; Columbia Studios, 207 E. 30th St. NYC.

[Information from Columbia archives.]

549. **VERDI:** *Il Trovatore—Stride la vampa!*
      Fedora Barbieri & Orchestra of the Metropolitan Opera Association of New York – Fausto Cleva.
             matrix: **XCO 43787**

78 rpm	**Columbia 73183-D** / released 12 March 1951 to ?
45 rpm	**Columbia 4-73183-D**
33⅓ rpm	**Columbia 3-73183-D**

550. **VERDI:** *Il Trovatore—Condotta ell'era in ceppi.*
      Fedora Barbieri & Orchestra of the Metropolitan Opera Association of New York – Fausto Cleva.
             matrix: **XCO 43788**

78 rpm	**Columbia 73183-D** / released 12 March 1951 to ?
45 rpm	**Columbia 4-73183-D**
33⅓ rpm	**Columbia 3-73183-D**

551. **VERDI:** *Don Carlos—O don fatale.*
      Fedora Barbieri & Orchestra of the Metropolitan Opera Association of New York – Fausto Cleva.
             matrix: **XCO 43789**

78 rpm	**Columbia 73184-D** / released 12 March 1951 to ?
45 rpm	**Columbia 4-73184-D**
33⅓ rpm	**Columbia 3-73184-D**

552. **VERDI:** *Un Ballo in Maschera—Re dell' abisso, affrettati.*
      Fedora Barbieri & Orchestra of the Metropolitan Opera Association of New York – Fausto Cleva.
             matrix: **XCO 43790**

78 rpm	**Columbia 73184-D** / released 12 March 1951 to ?
45 rpm	**Columbia 4-73184-D**
33⅓ rpm	**Columbia 3-73184-D**

Session of 24 December 1950, 2:00 to 6:30 P.M.; Columbia Studios, 207 E. 30th St. NYC.

[Information from Columbia archives.]

553. **JOHANN STRAUSS, II:** *Die Fledermaus.*
      During this session and the next two sessions, a complete recording of *Die Fledermaus* was made. For release information please see item #556.

Session of 29 December 1950, 3:00 to 5:30 P.M.; Columbia Studios, 207 E. 30th St. NYC.

[Information from Columbia archives.]

554. **JOHANN STRAUSS, II:** *Die Fledermaus.*
      During this session, the preceding session, and the next session, a complete recording of *Die Fledermaus* was made. For release information please see item #556.

<u>*Session of 7 January 1951, 12:00 to 4:30 P.M.; Columbia Studios, 207 E. 30th St. NYC.*</u>
[Information from Columbia archives.]

555. JOHANN STRAUSS, II: *Die Fledermaus.*

During this session and the preceding two sessions, a complete recording of *Die Fledermaus* was made. For release information please see item #556.

556. The recording sessions of 24 and 29 December 1950 and 7 January 1951 were devoted to a complete recording of *Die Fledermaus*. 78 rpm and 33⅓ rpm editions were released at the same time with the 45 rpm edition following in about two months. Given below are the side arrangements of the 78 rpm and 45 rpm editions. Following each side is the date of the issued take.

JOHANN STRAUSS, II: *Die Fledermaus.*
(English lyrics by Howard Dietz; English libretto by Garson Kanin)

Adele	**Lily Pons**
Rosalinda	**Ljuba Welitsch**
Alfred	**Richard Tucker**
Eisenstein	**Charles Kullman**
Prince Orlofsky	**Martha Lipton**
Dr. Falke	**John Brownlee**
Frank	**Clifford Harvuot**
Dr. Blind	**Paul Franke**

**Chorus of the Metropolitan Opera Association
(Kurt Adler, chorus master)
Orchestra of the Metropolitan Opera Association
Eugene Ormandy**

Side 1	matrix: **XCO 44827**	*Overture, part 1*	24 Dec 1950
Side 2	matrix: **XCO 44828**	*Overture, part 2*	24 Dec 1950
Side 3	matrix: **XCO 44829**	*Act I (beg.) Introduction, solo, duet*	24 Dec 1950
Side 4	matrix: **XCO 44830**	*Act I (continuation) Trio*	24 Dec 1950
Side 5	matrix: **XCO 44831**	*Act I (continuation) Duet*	24 Dec 1950
Side 6	matrix: **XCO 44832**	*Act I (continuation) Trio*	7 Jan 1951
Side 7	matrix: **XCO 44833**	*Act I (continuation) Finale (beginning)*	24 Dec 1950
Side 8	matrix: **XCO 44834**	*Act I (continuation) Finale (continuation)*	24 Dec 1950
Side 9	matrix: **XCO 44835**	*Act I (conclusion) Finale (conclusion)*	24 Dec 1950
Side 10	matrix: **XCO 44836**	*Act II (beginning)*	24 Dec 1950
Side 11	matrix: **XCO 44837**	*Act II (continuation) Laughing Song*	7 Jan 1951
Side 12	matrix: **XCO 44838**	*Act II (continuation) Watch Duet*	29 Dec 1950

Side 13	matrix: **XCO 44839**	*Act II (continuation) Czárdás*	7 Jan 1951
Side 14	matrix: **XCO 44840**	*Act II (continuation) Finale (beginning)*	7 Jan 1951
Side 15	matrix: **XCO 44841**	*Act II (continuation) Finale (continuation)*	7 Jan 1951
Side 16	matrix: **XCO 44842**	*Roses from the South, part 1*	7 Jan 1951
Side 17	matrix: **XCO 44843**	*Roses from the South, part 2*	7 Jan 1951
Side 18	matrix: **XCO 44844**	*Act II (conclusion) Finale (conclusion)*	7 Jan 1951
Side 19	matrix: **XCO 44845**	*Act III (beginning) Entr'acte*	29 Dec 1950
Side 20	matrix: **XCO 44846**	*Act III (continuation) Audition Song*	7 Jan 1951
Side 21	matrix: **XCO 44847**	*Act III (continuation) Trio (beginning)*	29 Dec 1950
Side 22	matrix: **XCO 44848**	*Act III (continuation) Trio (conclusion)*	29 Dec 1950
Side 23	matrix: **XCO 44849**	*Act III (conclusion) Finale*	7 Jan 1951

(Side 24 of the 78 rpm and 45 rpm sets contained the Alexander Schneider String Quintet's performance of Johann Strauss' *Die Unzertrennlichen, op. 108* recorded on 6 September 1948.)

78 rpm	**Columbia MOP-32** (73191/202-D) *automatic sequence* / released 29 January 1951 to ?
45 rpm	**Columbia MOP 4-32** (4-73191/202-D) / released 2 April 1951 to ?
33⅓ rpm	**Columbia SL 8** *manual sequence* / released 29 January 1951 to ?
	Columbia SL 108 (ML 54277/8) *automatic sequence*/ released 29 January 1951 to ?
	Odyssey Y2 32666 / released 4 January 1974 to ?
	Philips GBL 5643-4
	CBS 78245

Session of 17 January 1951, 3:00 to 6:00 P.M.; Columbia Studios, 207 E. 30th St. NYC.
[Information from Columbia archives.]

557. **PUCCINI:** *Gianni Schicchi—O mio babbino caro.*
    Dorothy Kirsten & Orchestra of the Metropolitan Opera Association – Fausto Cleva.

45 rpm	**Columbia A 1015** (4-73265-D) / released 19 October 1951 to ?
	Columbia A 1639 / released 6 April 1953 to ?
33⅓ rpm	**Columbia ML 2200** / released 19 October 1951 to ?
	Odyssey Y 31737 / released 25 October 1972 to ?

558. **PUCCINI:** *Madama Butterfly—Un bel dì, vedremo.*
    Dorothy Kirsten & Orchestra of the Metropolitan Opera Association – Fausto Cleva.

45 rpm	**Columbia A 1015** (4-73266-D) / released 19 October 1951 to ?
	Columbia A 1639 / released 6 April 1953 to ?
33⅓ rpm	**Columbia ML 2200** / released 19 October 1951 to ?
	Odyssey Y 31737 / released 25 October 1972 to ?

559. **PUCCINI:** *Madama Butterfly—Tu, tu piccolo Iddio!*
    Dorothy Kirsten & Orchestra of the Metropolitan Opera Association – Fausto Cleva.

45 rpm	**Columbia A 1015** (4-73267-D) / released 19 October 1951 to ?
	Columbia A 1639 / released 6 April 1953-?
33⅓ rpm	**Columbia ML 2200** / released 19 October 1951-?
	Odyssey Y 31737 / released 25 October 1972-?
_CD_	**MET 217-CD** / released 1993 to ?

560. **PUCCINI:** _Tosca—Vissi d'arte._
   Dorothy Kirsten & Orchestra of the Metropolitan Opera Association – Fausto Cleva.

45 rpm	**Columbia A 1015** (4-73265-D) / released 19 October 1951-?
	Columbia A 1639 / released 6 April 1953 to ?
33⅓ rpm	**Columbia ML 2200** / released 19 October 1951 to ?
	Odyssey Y 31737 / released 25 October 1972 to ?
_CD_	**MET 217-CD** / released 1993 to ?

Session of 18 January 1951, 3:00 to 6:00 P.M.; Columbia Studios, 207 E. 30ᵗʰ St. NYC.
[Information from Columbia archives.]

561. **PUCCINI:** _La Rondine—Ore liete divine._
   Dorothy Kirsten & Orchestra of the Metropolitan Opera Association – Fausto Cleva.

45 rpm	**Columbia A 1015** (4-73267-D) / released 19 October 1951 to ?
33⅓ rpm	**Columbia ML 2200** / released 19 October 1951 to ?
	Odyssey Y 31737 / released 25 October 1972 to ?

562. **PUCCINI:** _Turandot—Tu che di gel sei cinta._
   Dorothy Kirsten & Orchestra of the Metropolitan Opera Association – Fausto Cleva.

45 rpm	**Columbia A 1015** (4-73266-D) / released 19 October 1951 to ?
33⅓ rpm	**Columbia ML 2200** / released 19 October 1951 to ?

563. **PUCCINI:** _Manon Lescaut—Sola, perduta, abbandonata._
   Dorothy Kirsten & Orchestra of the Metropolitan Opera Association – Fausto Cleva.

45 rpm	**Columbia A 1015** (4-73265-D) / released 19 October 1951 to ?
33⅓ rpm	**Columbia ML 2200** / released 19 October 1951 to ?
	Columbia ML 4981 / released 4 April 1955 to ?
	Odyssey Y 31737 / released 25 October 1972 to ?
_CD_	**MET 217-CD** / released 1993 to ?
	Preiser 89637

__Session of 21 May 1951, 2:00 to 6:00 P.M.; Columbia Studios, 207 E. 30th St. NYC.__
[Information from Columbia archives.]

564. GOUNOD: *Faust.*

    During this session and the next two sessions, a complete recording of *Faust* was made. Act I was recorded during this session. For release information please see item #567.

__Session of 23 May 1951, 2:00 to 6:00 P.M.; Columbia Studios, 207 E. 30th St. NYC.__
[Information from Columbia archives.]

565. GOUNOD: *Faust.*

    During this session, the preceding session, and the next session, a complete recording of *Faust* was made. Act II was recorded during this session. For release information please see item #567.

__Session of 25 May 1951, 2:00 to 5:30 P.M.; Columbia Studios, 207 E. 30th St. NYC.__
[Information from Columbia archives.]

566. GOUNOD: *Faust.*

    During this session and the preceding two sessions, a complete recording of *Faust* was made. Acts III and IV were recorded during this session. For release information please see item #567.

567. The recording sessions of 21, 23 and 25 May 1951 were devoted to a complete recording of *Faust*. The cast and dates of recording of each act follow. In this Metropolitan Opera production of *Faust* in comparison to the traditional five act edition of *Faust*, Act I is in two scenes which correspond to Acts I and II of the original. The Metropolitan Opera Act II corresponds to Act III of the original. The Metropolitan Opera Act III is in two scenes, the Church Scene and the Public Square Scene which are both part of Act IV of the original. The Metropolitan Opera Act IV corresponds to the Prison Scene of Act V of the original. The Spinning Wheel Scene of Act IV and the Walpurgis Night Scene with ballet of Act V are omitted.

GOUNOD: *Faust.*

Marguerite	**Eleanor Steber**
Faust	**Eugene Conley**
Mephistophélès	**Cesare Siepi**
Valentine	**Frank Guarrera**
Siebel	**Margaret Roggero**
Marthe	**Thelma Votipka**

Wagner   **Lawrence Davidson**

Ernesto Barbini playing the Baldwin Organ
Chorus of the Metropolitan Opera Association
(Kurt Adler, chorus master)
Orchestra of the Metropolitan Opera Association
Fausto Cleva

Act I	21 May 1951
Act II	23 May 1951
Act III	25 May 1951
Act IV	25 May 1951

33⅓ rpm   **Columbia SL 112** (ML 4415/7)
Odyssey Y3 32103 / released 27 April 1973 to ?
Philips ABL 3096/8
Philips A 01165/7 L
CBS 77.360 (73.192/4) [This set was issued by CBS Inc. in 1975 in France in honor of a century of opera at the Palais Garnier. It contained a well-illustrated history of the Palais Garnier.]
CD   **Preiser 20015**

Selections from this set were also released as follows:

568. **GOUNOD:** *Faust—Le veau d'or.*
   CD   **Preiser 89642**

569. **GOUNOD:** *Faust—Ne permetterez-vous pas. ("Waltz finale")*
   Cassette   **MET 513-C** / released 1991 to ?
   CD   **MET 513-CD** / released 1991 to ?

570. **GOUNOD:** *Faust—Vous qui faites l'endormie. ("Sérénade")*
   CD   **Preiser 89642**

571. **GOUNOD:** *Faust—Que voulez-vous, messieurs? ("Duel trio")*
   Cassette   **MET 513-C** / released 1991 to ?
   CD   **MET 513-CD** / released 1991 to ?

___

Session of 4 June 1951, 2:00 to 5:30 P.M.; Columbia Studios, 207 E. 30ᵗʰ St. NYC.
[Information from Columbia archives.]

572. **LEONCAVALLO:** *Pagliacci.*

During this session and the next session, a complete recording of *Pagliacci* was made. Act I (with the exception of Scene 1) and the Intermezzo were recorded during this session. For release information please see item #574.

Session of 5 June 1951, 2:00 to 6:30 P.M.; Columbia Studios, 207 E. 30ᵗʰ St. NYC.
[Information from Columbia archives.]

573. LEONCAVALLO: *Pagliacci.*

During this session and the previous session, a complete recording of *Pagliacci* was made. Act I, Scene 1 and Act II were recorded during this session. For release information please see item #574.

574. The recording sessions of 4 and 5 June 1951 were devoted to a complete recording of *Pagliacci*. The cast and dates of recording of each act follow. This recording was first issued alone in a two disc set with the opera spread over four 33⅓ rpm sides. After the 1953 recording of *Cavalleria Rusticana* was made, *Pagliacci* was also made available in a three disc set with *Cavalleria Rusticana*, but then *Pagliacci* was spread over only three 33⅓ rpm sides.

LEONCAVALLO: *Pagliacci.*

Canio	**Richard Tucker**
Nedda	**Lucine Amara**
Tonio	**Giuseppe Valdengo**
Beppe	**Thomas Hayward**
Silvio	**Clifford Harvuot**

Chorus of the Metropolitan Opera Association
(Kurt Adler, chorus master)
Orchestra of the Metropolitan Opera Association
Fausto Cleva

Act I, Scene 1	5 June 1951
Act I (except Scene 1)	4 June 1951
Intermezzo	4 June 1951
Act II	5 June 1951

45 rpm   **Columbia A-1071** (7-1735/40) / released 10 October 1953 to ?
33⅓ rpm   **Columbia SL 113** (ML 4422/3) / released 17 August 1951 to ?
               Columbia SL 124 (ML 4659/61) / released 27 March 1953 to ?
               Odyssey Y3 33122 (Y 33123/5) / released 22 November 1974 to ?
               Philips ABL 3041/2
               Philips A 01102/3 L

_CD_   **Preiser 20030**

Selections from this set were also released as follows:

575. **LEONCAVALLO:** *Pagliacci—So ben che diforme.*
Cassette   **MET 512-C** / released 1991 to ?
_CD_   **MET 512-CD** / released 1991 to ?

576. **LEONCAVALLO:** *Pagliacci—Vesti la giubba.*
33⅓ rpm   **Columbia D3M 33448**

577. **LEONCAVALLO:** *Pagliacci—O Colombina.*
Cassette   **MET 512-C** / released 1991 to ?
_CD_   **MET 512-CD** / released 1991 to ?

Session of 18 June 1951, 2:00 to 5:30 P.M.; Columbia Studios, 207 E. 30ᵗʰ St. NYC.
[Information from Columbia archives.]

578. **VERDI:** *Otello—Tu?! Indietro! Fuggi!*
Ramon Vinay, Frank Guarrera & Orchestra of the Metropolitan Opera Association of New York –
Fausto Cleva.
33⅓ rpm   **Columbia ML 4499** / released 24 March 1952 to ? [This album, entitled "Great Scenes
                from Verdi's *Otello,*" combined separate recordings made during the sessions of 17 Febru-
                ary 1950, 16 August 1950, 31 December 1951 and this date.]
                Philips ABL 3005
                Philips N 02102 L
_CD_   **Preiser 90500**

579. **VERDI:** *Otello—Dio! mi potevi scagliar.*
Ramon Vinay & Orchestra of the Metropolitan Opera Association of New York – Fausto Cleva.
33⅓ rpm   **Columbia ML 4499** / released 24 March 1952 to ? [This album, entitled "Great Scenes
                from Verdi's *Otello,*" combined separate recordings made during the sessions of 17 Febru-
                ary 1950, 16 August 1950, 31 December 1951 and this date.]
                Philips ABL 3005
                Philips N 02102 L
_CD_   **Preiser 90500**

580. **VERDI:** *Otello—Niun mi tema.*
Ramon Vinay & Orchestra of the Metropolitan Opera Association of New York – Fausto Cleva.
33⅓ rpm   **Columbia ML 4499** / released 24 March 1952 to ? [This album, entitled "Great Scenes
                from Verdi's *Otello,*" combined separate recordings made during the sessions of 17 Febru-
                ary 1950, 16 August 1950, 31 December 1951 and this date.]
                Philips ABL 3005
                Philips N 02102 L
_CD_   **Preiser 90500**

Session of 11 July 1951, 1:00 to 4:30 P.M.; Columbia Studios, 207 E. 30th St. NYC.

[Information from Columbia archives.]

581. **VERDI: _Rigoletto—Caro nome._**
     Anna Maria Alberghetti & Members of the Metropolitan Opera Orchestra – Alfredo Antonini.
          matrix: **XCO 46599**

78 rpm	**Columbia 73264-D** / released 13 August 1951 to ?
45 rpm	**Columbia 4-73264-D** / released 13 August 1951 to ?
	Columbia 4-4804 / released July 1953 to ?
33⅓ rpm	**Columbia 3-73264-D** / released 13 August 1951 to ?

582. **FLOTOW: _Martha—Die letzte Rose._** (in English as _"The Last Rose of Summer"_)
     Anna Maria Alberghetti & Members of the Metropolitan Opera Orchestra – Alfredo Antonini.
          matrix: **XCO 46600**

78 rpm	**Columbia 73264-D** / released 13 August 1951 to ?
45 rpm	**Columbia 4-73264-D** / released 13 August 1951 to ?
	Columbia 4-4804 / released July 1953 to ?
33⅓ rpm	**Columbia 3-73264-D** / released 13 August 1951 to ?

583. **BISHOP: _Lo! Here the Gentle Lark._**
     Anna Maria Alberghetti with James B. Hosmer, (flute) & Members of the Metropolitan Opera Orchestra – Alfredo Antonini.
          matrix: **XCO 46601**
     Not released by Columbia.

Session of 15 November 1951, 2:00 to 5:00 P.M.; Columbia Studios, 207 E. 30th St. NYC.

[Information from Columbia archives.]

584. **VERDI: _Aïda—Prelude._**
     Orchestra of the Metropolitan Opera Association of New York – Fausto Cleva.

45 rpm	**Columbia 4-1551**
33⅓ rpm	**Columbia ML 4515** / released 18 April 1952 to ?
	Columbia ML 4886 / released 21 June 1954 to ?

585. **VERDI: _Aïda—Ballet Music (Danza Sacra delle Sacerdotesse; Danza di piccoli schiavi mori; Ballabile)._** _("Dance of the Priestesses; Dance of the Little Moorish Slaves; Triumphal March and Grand Ballet")_
     Orchestra of the Metropolitan Opera Association of New York – Fausto Cleva.

45 rpm	**Columbia 4-1551**
33⅓ rpm	**Columbia ML 4515** / released 18 April 1952 to ?
	Columbia ML 4886 / released 21 June 1954 to ?

586. **GOUNOD:** *Faust—Ballet Music (Les Nubiennes; Danse antique; Les Troyennes; Variations du Miroir; Danse de Phryné).* *("Dance of the Nubian Slaves; Dance Antique; Dance of the Trojan Maidens; Mirror Dance; Dance of Phryne")*
   Orchestra of the Metropolitan Opera Association of New York – Fausto Cleva.

45 rpm	**Columbia 4-1554** [The order of dances is altered on the 45 rpm edition with the *Variations du Miroir* played second.]
33⅓ rpm	**Columbia ML 4515** / released 18 April 1952 to ?
	Columbia ML 4886 / released 21 June 1954 to ?

Session of 10 December 1951, 2:00 to 5:00 P.M.; Columbia Studios, 207 E. 30th St. NYC.
[Information from Columbia archives.]

587. **BORODIN:** *Prince Igor—No sleep, no rest.* (in Russian) *("Aria of Prince Igor, Act II")*
   George London & Orchestra of the Metropolitan Opera Association – Kurt Adler.

33⅓ rpm	**Columbia ML 4489** / released 21 March 1952 to ?
CD	**Sony Classical MHK 62758** / released 1996 to ?

588. **RUBINSTEIN:** *The Demon—Do not weep, my child.* (in Russian)
   George London & Orchestra of the Metropolitan Opera Association – Kurt Adler.

33⅓ rpm	**Columbia ML 4489** / released 21 March 1952 to ?
	Columbia ML 4658 / released 23 March 1953 to ?
	Columbia Special Products P 14179 (synthetic stereo)
Cassette	**Columbia Special Products BT 14179** (synthetic stereo)
CD	**Sony Classical MHK 62758** / released 1996 to ?

Session of 13 December 1951, 2:00 to 5:00 P.M.; Columbia Studios, 207 E. 30th St. NYC.
[Information from Columbia archives.]

589. **MASSENET:** *Don Quichotte—Act V.* *("Mort de Don Quichotte" "Death of Don Quixote")*
   George London, Rosalind Nadell & Orchestra of the Metropolitan Opera Association – Jean Morel.
   [George London sings the rôles of both Don Quichotte and Sancho Panca.]

33⅓ rpm	**Columbia ML 4489** / released 21 March 1952 to ?
CD	**Sony Classical MHK 62758** [Rosalind Nadell's name is omitted.] / released 1996 to ?

590. **PALADILHE:** *Patrie—Pauvre martyr obscur.* *("Air de Rysoor")*
   George London & Orchestra of the Metropolitan Opera Association – Jean Morel.

33⅓ rpm	**Columbia ML 4489** / released 21 March 1952 to ?
CD	**Sony Classical MHK 62758** / released 1996 to ?

Session of 31 December 1951, 2:30 to 6:00 P.M.; Columbia Studios, 207 E. 30th St. NYC.
[Information from Columbia archives.]

591. **VERDI:** *Otello—Già nella notte densa.*
   Eleanor Steber, Ramon Vinay & Orchestra of the Metropolitan Opera Association of New York –
   Fausto Cleva.
   33⅓ rpm   **Columbia ML 4499** / released 24 March 1952 to ? [This album, entitled "Great Scenes
   from Verdi's *Otello,*" combined separate recordings made during the sessions of 17 February 1950, 16 August 1950, 18 June 1951 and this date.]
                Odyssey Y 31149 / released 8 March 1972 to ?
                Philips ABL 3005
                Philips N 02102 L
   CD   **Preiser 90500**

592. **VERDI:** *Otello—Dio ti giocondi.*
   Eleanor Steber, Ramon Vinay & Orchestra of the Metropolitan Opera Association of New York –
   Fausto Cleva.
   33⅓ rpm   **Columbia ML 4499** / released 24 March 1952 to ? [This album, entitled "Great Scenes
   from Verdi's *Otello,*" combined separate recordings made during the sessions of 17 February 1950, 16 August 1950, 18 June 1951 and this date.]
                Odyssey Y 31149 / released 8 March 1972 to ?
                Philips ABL 3005
                Philips N 02102 L
   CD   **Preiser 90500**

Session of 4 June 1952, 2:30 to 7:00 P.M.; Columbia Studios, 207 E. 30th St. NYC.
[Information from Columbia archives.]

593. **MOZART:** *Così Fan Tutte.*
   During this session and the next three sessions, a complete recording of *Così Fan Tutte* was made. For release
   information please see item #597.

Session of 5 June 1952, 2:30 to 7:00 P.M.; Columbia Studios, 207 E. 30th St. NYC.
[Information from Columbia archives.]

594. **MOZART:** *Così Fan Tutte.*
   During this session, the preceding session, and the next two sessions, a complete recording of *Così Fan Tutte*
   was made. For release information please see item #597.

Session of 6 June 1952, 2:30 to 6:00 P.M.; Columbia Studios, 207 E. 30th St. NYC.
This session was continued in the evening.
[Information from Columbia archives.]

595. **MOZART:** *Così Fan Tutte.*
    During this session, the preceding two sessions, and the next session, a complete recording of *Così Fan Tutte* was made. For release information please see item #597.

Session of 6 June 1952, 6:00 to 9:00 P.M.; Columbia Studios, 207 E. 30th St. NYC.
This session was a continuation of the afternoon session.
[Information from Columbia archives.]

596. **MOZART:** *Così Fan Tutte.*
    During this session, and the preceding three sessions, a complete recording of *Così Fan Tutte* was made. During this evening session, the recitatives were recorded. For release information please see item #597.

597. The recording sessions of 4 and 5 June 1952 and two sessions on 6 June 1952 were devoted to a complete recording in English of *Così Fan Tutte*. During the evening session of 6 June 1952, the recitatives were recorded.

MOZART: *Così Fan Tutte.*
(English version by Ruth and Thomas P. Martin)

Fiordiligi	**Eleanor Steber**
Dorabella	**Blanche Thebom**
Despina	**Roberta Peters**
Ferrando	**Richard Tucker**
Guglielmo	**Frank Guarrera**
Don Alfonso	**Lorenzo Alvary**

Josef Blatt, continuo
Chorus of the Metropolitan Opera Association
(Kurt Adler, chorus master)
Orchestra of the Metropolitan Opera Association
Fritz Stiedry

33⅓ rpm   **Columbia SL 122** (ML 4605/7) / released 13 October 1952 to ?
        Odyssey Y3 32670 (Y 32671/3) / released 4 January 1974 to ?
CD   **Sony Classical MH2K 60652** / released 1998 to ?

Selections from this set were also released as follows:

598. **MOZART:** *Così Fan Tutte—Un' aura amorosa.* (in English as *"My love is a flower"*)
        33⅓ rpm   **Columbia M 30118** / released 19 October 1974 to ?

599. **MOZART:** *Così Fan Tutte—Una donna a quindici anni.* (in English as *"Any girl fifteen or over"*)
        33⅓ rpm   **MET 405** / released 1985 to ?
        Cassette   **MET 405-C** / released 1985 to ?

Session of 30 November 1952, 2:30 to 5:30 P.M.; Columbia Studios, 207 E. 30ᵗʰ St. NYC.
[Information from Columbia archives.]

600. **GOUNOD:** *Faust—Il était un roi de Thulé.* (*"Ballade de Thulé"*)
        Dorothy Kirsten & Orchestra of the Metropolitan Opera Association of New York – Fausto Cleva.
        33⅓ rpm   **Columbia ML 4730** / released 14 September 1953 to ?
                        Columbia Special Products P 14183 (synthetic stereo)
        Cassette   **Columbia Special Products BT 14183** (synthetic stereo)

601. **GOUNOD:** *Faust—Air des bijoux.* (*"Jewel Song"*)
        Dorothy Kirsten & Orchestra of the Metropolitan Opera Association of New York – Fausto Cleva.
        33⅓ rpm   **Columbia ML 4730** / released 14 September 1953 to ?
                        Columbia Special Products P 14183 (synthetic stereo)
        Cassette   **Columbia Special Products BT 14183** (synthetic stereo)

602. **VERDI:** *La Traviata—Ah! fors' è lui ... Sempre libera.*
        Dorothy Kirsten & Orchestra of the Metropolitan Opera Association of New York – Fausto Cleva.
        33⅓ rpm   **Columbia ML 4730** / released 14 September 1953 to ?
                        Columbia Special Products P 14183 (synthetic stereo)
        Cassette   **Columbia Special Products BT 14183** (synthetic stereo)

Session of 17 December 1952, 2:00 to 5:00 P.M.; Columbia Studios, 207 E. 30ᵗʰ St. NYC.
[Information from Columbia archives.]

603. **VERDI:** *La Traviata—De' miei bollenti spiriti.*
        Richard Tucker & Metropolitan Opera Orchestra – Fausto Cleva.
        33⅓ rpm   **Columbia ML 4750** / released 19 October 1953 to ?
        CD   **Preiser 89637**

604. **PUCCINI:** *La Bohème—Che gelida manina.*
        Richard Tucker & Metropolitan Opera Orchestra – Fausto Cleva.

45 rpm	**Columbia A-1112** / released 4 April 1955 to ?
	Philips 409 523 NE
33⅓ rpm	**Columbia ML 4750** / released 19 October 1953 to ?
	Columbia ML 4981 / released 4 April 1955 to ?
	Philips 11053
	Philips N 02126 L
CD	**Preiser 89637**

605. **BIZET:** *Carmen—Air de fleur. ("La fleur que tu m'avais jetée")*
Richard Tucker & Metropolitan Opera Orchestra – Fausto Cleva.
33⅓ rpm   **Columbia ML 4750** / released 19 October 1953 to ?
CD   **Preiser 89637**

606. **MASCAGNI:** *Cavalleria Rusticana—Siciliana.*
Richard Tucker with Reinhardt Elster, (harp) & Metropolitan Opera Orchestra – Fausto Cleva.
Not released by Columbia.

Session of 18 January 1953, 11:00 A.M. to 3:00 P.M.; Columbia Studios, 207 E. 30ᵗʰ St. NYC.
[Information from Columbia archives.]

607. **MASCAGNI:** *Cavalleria Rusticana.*
During this session and the next session a complete recording of *Cavalleria Rusticana* was made. For release information please see item #609.

Session of 25 January 1953, 12:15 to 5:45 P.M.; Columbia Studios, 207 E. 30ᵗʰ St. NYC.
[Information from Columbia archives.]

608. **MASCAGNI:** *Cavalleria Rusticana.*
During this session and the preceding session a complete recording of *Cavalleria Rusticana* was made. For release information please see item #609.

609. The recording sessions of 18 and 25 January 1953 were devoted to a complete recording of *Cavalleria Rusticana*. The recording was first released in two separate sets. Columbia SL 123 contained the opera on three 33⅓ rpm sides in a two disc set. The fourth side contained four Verdi overtures and preludes which Cleva recorded with the Metropolitan Opera Orchestra in two sessions in February 1953. Columbia SL 124 contained the opera on three 33⅓ rpm sides in a three disc set. The other three sides of this set contained the 1951 recording of *Pagliacci*.

MASCAGNI: *Cavalleria Rusticana.*

Turiddu	**Richard Tucker**
Santuzza	**Margaret Harshaw**
Lola	**Mildred Miller**
Alfio	**Frank Guarrera**
Lucia	**Thelma Votipka**

**Chorus of the Metropolitan Opera Association
(Kurt Adler, chorus master)
Orchestra of the Metropolitan Opera Association**
Fausto Cleva

33⅓ rpm	**Columbia SL 123** (ML 4662/3) / released 27 March 1953 to ?
	Columbia SL 124 (ML 4659/61) / released 27 March 1953 to ?
	Odyssey Y3 33122 (Y 33123/5) / released 22 November 1974 to ?
	[An incorrect recording date of 29 January 1953 is given in this set.]
	Philips ABR 4000/1
	Philips A 01612/3 L
	CBS Classics 61640
Cassette	**CBS Classics 40-61640**

A selection from this set was also released as follows:

610. **MASCAGNI:** *Cavalleria Rusticana—Avete altro a dirmi?...Mamma, quel vino è generoso...Finale.*
Cassette	**MET 512-C** / released 1991 to ?
CD	**MET 512-CD** / released 1991 to ?

Session of 9 February 1953, 2:30 to 4:30 P.M.; Columbia Studios, 207 E. 30th St. NYC.
[Information from Columbia archives.]

611. **VERDI:** *La Forza del Destino—Overture.*
    Orchestra of the Metropolitan Opera Association of New York – Fausto Cleva.
33⅓ rpm	**Columbia SL 123** (ML 4662) / released 27 March 1953 to ?
	Columbia ML 4886 / released 21 June 1954 to ?

612. **VERDI:** *La Traviata—Prelude.*
    Orchestra of the Metropolitan Opera Association of New York – Fausto Cleva.
33⅓ rpm	**Columbia SL 123** (ML 4662) / released 27 March 1953 to ?
	Columbia ML 4886 / released 21 June 1954 to ?
	MET 408 / released 1986 to ?
Cassette	**MET 408-C** / released 1986 to ?

Session of 10 February 1953, 3:06 to 5:06 P.M.; Columbia Studios, 207 E. 30ᵗʰ St. NYC.
[Information from Columbia archives.]

613. **VERDI:** *La Traviata—Prelude to Act III.*
  Orchestra of the Metropolitan Opera Association of New York – Fausto Cleva.
  33⅓ rpm   **Columbia SL 123** (ML 4662) / released 27 March 1953 to ?
            Columbia ML 4886 / released 21 June 1954 to ?

614. **VERDI:** *Les Vêpres Siciliennes—Overture.*
  Orchestra of the Metropolitan Opera Association of New York – Fausto Cleva.
  33⅓ rpm   **Columbia SL 123** (ML 4662) / released 27 March 1953 to ?
            Columbia ML 4886 / released 21 June 1954 to ?

Session of 1 March 1953, 7:00 to 11:00 P.M.; Columbia Studios, 207 E. 30ᵗʰ St. NYC.
[Information from Columbia archives.]

615. **STRAVINSKY:** *The Rake's Progress.*
  During this session and the next two sessions a complete recording of *The Rake's Progress* was made. For release information please see item #618.

Session of 8 March 1953, 12:00 to 6:00 P.M.; Columbia Studios, 207 E. 30ᵗʰ St. NYC.
[Information from Columbia archives.]

616. **STRAVINSKY:** *The Rake's Progress.*
  During the preceding session, this session and the next session, a complete recording of *The Rake's Progress* was made. For release information please see item #618.

Session of 10 March 1953, 2:00 to 8:00 P.M.; Columbia Studios, 207 E. 30ᵗʰ St. NYC.
[Information from Columbia archives.]

617. **STRAVINSKY:** *The Rake's Progress.*
  During the preceding two sessions and this session, a complete recording of *The Rake's Progress* was made. For release information please see item #618.

618. The recording sessions of 1, 8 and 10 March 1953 were devoted to a complete recording of *The Rake's Progress*. Although Fritz Reiner conducted all the Metropolitan Opera performances of this work during the 1953-1953 season, the composer conducted for the recording sessions. In *"A Statement by the Composer"* that was included with the recording, Stravinsky wrote in part: "But of course, the chief value of a recording to the composer is in the fact that it is a 'record,' a document of his wishes respecting his own music. In view of this fact it becomes necessary to say a word abut the tempi of this recording. The musician will be able to detect discrepancies between certain metronome indications printed in the score and the recorded performance of these places. However, such discrepancies are the result of a restudy of the music undertaken with the object of finding the most suitable tempi for a purely musical reading, that is, a reading deprived of the theatre's time-scale and visual and histrionic elements."

STRAVINSKY: *The Rake's Progress.*

Anne Trulove	**Hilde Gueden**
Baba the Turk	**Blanche Thebom**
Tom Rakewell	**Eugene Conley**
Nick Shadow	**Mack Harrell**
Mother Goose	**Norman Scott**
Sellem, an Auctioneer	**Paul Franke**
Keeper of the Madhouse	**Lawrence Davidson**

**Chorus of the Metropolitan Opera Association
(Kurt Adler, chorus master)
Orchestra of the Metropolitan Opera Association
Igor Stravinsky**

33⅓ rpm	**Columbia SL-125** (ML 4723/5) / released 14 September 1953 to ?
	Philips ABL 3055/7
	Philips A 01181/3 L
CD	**Naxos 8.111266-67**

A selection from this set was also released as follows:

619. **STRAVINSKY:** *The Rake's Progress—Good people, just a moment. (Epilogue)*
33⅓ rpm	**MET 50** / released 1985 to ?
Cassette	**MET 50-C** / released 1985 to ?

Session of 17 June 1953, 6:00 to 9:30 P.M.; Columbia Studios, 207 E. 30ᵗʰ St. NYC.
[Information from Columbia archives.]

620. **VERDI:** *Un Ballo in Maschera—Ma se m'è forza perderti.*
    Richard Tucker & Metropolitan Opera Orchestra – Fausto Cleva.
33⅓ rpm	**Columbia ML 4750** / released 19 October 1953 to ?

CD   **Preiser 89637**

621. **GIORDANO:** *Andrea Chénier—Come un bel dì di Maggio.*
Richard Tucker & Metropolitan Opera Orchestra – Fausto Cleva.
33⅓ rpm   **Columbia ML 4750** / released 19 October 1953 to ?
CD   **Preiser 89637**

622. **GOUNOD:** *Faust—Salut! demeure.*
Richard Tucker & Metropolitan Opera Orchestra – Fausto Cleva.
33⅓ rpm   **Columbia ML 4750** / released 19 October 1953 to ?
CD   **Preiser 89637**

623. **DONIZETTI:** *L'Elisir d'Amore—Una furtiva lagrima.*
Richard Tucker & Metropolitan Opera Orchestra – Fausto Cleva.
33⅓ rpm   **Columbia ML 4750** / released 19 October 1953 to ?
CD   **Preiser 89637**

Session of 20 January 1954, 12:00 to 4:00 P.M.; Columbia Studios, 207 E. 30ᵗʰ St. NYC.
[Information from Columbia archives.]

624. **DONIZETTI:** *Lucia di Lammermoor.*
During this session and the next two sessions a complete recording of *Lucia di Lammermoor* was made. For release information please see item #627.

Session of 26 January 1954, 2:00 to 5:00 P.M.; Columbia Studios, 207 E. 30ᵗʰ St. NYC.
[Information from Columbia archives.]

625. **DONIZETTI:** *Lucia di Lammermoor.*
During the preceding session, this session and the next session a complete recording of *Lucia di Lammermoor* was made. For release information please see item #627.

Session of 1 February 1954, 3:30 to 6:30 P.M.; Columbia Studios, 207 E. 30ᵗʰ St. NYC.
[Information from Columbia archives.]

626. **DONIZETTI:** *Lucia di Lammermoor.*
During the preceding two sessions and this session a complete recording of *Lucia di Lammermoor* was made. For release information please see item #627.

627. **The recording sessions of 20, 26 January and 1 February 1954 were devoted to a complete recording of *Lucia di Lammermoor*.**

DONIZETTI: *Lucia di Lammermoor.*

Lucia	**Lily Pons**
Alisa	**Thelma Votipka**
Edgardo	**Richard Tucker**
Arturo	**Thomas Hayward**
Normanno	**James McCracken**
Enrico	**Frank Guarrera**
Raimondo	**Norman Scott**

Chorus of the Metropolitan Opera Association
(Kurt Adler, chorus master)
Orchestra of the Metropolitan Opera Association
Fausto Cleva

33⅓ rpm   **Columbia SL-127** (ML 4933/4) / released 25 October 1954 to ?
Odyssey Y2 32361 (Y 32362/3) / released 7 September 1973 to ?
Philips A 01161/2 L

A selection from this set was also released as follows:

628. **DONIZETTI: *Lucia di Lammermoor—T'allontana, sciagurato.* *(Act II Finale)***
Cassette   **MET 521-C** / released 1993 to ?
CD   **MET 521-CD** / released 1993 to ?

Sessions of 14 & 16 June 1954; Columbia Studios, 207 E. 30th St. NYC.

[Information from Columbia archives.]
There is a bit of confusion in the archives regarding these sessions. In several places "June 1954" is the only date given, but on an artist's card the exact dates of 14 and 16 June 1954 are listed.

There is also a lack of clarity on the disc on which these selections first appeared. Columbia ML 4981 which had the title "Great Love Duets" gave the impression that it was all newly recorded by Kirsten and Tucker with the Orchestra of the Metropolitan Opera Association of New York directed by Fausto Cleva. A minor bit of confusion with this disc was added with all the selections given only English titles, although everything was sung in the original language. Actually several sections had been recorded and released earlier in different collections, and two of these selections did not even employ the orchestra of the Metropolitan Opera but used the Columbia Symphony Orchestra which was clearly indicated on the earlier release.

Here is a summary of what is actually on Columbia ML 4981 with the parts not recorded during these June 1954 sessions given their actual recording dates.

Side 1 contains excerpts from Puccini's *La Bohème* and lists the contents as follows:

Act I:	**Duet Music**
	"Your Tiny Hand Is Frozen"
	"My Name Is Mimi"
	"O Beautiful Maiden"
Act II:	**"Musetta's Waltz"**
Act III:	**"Mimi's Farewell"**

The "Duet Music" is actually the last part of the first act but with only the rôles of Rodolfo and Mimì. It begins with:

Non sono in vena (sung by Kirsten and Tucker) and continues with

Che gelida manina (sung by Tucker and recorded on <u>17 December 1952</u>), and

Sì, mi chiamano Mimì (sung by Kirsten, but without Rodolfo's single word "Sì"), and concludes with

O soave fanciulla (sung by Kirsten and Tucker without Marcello's, Schaunard's and Colline's parts).

"Musetta's Waltz" is, of course:

Quando me'n vo' (sung by Kirsten with Cleva directing the <u>Columbia Symphony Orchestra</u> and recorded on <u>24 February 1953</u>. This was first released on Columbia ML 4730.

"Mimi's Farewell" is:

Donde lieta usci (sung by Kirsten with Cleva directing the <u>Columbia Symphony Orchestra</u> and recorded on <u>24 February 1953</u>. This was first released on Columbia ML 4730.

Side 2 begins with excerpts from Puccini's *Manon Lescaut* and lists the contents as follows with the English titles from Mowbray Marras' English version:

Act II:	**"These Are Hours of Joy's Creating"**
	"You, You, My Love"
Act IV:	**"Lonely, Forsaken and Abandoned"**
	Duet Music

"These Are Hours of Joy's Creating" is:

L'ora, o Tirsi (sung by Kirsten solo without the other vocal parts)

"You, You, My Love" is

Tu, tu, amore? (sung by Kirsten and Tucker)

"Lonely, Forsaken and Abandoned" is

Sola, perduta, abbandonato (sung by Kirsten and recorded on <u>18 January 1951</u>)

The "Duet Music" which follows is:

Fra le tue braccia (sung by Kirsten and Tucker)

Side 2 concludes with an excerpt from Massenet's *Manon* and lists the title as follows:

Act III:	**"Thou, You"**

"Thou, You" is

Toi! Vous! (sung by Kirsten and Tucker)

629. PUCCINI: *La Bohème—Non sono in vena.*

Dorothy Kirsten, Richard Tucker & Orchestra of the Metropolitan Opera Association of New York – Fausto Cleva.

<u>*33⅓ rpm*</u>	**Columbia ML 4981** / released 4 April 1955 to ?
<u>*CD*</u>	**Preiser 89637**

630. PUCCINI: *La Bohème—Sì, mi chiamano Mimì.*

Dorothy Kirsten & Orchestra of the Metropolitan Opera Association of New York – Fausto Cleva.

45 rpm	**Columbia A-1112** / released 4 April 1955 to ?
	Philips 409 523 NE
<u>*33⅓ rpm*</u>	**Columbia ML 4981** / released 4 April 1955 to ?
	Philips NBE 11053

Philips N 02126 E
CD   **Preiser 89637**

631. **PUCCINI:** *La Bohème—O soave fanciulla.*
Dorothy Kirsten, Richard Tucker & Orchestra of the Metropolitan Opera Association of New York – Fausto Cleva.
45 rpm   **Columbia A-1112** / released 4 April 1955 to ?
            Philips 409 523 NE
33⅓ rpm   **Columbia ML 4981** / released 4 April 1955 to ?
            Philips NBE 11053
            Philips N 02126 E
CD   **Preiser 89637**

632. **PUCCINI:** *Manon Lescaut—L'ora, o Tirsi.*
Dorothy Kirsten & Orchestra of the Metropolitan Opera Association of New York – Fausto Cleva.
33⅓ rpm   **Columbia ML 4981** / released 4 April 1955 to ?
CD   **Preiser 89637**

633. **PUCCINI:** *Manon Lescaut—Tu, tu amore?*
Dorothy Kirsten, Richard Tucker & Orchestra of the Metropolitan Opera Association of New York – Fausto Cleva.
33⅓ rpm   **Columbia ML 4981** / released 4 April 1955 to ?
            Odyssey Y 31737 / released 25 October 1972 to ?
CD   **Preiser 89637**

634. **PUCCINI:** *Manon Lescaut—Fra le tue braccia.*
Dorothy Kirsten, Richard Tucker & Orchestra of the Metropolitan Opera Association of New York – Fausto Cleva.
33⅓ rpm   **Columbia ML 4981** / released 4 April 1955 to ?
CD   **Preiser 89637**

635. **MASSENET:** *Manon—Toi! Vous!*
Dorothy Kirsten, Richard Tucker & Orchestra of the Metropolitan Opera Association of New York – Fausto Cleva.
33⅓ rpm   **Columbia ML 4981** / released 4 April 1955 to ?
CD   **MET 217-CD** / released 1993 to ?
            Preiser 89637

Session of 9 January 1955, 12:00 to 3:07 P.M.; Manhattan Center, NYC.
This session was the first of three held this day.
[Information from Victor archives.]

636. **VERDI:** *Un Ballo in Maschera—Excerpts.*

During this session and the next three sessions, excerpts from *Un Ballo in Maschera* were recorded. During this session the following excerpts were recorded. For release information please see item #640.

Alla vite che t'arride / Leonard Warren
Ecco l'orrido campo (*recitative to* **Ma dall'arrido stelo divulsa**) / Zinka Milanov
Teco io sto / Zinka Milanov, Jan Peerce

Session of 9 January 1955, 4:00 to 7:00 P.M.; Manhattan Center, NYC.
This session was the second of three held this day.
[Information from Victor archives.]

637. VERDI: *Un Ballo in Maschera—Excerpts.*
During the previous session, this session and the next two sessions, excerpts from *Un Ballo in Maschera* were recorded. During this session the following excerpts were recorded. For release information please see item #640.

Re dell' abisso, affrettati / Marian Anderson
Eri tu / Leonard Warren
Saper vorreste / Roberta Peters

Session of 9 January 1955, 8:00 to 11:00 P.M.; Manhattan Center, NYC.
This session was the third of three held this day.
[Information from Victor archives.]

638. VERDI: *Un Ballo in Maschera—Excerpts.*
During the previous two sessions, this session and the next session, excerpts from *Un Ballo in Maschera* were recorded. During this session the following excerpts were recorded. For release information please see item #640.

Ahimé! S'appressa alcun / Zinka Milanov, Jan Peerce, Leonard Warren
Morrò, ma prima in grazia / Zinka Milanov
Overture

Session of 21 January 1955, 1:00 to 4:00 P.M.; Manhattan Center, NYC.
[Information from Victor archives.]

639. VERDI: *Un Ballo in Maschera—Excerpts.*
During the previous three sessions and this session, excerpts from *Un Ballo in Maschera* were recorded. During this session the following excerpts were recorded. For release information please see item #640.

Ma dall'arrido stelo divulsa (aria only) / Zinka Milanov
Ma se m'è forza perderti / Jan Peerce

640. The three recording sessions of 9 January 1955 and the session of 21 January 1955 were devoted to a recording of excerpts from *Un Ballo in Maschera*. The excerpts followed by the recording dates are listed below.

VERDI: *Un Ballo in Maschera — Excerpts*

Amelia	**Zinka Milanov**
Riccardo	**Jan Peerce**
Renato	**Leonard Warren**
Ulrica	**Marian Anderson**
Oscar	**Roberta Peters**

Metropolitan Opera Orchestra
Dimitri Mitropoulos

Overture (9 January 1955)
Alla vita che t'arride / Warren (9 January 1955)
Re dell' abisso, affrettati/ Anderson (9 January 1955)
Ecco l'orrido campo…Ma dall'arido stelo divulsa / Milanov
   (9 & 21 January 1955)
Teco io sto/ Milanov, Peerce (9 January 1955)
Ahimé! S'appressa alcun / Milanov, Peerce, Warren (9 January 1955)
Morrò, ma prima in grazia / Milanov (9 January 1955)
Alzati! là tuo figlio…Eri tu / Warren (9 January 1955)
Forse la soglia attinse…Ma se m'è forza perderti / Peerce (21 January 1955)
Saper vorreste / Peters (9 January 1955)

33⅓ rpm   **RCA Victor LM-1911** / released March 1955 to 1 April 1961 [There are two editions of this recording, and both used the same record number, LM-1911, and contained exactly the same musical content. The first edition released in 1955 had a photograph of boxes at the Metropolitan Opera House on the cover and notes on the back by Francis Robinson highlighting the debut of Marian Anderson. The second edition released in 1959 had an art work by Eugene Karlin of two maskers on the front cover. Francis Robinson's notes have been removed from the back. It included a libretto of some eighteen pages with the story of the opera and an essay by Henry W. Simon.]
HMV ALP 1476 / released July 1957 to ?
CD   **Naxos 8.111042-44**

Selections from this set were also released as follows:

641. **VERDI:** *Un Ballo in Maschera—Re dell' abisso, affrettati.*
    33⅓ rpm **RCA Red Seal CRM8-5177** / released 1984 to ?
    Cassette **RCA Red Seal CRK8-5177** / released 1984 to ?
         RCA Victor 7911-4-RG
    CD   **RCA Victor Red Seal 09026-61580-2** / released 1993 to ?
         RCA Victor 7911-2-RG / released 1989 to ?
         RCA Victor Red Seal 09026-68921-2 / released 1997 to ?

642. **VERDI:** *Un Ballo in Maschera—Ma dall'arido stelo divulsa.*
    33⅓ rpm **MET 107** / released 1980 to ?
    Cassette **MET 107-C** / released 1980 to ?
    CD   **MET 107-CD** / released 1989 to ?

643. **VERDI:** *Un Ballo in Maschera—Morrò, ma prima in grazia.*
    33⅓ rpm **RCA Victrola VICS-1336(e)** (synthetic stereo) / released May 1968 to ?
    CD   **MET 525-CD** / released 1995 to ?

644. **VERDI:** *Un Ballo in Maschera—Eri tu.*
    33⅓ rpm **RCA Victor LM-6061** / released 19 September 1958 to 1 March 1964

645. **VERDI:** *Un Ballo in Maschera—Ma se m'è forza perderti.*
    33⅓ rpm **RCA Victor LM-2055** / released January 1957 to 1 April 1960
         RCA Victor LM-6061 / released 19 September 1958 to 1 March 1964

646. **VERDI:** *Un Ballo in Maschera—Saper vorreste.*
    33⅓ rpm **RCA Victor LM-6061** / released 19 September 1958 to 1 March 1964

There is very little official information to be found on the twenty recordings listed in this section, however, we can be sure they all were made after the January 1955 recording of excerpts from *Un Ballo in Maschera* listed just above and before the February and April 1958 recording of *Vanessa* listed after this section. The first nineteen recordings of abridged operas were made jointly by the Metropolitan Opera and the Book-of-the-Month Club. Neither organization now has any of the actual recording information or even the master tapes which have apparently gone missing. Also the company that made the Ravel concerto is no longer in existence, and its former owner could not supply any information. Thankfully Max Rudolf still had the exact information for the concerto in his files and was able to provide it. We have arranged the opera recordings alphabetically by the name of the composer with the Ravel concerto listed last. Following the artists for each abridged opera, a summary of the contents is given. Some operas were almost complete and were lacking only brief passages while others were severely cut. Some used narrators to stitch the plot together. The forms of the summaries are as diverse as the forms of the abridgements. The recording dates and locations of sessions that are given here came from correspondence found in the Metropolitan archives and from information provided by Max Rudolf. The recording dates for *Tosca* and *Eugene Onegin* came from the compact disc set of highlights of these abridged operas released by The Metropolitan Opera Guild in 2006.

Sessions of 4, 5 & 6 January 1956; Metropolitan Opera House, NYC.
[Although Max Rudolf thought this might have been recorded at the Columbia Studios, information in the Metropolitan archives points to it being made at the Metropolitan Opera House.]

647.   **BIZET:** *Carmen – Excerpts*

Carmen	**Rosalind Elias**
Don José	**Kurt Baum**
Micaëla	**Lucine Amara**
Escamillo	**Walter Cassel**
Frasquita	**Heidi Krall**
Mercédès	**Margaret Roggero**
Moralès	**Clifford Harvuot**
Le Dancaïre	**George Cehanovsky**
Le Remendado	**Paul Franke**

Metropolitan Opera Chorus
(Kurt Adler, chorus master)
Metropolitan Opera Orchestra
Max Rudolf

Act I
Sur la place.
Avec la garde montante.
Voyez-les. Regards impudents.
Dans l'air. ("Chœur des cigarières")
Habañera. ("L'amour est un oiseau rebelle") [one verse]
Votre mere avec moi sortait de la chapelle. [abridged]
Séguedille. ("Près des remparts de Séville")
Tais-toi, je t'avais dit de ne pas me parler!

Act II
Chanson du Toréador. ("Toreador Song")
Nous avons en tête une affaire. ("Quintet")
Air de fleur. ("La fleur que tu m'avais jetée")
Non, tu ne m'aimes pas.
Le ciel ouvert, la vie errante.

Act III
Mêlons! Coupons! [abridged]
Air des cartes. ("En vain pour éviter")
Air de Micaëla. ("Je dis que rien ne m'épouvante")
En route, en route

Act IV
Entr'acte
C'est toi? C'est moi. [abridged]

33⅓ rpm   **Metropolitan Opera Record Club MO 113**

Selections from this set were also released as follows:

648. **BIZET:** *Carmen—Séguedille. ("Près des remparts de Séville")*
     <u>CD</u>   **MET 258** / released 2006 to ?

649. **BIZET:** *Carmen—Chanson du Toréador. ("Toreador Song")*
     <u>CD</u>   **MET 258** / released 2006 to ?

650. **BIZET:** *Carmen—Nous avons en tête une affaire. ("Quintet")*
     <u>CD</u>   **MET 258** / released 2006 to ?

651. **BIZET:** *Carmen—Air de Micaëla. ("Je dis que rien ne m'épouvante")*
     <u>Cassette</u>   **MET 502-C** / released 1988 to ?
     <u>CD</u>   **MET 502-CD** / released 1988 to ?

<u>*Session(s) of ?*</u>

652.   **DONIZETTI:** *Don Pasquale –Excerpts*

Don Pasquale	**Salvatore Baccaloni**
Ernesto	**Charles Anthony**
Norina	**Dolores Wilson**
Dr. Malatesta	**Frank Guarrera**

Metropolitan Opera Chorus
(Walter Taussig, chorus master)
Metropolitan Opera Orchestra
Tibor Kozma
(Corrado Muccini, assistant conductor)

Overture.
<u>**Act I, Scene 1**</u>
The opening scene with Don Pasquale and Dr. Malatesta is given with cuts. The following scene with Ernesto is cut completely.
<u>**Act I, Scene 2**</u>
The duet of Norina with Dr. Malatesta is given with cuts.

Act II
Ernesto's opening aria is given, but then there is a cut until Dr. Malatesta and Norina enter. The first part of the scene with Dr. Malatesta, Norian and Don Pasquale is given, but the second part is cut completely until the arrival of Ernesto. The rest of the act continues with several cuts.

Act III, Scene 1
The first part is cut completely until the appearance of Norina. The scene with Norina and Don Pasquale is given with several cuts. The scene with the servants is cut completely as is the scene with Ernesto and Dr. Malatesta. The recording begins again with Don Pasquale's Cheti, cheti, immantinente *and continues with cuts until the end of Scene 1.*

Act III, Scene 2
This opens with Ernesto's Com'è gentil *and continues with* Tornami a dir *and the appearance of Don Pasquale and Dr. Malatesta. The dialogue between Norina and Dr. Malatesta beginning with* Il bello adesso viene *is cut completely. The recording begins again with Dr. Malatesta's* Ehi! di casa, qualcuno *and continues to the end of the opera.*

33⅓ rpm   **Metropolitan Opera Record Club MO 715**
               RCA Victor LM-2358 / released December 1959 to 1 March 1962

        Selections from this set were also released as follows:

653. **DONIZETTI:** *Don Pasquale—Via, da brava.*
     CD   **MET 258** / released 2006 to ?

654. **DONIZETTI:** *Don Pasquale—Com'è gentil.*
     CD   **MET 258** / released 2006 to ?

Sessions of 25 November, 23 & 27 December 1957; Columbia Studios, 207 E. 30ᵗʰ St. NYC.

655.   **GIORDANO:** *Andrea Chénier – Excerpts*

                  Andrea Chénier   **Richard Tucker**
                  Maddalena di Coigny   **Mary Curtis-Verna**
                  Carlo Gérard   **Mario Sereni**
                  La Bersi   **Rosalind Elias**
                  Madelon   **Belen Amparan**
                  Countess di Coigny   **Martha Lipton**
                  The Abbé   **Gabor Carelli**
                  The Spy ("L'Incroyable")   **Alessio De Paolis**

Pietro Fléville	**George Cehanovsky**
Dumas	**Osie Hawkins**
Roucher	**Frank Valentino**
Mathieu	**Gerhard Pechner**
Fouquier-Tinville	**Norman Scott**
Schmidt	**Louis Sgarro**
Major-Domo	**Louis Sgarro**

Metropolitan Opera Chorus
(Kurt Adler, chorus master)
Metropolitan Opera Orchestra
Fausto Cleva
(Victor Trucco, assistant conductor)

Act I
This act is given complete without cuts.

Act II
Eleven measures of the orchestra alone (pages 106-107 of the Sonzogno piano vocal score) are cut between Roucher's word Guarda *and Bersi's* Non mi saluti?.

Act III
There is an unfortunate cut in Nemico della Patria?!. *This includes all fourteen measures on page 166 of the piano vocal score beginning with* Io della Redentrice *and ending with* il mio cammino!. *(This cut is not made in the Cleva directed Metropolitan Opera broadcast of 4 December 1954).*

Act IV
After Mathieu hums the first phrase of La Marseillaise, *there is a cut of ten measures until the five measures sung by Gérard and Schmidt beginning* Viene a costei concesso *and ending with* Sta ben!. *Then there is a cut of thirty-seven measures before beginning again with Maddalena's* Benedico il destino!.

33⅓ rpm   **Metropolitan Opera Record Club MO 826**

Selections from this set were also released as follows:

656. **GIORDANO:** *Andrea Chénier—Nemico della patria?!*
    CD   **MET 258** / released 2006 to ?

657. **GIORDANO:** *Andrea Chénier—Come un bel dì di maggio.*
    CD   **MET 258** / released 2006 to ?

658. GIORDANO: *Andrea Chénier—Vicino a te.*
    CD   **MET 258** / released 2006 to ?

Sessions of 7 & 8 February 1957, 1:00 P.M. to ? each day; Columbia Studios, 207 E. 30th St. NYC.

659.   **HUMPERDINCK:** *Hänsel und Gretel – Excerpts*
                      (Sung in English to a Text by John Gutman)

Hänsel	**Mildred Miller**
Gretel	**Laurel Hurley**
Witch	**Regina Resnik**
Sandman	**Emilia Cundari**
Father	**Calvin Marsh**
Mother	**Thelma Votipka**

Metropolitan Opera Chorus
(Walter Taussig, chorus master)
Metropolitan Opera Orchestra
Max Rudolf
(Julius Burger, assistant conductor)

Prelude. [abridged]
Act I
The opening scene with Hänsel and Gretel is basically complete with a few minor cuts. The scene with the Mother is complete until the children run into the forest. There is a cut until the Father is heard. The duet between the Father and Mother has several cuts.

Act II
The Act II Prelude is abridged. The scene with the children in the forest has several cuts. The Sandman's scene is complete as is the Evening Prayer, but the Dream Pantomime is heavily abridged.

Act III
The Act III Prelude is abridged. The scene with the Dew Fairy is cut completely. The following scene with the children and then with the witch is heavily abridged. The Witch's song is complete. The remaining part of the opera is mostly complete with a few cuts.

   33⅓ rpm   **Metropolitan Opera Record Club MO 717** [on record label]
                       MO 214 [on back of album]
             RCA Victor LM-2457 / released November 1960 to 1 March 1962

Selections from this set were also released as follows:

660. **HUMPERDINCK:** *Hänsel und Gretel—Prelude.* [abridged]
  CD   **MET 258** / released 2006 to ?

661. **HUMPERDINCK:** *Hänsel und Gretel—Forest Scene and Pantomime.*
  Includes: ***Ein Männlein steht im Walde*** (in English as *"A little follow stands in the wood"*)
          Der kleine Sandmann bin ich, s-t! (in English as *"I carry sand for sleeping, sh!"*)
          Abends, will ich schlafen geh'n (in English as *"Now I lay me down to sleep"*)
          ("Abendsegen" "Evening Prayer")
          Dream Pantomime [abridged]
  CD   **MET 258** / released 2006 to ?

662. **HUMPERDINCK:** *Hänsel und Gretel—Halt! Hokuspokus, Hexenschuß!*
  (in English as *"Stay! Hocus-pocus, witch's brew"*)
  CD   **MET 258** / released 2006 to ?

Session(s) of ?; Columbia Studios, 207 E. 30ᵗʰ St. NYC.

663.   **LEONCAVALLO:** *Pagliacci – Excerpts*

Canio	**Albert Da Costa**
Nedda	**Lucine Amara**
Tonio	**Frank Guarrera**
Beppe	**Charles Anthony**
Silvio	**Calvin Marsh**

Metropolitan Opera Chorus
(Kurt Adler, chorus master)
Metropolitan Opera Orchestra
Fausto Cleva
(Victor Trucco, assistant conductor)

Prologue
The orchestral introduction to Si può? *is abbreviated.*

Act I
The opening chorus is given with cuts followed by Un grande spettacolo.
Following this there is a cut of some twenty measures before recording begins again with a Villager singing Di', con noi vuoi bevere *and continuing through* Un tal gioco. *The scene before the Chorus of the Bells is cut completely with recording beginning again with* Andiam! *and the chorus. This*

is followed by Nedda's ballatella. The following scene with Tonio is cut completely. The duet with Nedda and Silvio is then given, but this has a longer cut than the standard cut and misses everything from Decidi il mio destin *before beginning again with* E allor perchè. *Eighteen measures are cut following the duet before beginning again with* Ah! Fuggi!. *The some fifteen measures with Beppe and Canio are cut before recording begins again with Canio's* Infamia! Infamia! *and then continues through the end of the act except the orchestral conclusion is abbreviated.*

Act II
The intermezzo and beginning of Act II are cut completely. Recording begins in The Play with the words E quello seimunito di Taddeo *and continues through Harlequin's Serenade. Then the Scena Comica is cut completely before recording begins again with the duet* Arlecchin! Colombina! *and continues to the end of the opera.*

33⅓ rpm   **Metropolitan Opera Record Club MO 811**

Selections from this set were also released as follows:

664. **LEONCAVALLO:** *Pagliacci—Prologue.*
   CD   **MET 258** / released 2006 to ?

665. **LEONCAVALLO:** *Pagliacci—Qual fiamma avea nel guardo. ("Ballatella")*
   CD   **MET 258** / released 2006 to ?

666. **LEONCAVALLO:** *Pagliacci—Vesti la giubba.*
   CD   **MET 258** / released 2006 to ?

Session of 15 November 1955; Metropolitan Opera House, NYC.
[Although Max Rudolf thought this might have been recorded at the Columbia Studios, information in the Metropolitan archives points to it being made at the Metropolitan Opera House.]

667.   **MOZART:** *Le Nozze di Figaro – Excerpts*

Count Almaviva	**Martial Singher**
Figaro	**Giorgio Tozzi**
Countess Almaviva	**Lucine Amara**
Cherubino	**Mildred Miller**
Susanna	**Nadine Conner**
Marcellina	**Herta Glaz**
Dr. Bartolo	**Salvatore Baccaloni**

Antonio	**Lawrence Davidson**
Don Basilio	**Alessio De Paolis**
Barbarina	**Emilia Cundari**
Don Curzio	**Gabor Carelli**

Narration by Milton Cross
Metropolitan Opera Orchestra
Max Rudolf

Overture.
Narration by Milton Cross
<u>**Act I**</u>
Cinque, dieci, venti, trenta.
Se vuol ballare.
Non so più cosa son.
Non più andrai.

Narration by Milton Cross
<u>**Act II**</u>
Voi, che sapete.
Esci omai, garzon malnato.

Narration by Milton Cross
<u>**Act III**</u>
Crudel! perchè finora.
E Susanna non vien!...Dove sono.
Sull' aria. Che soave zefiretto.

Narration by Milton Cross
<u>**Act IV**</u>
Deh vieni, non tardar.
Gente, gente! all'armi, all'armi!

33⅓ rpm   **Metropolitan Opera Record Club MO 315**

<u>Selections from this set were also released as follows:</u>

668. **MOZART:** *Le Nozze di Figaro—Overture.*
   <u>*CD*</u>   **MET 258** / released 2006 to ?

669. **MOZART:** *Le Nozze di Figaro—Se vuol ballare.*
   <u>*CD*</u>   **MET 258** / released 2006 to ?

670. **MOZART:** *Le Nozze di Figaro—Non so più cosa son.*
   <u>*Cassette*</u>   **MET 504-C** / released 1989 to ?
   <u>*CD*</u>   **MET 504-CD** / released 1989 to ?

671. MOZART: *Le Nozze di Figaro—Gente, gente! all'armi, all'armi!*
    CD   **MET 258** / released 2006 to ?

Sessions of 4, 15 & 16 April 1957; Columbia Studios, 207 E. 30ᵗʰ St. NYC.

672.   **MOZART:** *Die Zauberföte – Excerpts*
(Sung in English to a Text by Ruth and Thomas Martin)

Pamina	**Lucine Amara**
Tamino	**Brian Sullivan**
Papageno	**Theodor Uppman**
Sarastro	**Jerome Hines**
Queen of the Night	**Laurel Hurley**
Monostatos	**Paul Franke**
High Priest	**Clifford Harvuot**
Priest	**Osie Hawkins**
Three Ladies	**Madelaine Chambers**
	Sandra Warfield
	Heidi Krall
Three Genii	**Emilia Cundari**
	Rosalind Elias
	Margaret Roggero
Two Men in Amour	**Albert Da Costa**
	Louis Sgarro

Metropolitan Opera Chorus
(Kurt Adler, chorus master)
Metropolitan Opera Orchestra
Tibor Kozma
(Ignace Strasfogel, assistant conductor)

Contains spoken dialogue
Overture.
Act I
The first five parts, the introduction **Zu Hilfe! zu Hilfe!** (O help me, protect me) *through the quintet* **Hm! hm! hm!** (Hm! hm! hm!), *are given complete. The trio* **Du feines Täubchen** (My dainty lambkin) *is cut completely. The duet* **Bei Männern, welche Liebe fühlen** (The man who feels sweet love's emotion) *is given complete as is the Act I finale,* **Zum Ziele führt dich diese Bahn** (Your journey's end you soon will reach), *except that nineteen measures in the finale are cut before* **Es lebe Sarastro! Sarastro soll leben!** (We praise thee, Sarastro, with great exultation!).

Act II

This act's first part, the March of the Priests, is cut completely. The next part, the aria and chorus **O Isis und Osiris** (O Isis and Osiris) *is given, but the following duet* **Bewahret euch vor Weibertücken** (Beware of woman's crafty scheming) *is cut completely. Recording begins again with the quintet* **Wie? Wie? Wie?** (Ye? Ye? Ye?) *and continues with the aria* **Alles fühlt der Liebe Freuden** (All the world is full of lovers) *but only the first verse is heard. This is followed by the aria* **Die Hölle Rache kocht in meinem Herzen** (The wrath of hell within my breast I cherish) *and the aria* **In diesen heil'gen Hallen** (Within these holy portals) *but only the first verse of this is recorded. The trio* **Seid uns zum zweitenmal willkommen** (Here in Sarastro's hallowed border) *is cut completely. Recording begins again with the aria* **Ach, ich fühl's** (Ah, I feel, to grief and sadness), *but the following Chorus of the Priests* **O Isis und Osiris** (O Isis and Osiris!) *is cut completely. Recording begins again with the trio* **Soll ich dich, Teurer, nicht mehr sehn?** (Must I from thee forever part?) *and continues with the aria* **Ein Mädchen oder Weibchen** (A sweetheart or a maiden) *but only the first verse of this aria is heard. The finale,* **Bald prangt, den Morgen zu verkünden** (Soon speeds the morning light proclaiming), *is given complete except that the duet between Pamina and Tamino,* **Wir wandelten durch Feuergluten** (The fire's flames we have transcended), *is abbreviated and the following chorus,* **Triumph, Triumph, Triumph! Du edles Paar!** (Rejoice! The victory is gained!), *is cut completely.*

33⅓ rpm   **Metropolitan Opera Record Club MO 823**
RCA Victor LM-6089 / released July 1960 to 1 March 1962

Selections from this set were also released as follows:

673. **MOZART:** *Die Zauberföte—Bei Männern, welche Liebe fühlen.*
(in English as *"The man who feels sweet love's emotion"*)
33⅓ rpm   **MET 50** / released 1985 to ?
Cassette   **MET 50-C** / released 1985 to ?

674. **MOZART:** *Die Zauberföte—Schnelle Füsse, rascher Mut.*
(in English as *"Nothing ventured, nothing won!"*)
Cassette   **MET 517-C** / released 1992 to ?
CD   **MET 517-CD** / released 1992 to ?

675. **MOZART:** *Die Zauberföte—O Isis und Osiris.* (*"Possenti Numi"*)
(in English as *"O Isis and Osiris"*)
33⅓ rpm   **MET 50** / released 1985 to ?
Cassette   **MET 50-C** / released 1985 to ?

676. **MOZART:** *Die Zauberföte—Die Hölle Rache kocht in meinem Herzen.*
     (in English as *"The wrath of hell within my breast I cherish"*)
     CD   **MET 258** / released 2006 to ?

677. **MOZART:** *Die Zauberföte—In diesen heil'gen Hallen.*
     (in English as *"Within these holy portals"*)
     CD   **MET 258** / released 2006 to ?

678. **MOZART:** *Die Zauberföte—Soll ich dich, Teurer, nicht mehr sehn?*
     (in English as *"Must I from thee forever part?"*)
     CD   **MET 258** / released 2006 to ?

679. **MOZART:** *Die Zauberföte—Ein Mädchen oder Weibchen.*
     (in English as *"A sweetheart or a maiden"*)
     CD   **MET 258** / released 2006 to ?

680. **MOZART:** *Die Zauberföte—Papagena! Papagena!*
     (in English as *"Papagena! Papagena!"*)
     Cassette   **MET 517-C** / released 1992 to ?
     CD   **MET 517-CD** / released 1992 to ?

Sessions of 5, 6 & 7 March 1956; Metropolitan Opera House, NYC.

681.   **MUSSORGSKY:** *Boris Godunov – Excerpts*
                    (Sung in English to a Text by John Gutman)
            (The orchestral score was revised and edited by Karol Rathaus)

Boris Godunov	**Giorgio Tozzi**
Marina	**Nell Rankin**
Prince Shuiski	**Charles Kullman**
Grigori, later *Dimitri*	**Albert Da Costa**
Brother Pimen	**Norman Scott**
The Simpleton	**Paul Franke**
Rangoni	**Frank Valentino**
Fyodor	**Margaret Roggero**
Xenia	**Laurel Hurley**
Xenia's Nurse	**Sandra Warfield**
Shchelkalov	**Arthur Budney**
Mityukh	**Arthur Budney**

Metropolitan Opera Chorus
(Kurt Adler, chorus master)
Metropolitan Opera Orchestra
Dimitri Mitropoulos

Act I
Scene 1 – "Outside a Monastery near Moscow"
  This scene is cut completely.
Scene 2 – "The Square in the Kremlin" – Coronation Scene
  This scene is given without cuts.
Scene 3 – "A Cell in a Monastery"
  This scene begins with narration by Norman Scott in the rôle of Brother Pimen. There are several cuts.
Scene 4 – "An Inn near the Lithuanian Border"
  This scene is cut completely.

Act II
"A Room in the Tsar's Palace in the Kremlin"
  This scene begins with narration by Norman Scott in the rôle of Brother Pimen. There are several cuts and several parts are shortened.

Act III
Scene 1 – "A Castle in Poland. Marina's Room"
  This scene begins with narration by Norman Scott in the rôle of Brother Pimen. The beginning of the scene until the appearance of Rangoni is cut completely. There is also a cut in the dialogue between Marina and Rangoni.
Scene 2 – "A Hall in the Castle"
  The Polonaise is performed but in a version for orchestra alone. The duet with Grigori and Marina is slightly abbreviated.

Act IV
Scene 1 – "Outside a Convent near Moscow"
  This scene begins with narration by Norman Scott in the rôle of Brother Pimen. This scene is given without cuts.
Scene 2 – "The Great Hall in the Kremlin"
  This scene begins with narration by Norman Scott in the rôle of Brother Pimen. This scene is given without cuts.
Scene 3 – "A Forest near Kromy" – Revolutionary Scene
  This scene is cut completely.

33⅓ rpm   **Metropolitan Opera Record Club MO 417**
RCA Victor LM-6063 / released October 1958 to 1 March 1963

Selections from this set were also released as follows:

682. **MUSSORGSKY:** *Boris Godunov—Coronation Scene.* (in English)
  CD   **MET 258** / released 2006 to ?

683. **MUSSORGSKY:** *Boris Godunov—Polonaise.*
  33⅓ rpm **MET 408** / released 1986 to ?
  Cassette **MET 408-C** / released 1986 to ?

684. **MUSSORGSKY:** *Boris Godunov—You have come, beloved.* *("Garden Scene")* (in English)
  CD   **MET 258** / released 2006 to ?

Sessions of 22 & 26 October 1956, 7:00 to 11:00 P.M. each day; Columbia Studios, 207 E. 30ᵗʰ St. NYC.

685.   **OFFENBACH:** *Les Contes d'Hoffmann – Excerpts*
     (Sung in English to a Text by John Gutman)

Hoffmann	**Jon Crain**
Nicklausse	**Helen Vanni**
Olympia	**Laurel Hurley**
Giulietta	**Rosalind Elias**
Antonia	**Lucine Amara**
Coppelius	**Martial Singher**
Dappertutto	**Martial Singher**
Dr. Miracle	**Martial Singher**
Spalanzani	**Paul Franke**
Cochenille	**Charles Anthony**
Pitichinaccio	**Charles Anthony**
Schlemil	**Clifford Harvuot**
Crespel	**Norman Scott**
The Voice of Antonia's Mother	**Sandra Warfield**

Metropolitan Opera Chorus
(Kurt Adler, chorus master)
Metropolitan Opera Orchestra
Jean Morel

There are many cuts throughout these selections
Prélude.
Prologue
Dear master Luther (Drig, drig, drig, drig)
Narration by Jon Crain in the rôle of Hoffmann.

> **In times of yore, well over a century back** (Il était une fois à la cour d'Eisenach) [one verse]
> **Beer? I would sooner give up drinking!** (Peuh! cette bière est detestable!)
> *("Finale of Prologue")* [abbreviated]

Act I
Narration by Jon Crain in the rôle of Hoffmann.
> **No one, but no one at all** (Non, aucun hôte vraiment)
> **When the bird begin their singing** (Les oiseaux dans la charmille) [one verse]
> **I like to watch when they're dancing** (Voici la ritournelle!)
Narration by Jon Crain in the role of Hoffmann.

Act II
> **Dream of love** (Belle nuit) *("Barcarolle")*
> **I say- No time to lose. Let's play.** (Morbleu! au jeu! au jeu! Messieurs)
> **Shine and glitter** (Scintille diamant)
> **Giulietta! What is your wish?** (Cher ange! Qu'attendez vous de votre servant?)
> **Enchanting revelation** (O Dieu! de quelle ivresse) [abbreviated]
Narration by Jon Crain in the rôle of Hoffmann.
> **Schlemil! Just as I thought: together.** (Schlemil! J'en étais sûr! Ensemble!)
> **My heart is filled with trepidation** (Hélas! mon cœur s'égare encore)
> *("Septet" "Finale of Act II")*

Act III
Narration by Jon Crain in the rôle of Hoffmann.
> **Flown away, dove that I cherished** (Elle a fui, la touterelle!) [one verse]
> **Song of my love I will sing you again** (C'est une chanson d'amour qui s'envole) [abbreviated]
Narration by Jon Crain in the rôle of Hoffmann.
> **You'll never sing again?** (Tu ne chanteras plus?) [abbreviated]
> **Ah, my child!** (Mon enfant!) *("Finale of Act III")*

Epilogue
This is not recorded.

33⅓ rpm   **Metropolitan Opera Record Club MO 710**
                RCA Victor LM-2310 / released April 1959 to ?

A selection from this set was also released as follows:

686. **OFFENBACH:** *Les Contes d'Hoffmann—Hélas! mon cœur s'égare encore.*
(in English as *"My heart is filled with trepidation"*)
CD   **MET 258** / released 2006 to ?

Session(s) of January 1957; Columbia Studios, 207 E. 30ᵗʰ St. NYC.

687.   **OFFENBACH:** *La Périchole – Excerpts*
                    (Sung in English to a Text by Maurice Valency)
                    (Musical Version by Jean Morel and Ignace Strasfogel)
                    (Orchestration revised and adapted by Julius Burger)

La Périchole	**Patrice Munsel**
Paquillo	**Theodor Uppman**
Don Andres	**Cyril Ritchard**
Don Pedro	**Ralph Herbert**
Panatellas	**Paul Franke**
Guadalena	**Heidi Krall**
Estrella	**Madelaine Chambers**
Virginella	**Rosalind Elias**
The Old Prisoner	**Alessio De Paolis**
First Notary	**Charles Anthony**
Second Notary	**Calvin Marsh**

Metropolitan Opera Chorus
(Kurt Adler, chorus master)
Metropolitan Opera Orchestra
Jean Morel
(Ignace Strasfogel, assistant conductor)

Cyril Ritchard as Don Andres provides the spoken narration. A special delight is the spoken part of the Old Prisoner as portrayed by Alessio De Paolis at the beginning of the Third Act. Some of the highlights of this recording include the following.

Act I
We are three cousins (sung by Guadalena, Estrella, Virginella)
Without a word to anybody (Don Andres)
The soldier wooed the maiden (Paquillo, Périchole)
Oh, my dearest, from my heart I swear it (Périchole)
I've dined so well (Périchole)
I have to tell you, pretty lady (Paquillo)

Act II
This truth is great (Panatellas, Paquillo, Don Pedro)
I humbly bow before your graces (Périchole)
And now, O ruler (Paquillo)

Act III, Scene 1
Were I rogue, I'd own the city (Paquillo)

You are not rich, you are no beauty (Périchole)
A jolly jailer, I (Don Andres)
<u>**Act III, Scene 2**</u>
Forward, dragoons! (Don Pedro, chorus)
Of all the wealth and all the treasure (Périchole)

33⅓ rpm   **Metropolitan Opera Record Club MO 713**
RCA Victor LOC-1029 / released July 1957 to 1 September 1961
[While all the other Metropolitan Opera Record Club recordings that appeared later on the RCA Victor label were given record numbers that began with the LM prefix that RCA Victor used for their long playing classical "Red Seal" recordings, this recording of *La Périchole* was the only one to appear in the LOC series which was used for long playing original cast show recordings.]

<u>Selections from this set were also released as follows:</u>

688. **OFFENBACH:** *La Périchole—Le conquérant dit à la jeune Indienne.* (in English as *"The soldier wooed the maiden"*)
   CD   **MET 258** / released 2006 to ?

689. **OFFENBACH:** *La Périchole—O mon cher amant, je te jure.* (in English as *"Oh, my dearest, from my heart I swear it"*)
   CD   **MET 258** / released 2006 to ?

<u>*Session(s) of ?; Metropolitan Opera House, NYC.*</u>

690.   **PUCCINI:** *La Bohème – Excerpts*

Mimì	**Lucine Amara**
Rodolfo	**Daniele Barioni**
Musetta	**Heidi Krall**
Marcello	**Frank Valentino**
Colline	**Nicola Moscona**
Schaunard	**Clifford Harvuot**
Alcindoro	**Alessio De Paolis**
Parpignol	**Frank D'Elia**
Officer	**Carlo Tomanelli**

Metropolitan Opera Chorus
(Kurt Adler, chorus master)
Metropolitan Opera Orchestra
Fausto Cleva

Act I

The recording goes from the beginning through Eureka! Trovasti! Sì. *Then there is a cut of some 140 measures before beginning again with* Legna! Sigari! Bordò!. *This section lasts only thirty-one measures and ends with* Sta Luigi Filippo ai nostri piè!. *Then there is a large cut of some 312 measures before beginning again with* Au Quartiere Latin ci attende Momus. *After Mimì's aria,* Sì. Mi chiamano Mimì, *twenty-eight measures are cut before beginning again with* O soave fanciulla *which omits Marcello's short phrase at the beginning.*

Act II

After the opening chorus and a few words of Schaunard ending with Pipa e corno quant'è?, *there is a cut of some eighty measures before beginning again with Rodolo's* Chi guardi?. *This continues only through Rodolfo's presentation of Mimì to his friends ending with his words* sboccia l'amor *and his friends'* Ah! Ah! Ah! Ah!. *Then there is cut of some 260 measures before beginning again with Musetta's* Quando me'n vo'. *Then shortly after the beginning of the Allegro alla Marcia section and after Schaunard's* Ma il mio Tesoro ov'è!, *there is a cut of some seventy-six measures to the closing part of the chorus* Eccolo là! Il bel tambur maggior!.

Act III

After the forty-seven measures of the orchestral introduction of the act, there is a cut of some 126 measures beginning again with Mimì's Sa dirmi, scusi. *In the duet of Mimì and Marcello there is a cut of twenty-nine measures between Mimì's* Il mio Rodolfo si strugge per gelosia *and her* Fate voi per il meglio. *This continues for only ten(!) measures before there is a cut of some twenty-six measures beginning again with Rodolfo's* Marcello, finalmente!. *This continues through Marcello's* l'amore è fiacco e roco *and then there is a cut of eleven measures before beginning again with Rodolfo's* Mimì è una civetta. *This continues for only fifty-five measures before there is a cut of twenty-seven measures beginning in the concerted passage of Rodolfo, Mimì and Marcello with Roldolfo's* Mimì di serra è fiore. *Following Mimì's Farwell and Rodolfo's* Addio sogni d'amor!, *there is a cut of twenty-seven measures which includes the beginning of the Quartet and resumes in the Quartet with Marcello's* Che facevi? Che dicevi.

Act IV

The beginning of Rodolfo's and Marcello's duet is cut, and recording begins with Rodolfo's O Mimì, tu più non torni. *After the duet there is a cut until the appearance of Musetta and with Marcello's word* Musetta!. *Recording continues through Mimì's* Queste mie mani riscaldare non si potranno mai?. *Then after a cut of thirty-one measures, recording begins again with Musetta's* Ascolta! Forse è l'ultima volta, *but this lasts for only twelve measures before a cut of forty measures eliminates Colline's Coat*

Aria. Recording begins again with Mimì's Sono andati?, *but this lasts only through Mimì's* bella come un tramonto. *Then there is a cut of ninety-three measures until Musetta's* Dorme?.

33⅓ rpm   **Metropolitan Opera Record Club MO 610**

A selection from this set was also released as follows:

691. **PUCCINI:** *La Bohème—Sì, mi chiamano Mimì .*
     CD   **MET 258** / released 2006 to ?

Sessions of 10, 11 & 13 December 1957, 2:00 to 5:00 P.M. each day; Columbia Studios, 207 E. 30ᵗʰ St. NYC.

692.   **PUCCINI:** *Madama Butterfly – Excerpts*

Cio-cio-san	**Dorothy Kirsten**
B. F. Pinkerton	**Daniele Barioni**
Sharpless	**Clifford Harvuot**
Suzuki	**Mildred Miller**
Kate Pinkerton	**Madelaine Chambers**
Goro	**Alessio De Paolis**
The Bonze	**Osie Hawkins**
The Imperial Commissioner	**Calvin Marsh**
The Registrar	**Luigi De Cesare**

**Metropolitan Opera Chorus
(Kurt Adler, chorus master)
Metropolitan Opera Orchestra
Dimitri Mitropoulos**

Act I
After Pinkerton's È una casa a soffietto, *there is a cut of fifty-nine measures before resuming with his* Che guardi?. *This bridge is made a bit less abrupt by playing a couple intervening measures about nine measures before the* Che guardi? *section begins. After Pinkerton's* Dipende dal grado di cottura!, *there is a cut of forty-seven measures, which eliminates* Amore o grillo, *before beginning again with Sharpless'* Ier l'altro, il Consolato. *After the duet passage with Sharpless in which Pinkerton's part ends with* drizzare ai dolci voli dell'amor!, *there is a cut of nineteen measures before beginning again with Goro's* Ecco! Son giunte *which is sung along with But-*

terfly's friends singing Ah! Ah! Ah!. *After Butterfly's* B. F. Pinkerton. Giù, *which is echoed with her friends'* Giù, *there is a cut of 124 measures before resuming with Goro's* L'Imperial Commissario. *Thirty-six measures later the standard cut of forty-two measures is observed between Pinkerton's* della nova parentela *and Butterfly's Mother's* Mi pare un re! *in the concerted passage with friends and relatives. Next there is a cut of seventy measures between Butterfly's* uno, due, tre e tutti giù *and her* Ieri son salita. *After the last chorus singing of* Hou! Cio-cio-san!, *there is a cut of forty-three measures before beginning again with Pinkerton's* Viene la sera. *This section continues for only thirty measures. It should have ended with Suzuki's* Buona note, *but her vocal part is omitted. After a cut of forty-five measures, recording begins again with Pinkerton's* Ma intanto finor non m'hai detto.

Act II
The twenty-nine measures of orchestral introduction to the act are omitted. After Suzuki's opening prayer, twenty measures are cut before Butterfly begins with Suzuki è lungi la miseria?. *After Sharpless'* Grazie, *there is a cut of thirty-one measures before continuing with his* Ho da mostrarvi. *This continues for thirty measures through Butterfly's* Quando fanno il lor nido in America i pettirossi?. *Then there is a cut of forty-four measures beginning again with Sharpless'* Mi rincresce, ma ignore *which continues for only nine measures. After this there is a large cut of 260 measures which eliminates the scene with Prince Yamadori. Recording resumes with Sharpless'* Ora a noi. *After Butterfly's* A un infelice madre la carità, muovetevi a pietà!, *there is a cut of only nine measures before beginning again with her* E la canzon giuliva. *After Sharpless'* Tuo padre lo saprà, te lo prometto, *there is a cut of 104 measures before beginning again with Butterfly's* Vedrai, piccolo amor. *In the Flower Duet some eighteen measures for orchestra alone are cut before* Spoglio è l'orto. *After the duet there is a cut of sixty-three measures beginning where Butterfly would have sung* Or vienmi ad adornar *and beginning again with the Humming Chorus.*

Act III
After just sixteen measures of the orchestral introduction, forty measures are cut. Recording begins again with the chorus singing Oh eh! Oh eh!. *Before Suzuki's first word* Cio-cio-san, *four measures are cut. The first verse of Buttefly's* Dormi amor mio *is cut. After Pinkerton's* Sharpless, v'aspetto per via, *there is a cut of forty-one measures before beginning again with Sharpless'* Andate: il triste vero. *After Butterfly's* Che vuol da me?, *there is a cut of fifty-seven measures before resuming with her* Vespa!. *After Butterfly's* A lui devo obbedir!, *there is a cut of fifteen measures before beginning again with Suzuki's* Come una mosca prigioniera.

33⅓ rpm   **Metropolitan Opera Record Club MO 722**

Selections from this set were also released as follows:

693. **PUCCINI:** *Madama Butterfly—Dovunque al mondo.*
  Cassette   **MET 507-C** / released 1989 to ?
  CD   **MET 507-CD** / released 1989 to ?

694. **PUCCINI:** *Madama Butterfly—Ieri son salita … Bonze Scene.*
  Cassette   **MET 507-C** / released 1989 to ?
  CD   **MET 507-CD** / released 1989 to ?

695. **PUCCINI:** *Madama Butterfly—Viene la sera.*
  CD   **MET 258** / released 2006 to ?

696. **PUCCINI:** *Madama Butterfly—Letter Scene.*
  Cassette   **MET 507-C** / released 1989 to ?
  CD   **MET 507-CD** / released 1989 to ?

697. **PUCCINI:** *Madama Butterfly—Sai cos'ebbe cuore … Vedrai, piccolo amor.*
  CD   **MET 217-CD** / released 1993 to ?

698. **PUCCINI:** *Madama Butterfly—Humming Chorus.*
  Cassette   **MET 507-C** / released 1989 to ?
  CD   **MET 507-CD** / released 1989 to ?

699. **PUCCINI:** *Madama Butterfly—Tu, tu, piccolo Iddio!*
  CD   **MET 258** / released 2006 to ?

Session(s) of March 1957; Columbia Studios, 207 E. 30th St. NYC.

700.   **PUCCINI:** *Tosca – Excerpts*

Floria Tosca	**Dorothy Kirsten**
Mario Cavaradossi	**Daniele Barioni**
Baron Scarpia	**Frank Guarrera**
Cesare Angelotti	**Clifford Harvuot**
The Sacristan	**Salvatore Baccaloni**
Spoletta	**Alessio De Paolis**
Sciarrone	**George Cehanovsky**
A Jailer	**Louis Sgarro**

Metropolitan Opera Chorus
(Kurt Adler, chorus master)

Metropolitan Opera Orchestra
Dimitri Mitropoulos
(Martin Rich, assistant conductor)

Act I
Before the Sacristan begins with E sempre lava!*, forty-eight measures of orchestral music are cut. After Scarpia's* Buon indizio*, two more measures are played that should have had Scarpia singing the word* Entriamo*, but the vocal part is omitted. Ninety-three measures are then cut before resuming with Scarpia's* Tosca? Che non mi veda.

Act II
After Scarpia's E che là sia nascosto? *and Cavaradossi's* Nego! Nego!*, there is a cut of nineteen measures before beginning again with Spoletta's* O bei tratti di corda!*. Before Scarpia's* Ed or fra noi parliam da buoni amici*, there is a cut of seventeen measures of orchestral music. After Tosca's* ah! non posso più! *and Cavaradossi's* Ahimè!*, there is a cut of just fifteen measures before beginning with the last time that Spoletta says* Nil inultum remanebit!*. The usual cut of three measures is taken at the end of the aria* Vissi d'arte. *After Scarpi's* Si adempia il voler vostro*, there is a cut of fifteen measures before resuming with his* Tosca, finalmente mia!*. After Tosca's* E avanti a lui tremava tutta Roma!*, the next six measures are cut before returning to the closing orchestral passage.*

Act III
After the first fourteen measures of the introduction to this act, there is a cut of 126 measure which eliminates the scene with the Young Shepherd. The recording resumes with the Jailer's Mario Cavaradossi?.

33⅓ rpm   **Metropolitan Opera Record Club MO 724**

Selections from this set were also released as follows:

701. **PUCCINI:** *Tosca—Recondita armonia.*
    CD   **MET 258** / released 2006 to ?

702. **PUCCINI:** *Tosca—Mario! Mario! Mario! ("Love Duet")*
    CD   **MET 258** / released 2006 to ?

703. **PUCCINI:** *Tosca—La povera mia cena fu interrotta … Vissi d'arte.*
    CD   **MET 258** / released 2006 to ?

704. **PUCCINI:** *Tosca—Senti, l'ora è vicina.*
    Cassette   **MET 516-C** / released 1992 to ?
    CD   **MET 516-CD** / released 1992 to ?

Session(s) of ?; Metropolitan Opera House, NYC.

705.   **JOHANN STRAUSS, II:** *Die Fledermaus – Excerpts*
                                  (English Lyrics by Howard Dietz)

Gabriel von Eisenstein	**Brian Sullivan**
Rosalinda	**Heidi Krall**
Adele	**Laurel Hurley**
Alfred	**Thomas Hayward**
Prince Orlofsky	**Mildred Miller**
Dr. Falke	**John Brownlee**
Frank	**Clifford Harvuot**

Metropolitan Opera Chorus
(Walter Taussig, chorus master)
Metropolitan Opera Orchestra
Tibor Kozma

Several of the sections chosen for recording are abbreviated.
Overture.
Act I
Do you still belong to me (Täubchen, das entflattert ist)
I've a sister rarely writes me (Da schreibt meine Schwester Ida)
Narration by John Brownlee in the rôle of Dr. Falke.
The graying sea, the leaden sky (So muss allein ich bleiben)
Narration by John Brownlee in the rôle of Dr. Falke.
What a lovely rendezvous! (Trinke, Liebchen, trinke schnell)
Dialogue
If this affair were clandestine (Mein Herr, was dächten Sie von mir)
Oh, come with me and you'll agree (Mein schönes, grosses Vogelhaus)

Act II
You will find, if you mind (Ein Souper heut uns winkt)
Dialogue
I've many peculiarities (Ich lade gern mir Gäste ein)
Narration by John Brownlee in the rôle of Dr. Falke.
It seems we're entertaining (Ach, meine Herr'n und Damen)
Look me over once (Mein Herr Marquis)
Dialogue
A Bacchanalian revel (Im Feuerstrom der Reben)
Happy Days! (Brüderlein)
Let's hope this never halts (Genug, damit, genug!)

Act III
Narration by John Brownlee in the rôle of Dr. Falke.

Dialogue
I am portraying a farm girl (Spiel' ich die Unschuld vom Lande)
Narration by John Brownlee in the rôle of Dr. Falke.
Dialogue
Narration by John Brownlee in the rôle of Dr. Falke.
Dialogue
The case that you take up (Ich stehe voll Zagen)
I went to her apartment (Ein seltsam Abendteuer)
Dialogue
Narration by John Brownlee in the rôle of Dr. Falke.
And now to a brief conclusion (Champagner hat's verschuldet)

33⅓ rpm   **Metropolitan Opera Record Club MO 518**

Selections from this set were also released as follows:

706. **JOHANN STRAUSS, II:** *Die Fledermaus—So muss allein ich bleiben.* (in English as *"The graying sea, the leaden sky"*)
    CD   **MET 258** / released 2006 to ?

707. **JOHANN STRAUSS, II:** *Die Fledermaus—Ich lade gern mir Gäste ein.* (in English as *"I've many peculiarities"*)
    CD   **MET 258** / released 2006 to ?

708. **JOHANN STRAUSS, II:** *Die Fledermaus—Mein Herr Marquis.* (in English as *"Look me over once"*)
    CD   **MET 258** / released 2006 to ?

Session(s) of December 1957; Columbia Studios, 207 E. 30ᵗʰ St. NYC.

709.   **TCHAIKOVSKY:** *Eugene Onegin – Excerpts*
                        (English Text by Henry Reese)

Tatyana	**Lucine Amara**
Lenski	**Richard Tucker**
Olga	**Rosalind Elias**
Eugene Onegin	**Frank Guarrera**
Madame Larina	**Martha Lipton**
Prince Gremin	**Giorgio Tozzi**
Filippyevna	**Belen Amparan**
Zaretski	**George Cehanovsky**

Metropolitan Opera Chorus
(Kurt Adler, chorus master)
Metropolitan Opera Orchestra
Dimitri Mitropoulos
(Ignace Strasfogel, assistant conductor)

Introduction. *The introduction is cut completely.*
Act I
Scene 1 – "A Garden"
No. 1 Duet and Quartet *"And did you hear"*
   This number is given without cuts.
No. 2 Chorus and Dance of Reapers *"My tottering legs"*
   This number is given without cuts.
No. 3 Scene and Aria *"Cross the little bridge"*
   This number is given without cuts.
No. 4 Scene *"My merry little daughter"*
   This first thirty-six measures are cut. Recording begins with Olga's
   There! I hear a carriage now.
No. 5 Scene and Quartet *"Madame, I've brought Eugene Onegin"*
   This number is complete only through the first twenty-four measures and
   eliminates the quartet. It ends with Larina's **You make our guests at**
   home here. I'll be back. [*Instead of* "I'll be back," "I'll be quick" *is*
   printed in the G. Schirmer vocal score which was published in 1957 with
   Henry Reese' English version].
No. 6 Scene and Arioso *"How happy, how pleased am I"*
   This number is given without cuts.
No. 7 Closing Scene *"Ah, here you are"*
   This number is cut completely.
Scene 2 – "Tatyana's Room"
No. 8 Introduction and Scene *"Oh how I've babbled on!"*
   This number is cut completely.
No. 9 The Letter Scene *"Though it destroy my soul"*
   This number is given with several cuts.
No. 10 Scene and Duet *"Ah, the sun is rising"*
   This number is cut completely.
Scene 3 – "Another Part of the Garden"
No. 11 Chorus of Country Girls *"Come, sweet maidens"*
   This number is given without cuts.
No. 12 Scene and Aria *"He comes! He! Onegin"*
   The final thirty-two measures which comprise Onegin singing **So you**
   must learn more self control *with chorus are cut.*

Act II
Scene 1 – "A Lighted Ball-Room in the house of Larina"

No. 13 Entr'acte and Waltz *"We are surprised"*
> *The first thirty-one measures of the orchestral introduction are cut. The text of the G. Schirmer vocal score begins* **What a surprise,** *but the text as sung in the recording begins* **We are surprised.**

No. 14 Scene and Couplets *"Now how have I deserved your cruel mockery?"*
> *This number is cut completely.*

No. 15 Mazurka and Scene *"Messieurs! Mesdames!"*
> *The first seventy-six measures are cut.*

No. 16 Finale *"In your house here"*
> *This number is given with several cuts.*

Scene 2 – "A Village Mill on the Banks of a Wooded Stream"

No. 17 Introduction, Scene and Aria *"Well Lenski, where can your opponent be?"*
> *The first twenty-eight measures are cut.*

No. 18 Duel Scene *"He's coming now"*
> *This number is given without cuts.*

Act III

Scene 1 – "Ballroom of Prince Gremin's Palace"

No. 19 Polonaise
> *This number is given without cuts.*

No. 20 Scene and Aria *"Here too I'm bored"*
> *This number is given without cuts.*

No. 21 Scene and Aria *"Now come, and let me introduce my wife"*
> *This number is given without cuts.*

Scene 2 – "A Park"

No. 22 Final Scene *"My heart is worn with fear"*
> *The first fifty-two measures are cut.*

33⅓ rpm   **Metropolitan Opera Record Club MO 824**

Selections from this set were also released as follows:

710. **TCHAIKOVSKY:** *Eugene Onegin—How happy, how pleased am I.* (in English)
    CD   **MET 258** / released 2006 to ?

711. **TCHAIKOVSKY:** *Eugene Onegin—Letter Scene.* (in English)
    CD   **MET 258** / released 2006 to ?

712. **TCHAIKOVSKY:** *Eugene Onegin—Oh where, oh where have flown my days of Springtime.* (in English)
    CD   **MET 258** / released 2006 to ?

713.   **VERDI:** *Aïda – Excerpts*

Aïda	**Lucine Amara**
Radamès	**Albert Da Costa**
Amneris	**Rosalind Elias**
Amonasro	**Frank Guarrera**
Ramfis	**Giorgio Tozzi**
The King	**Louis Sgarro**
Messenger	**James McCracken**
Priestess	**Shakeh Vartenissian**

Metropolitan Opera Chorus
(Kurt Adler, chorus master)
Metropolitan Opera Orchestra
Fausto Cleva

Prelude.
Act I, Scene 1
After Amneris' E quale sguardo rivolse a lei!, *there is a cut of thirty-three measures before beginning again with her* Trema! or rea schiava!. *In the concerted passage which begins with the King's* Su! del Nilo, *there is a cut of twenty-four measures that begins just before Aïda would have sung* Per chi piano?. *The music resumes with the cries of* Guerra! *by the King, Ramfis and the chorus.*
Act I, Scene 2
After the first invocation of the High Priestess and the response of Ramfis and the chorus of the Priests which is a passage of only seventeen measures, there is a cut to the Sacred Dance of Priestesses.

Act II, Scene 1
After Amneris first sings the phrase beginning Ah! vieni *and ending with* fammi beato il cor, *there is a cut to the Dance of Young Moorish Slaves. After Aïda's* che dissi mai? pietà! perdono! Ah!, *there is a cut of fourteen measures before resuming with her* Tu sei felice. *After Amneris'* Io sul trono accanto al Re *with the chorus, there is a cut of twenty-three measures before beginning again with Aïda's* Numi, pieta.
Act II, Scene 2
In the opening chorus after le mistiche carole, *there is a cut of twenty measures going to the last four measures of the chorus before the trumpets begin the Grand March. After the march, all of the ballet music is cut. Recording begins again with the chorus* Vieni, o guerriero vindice. *After* i fior versiam!, *there is a cut of thirty-two measures before beginning again with*

Gloria!. **Before Amonasro begins** Fa' cor: della tua patria, *there is a cut of nine measures.*

Act III
After the sixteen measures of the orchestral introduction to the act, the entire scene with chorus, Amneris and Ramfis is cut. Recording begins again with the twelve measures of introduction to Qui Radamès verrà!. *Twenty-two measures are cut from where Radamès should have sung* Sovra una terra estrania *before beginning again with his* il ciel de' nostri amori. *After Radamès'* Di più limpido fulgor, *there is a cut of sixteen measures before resuming with Aïda and Radamès singing* Vieni meco.

Act IV, Scene 1
Only the first half of this scene, the duet with Amneris and Radamès, is given. The judgment scene is cut completely.
Act IV, Scene 2
This is given without cuts.

33⅓ rpm   **Metropolitan Opera Record Club MO 721**

Selections from this set were also released as follows:

714. **VERDI:** *Aïda—Quest'assisa ch'io vesto vi dica ... Ma tu, re.*
     CD   **MET 258** / released 2006 to ?

715. **VERDI:** *Aïda—Qui Radamès verrà ... O patria mio.*
     CD   **MET 258** / released 2006 to ?

Session(s) of ?; Metropolitan Opera House, NYC.

716.   **VERDI:** *Rigoletto – Excerpts*

Rigoletto	**Robert McFerrin**
Duke of Mantua	**Daniele Barioni**
Gilda	**Laurel Hurley**
Giovanna	**Thelma Votipka**
Maddalena	**Sandra Warfield**
Monterone	**Louis Sgarro**

Metropolitan Opera Chorus
(Kurt Adler, chorus master)
Metropolitan Opera Orchestra
Fausto Cleva

Act I

After the Prelude is played, the introductory scene with the Duke and Borsa is cut, and the recording resumes with Questa o quella. *This is followed at once by Monterone's* Ch'io gli parli *and continues to the end of the act.*

Act II

The opening scene with Rigoletto and Sparafucile is cut, and the recording begins with Rigoletto's Pari siamo!. *This continues through the beginning of the duet with Gilda. A cut that begins where Gilda would have sung* Il nome vostro ditemi *continues until Gilda sings* Cielo! Sempre novel sospetto. *The rest of their duet continues through Rigoletto's departure. The next part is cut until the Duke begins* E il sol dell'anima. *A cut begins where the Duke would have sung* Che m'ami deh!. *Recording resumes with* Caro nome *which concludes before the section that begins* Gualtier Maldè!. *Then there is a quick cut to the closing of the act and Gilda's* Soccorso, padre mio!.

Act III

The first part of the act is cut and recording begins with Povero Rigoletto!. *After just fifteen measures, there is a cut of twenty-one measures beginning again with Rigoletto's* Dorme il Duca tuttor?. *This continues through the end of* Cortigiani, vil razza dannata. *Then there is a cut of sixty-eight measures resuming with Gilda's* Tutte le feste. *After she sings* dagl'occhi il cor, il cor parlò, *there is a cut of fourteen measures before continuing with* Partì, partì. *From the end of* Tutte le feste, *there is an abrupt cut of fifty-nine measures to Monterone's* Poichè *and from there recording continues to the end of the act.*

Act IV

The opening of the act is cut. Recording begins with La donna è mobile. *From the end of this canzone, there is a cut of thirty measures before beginning again with the Duke's* Un dì, se ben rammentomi. *From the end of the quartet, there is a major cut to the recitative and final duet of the opera beginning with Rigoletto's* Chi è mai, chi è qui in sua vece?. *In the final duet the first eight measures of Gilda's* Lassù in cielo *are cut.*

33⅓ rpm   **Metropolitan Opera Record Club MO 214**

A selection from this set was also released as follows:

717. **VERDI:** *Rigoletto—Pari siamo! … Figlia! Mio padre!.*
     CD   **MET 258** / released 2006 to ?

Sessions of 18, 25 & 26 March 1957, 2:00 P.M. to ? each day; Columbia Studios, 207 E. 30th St. NYC.

718.   **VERDI:** *Il Trovatore – Excerpts*

Manrico	**Kurt Baum**
Leonora	**Mary Curtis-Verna**
Azucena	**Rosalind Elias**
Count di Luna	**Frank Guarrera**
Ferrando	**Norman Scott**
Inez	**Helen Vanni**
Ruiz	**James McCracken**
A Messenger	**James McCracken**

Metropolitan Opera Chorus
(Kurt Adler, chorus master)
Metropolitan Opera Orchestra
Max Rudolf
(Victor Trucco, assistant conductor)

This recording follows most standard performance practices and cuts. Additional variants are listed here.

Act I
In the Tacea la note placida *scene, before Inez'* Quanto narrasti *seven measures are cut. The first verse of* Di tale amor *is cut, as is the second verse of* Deserto sulla terra.

Act II
The second verse of the Anvil Chorus is cut as is the second verse of Stride la vampa. *The entire chorus of Gipsies,* Mesta è la tua canzon!*, is cut.*

Act III
The chorus Squilli, echeggi la tromba *is abbreviated. After* Ah, sì, ben mio, *the short duet of twenty-two measures,* L'onda de' suoni mistici *is cut.*

Act IV
The opening recitative with Ruiz and Leonora is cut and the recording of the act begins with Leonora's Timor di me?. *The Miserere is abbreviated. Leonora's* Tu vedrai che amore in terra *is cut completely.*

33⅓ rpm   **Metropolitan Opera Record Club MO 726**

Selections from this set were also released as follows:

719. **VERDI:** *Il Trovatore—Condotta ell'era in ceppi.*
    <u>CD</u>   **MET 258** / released 2006 to ?

720. **VERDI:** *Il Trovatore—Il balen del suo sorriso.*
    <u>CD</u>   **MET 258** / released 2006 to ?

<u>Sessions of 11 February 1957, 3:00 to 6:00 P.M., 14 February 1957, 2:00 to 6:00 P.M.,</u>
<u>6 March 1957, 2:00 to 6:00 P.M.; Columbia Studios, 207 E. 30th St. NYC.</u>

721.   **WAGNER:** *Die Walküre – Excerpts*

Brünnhilde	**Margaret Harshaw**
Sieglinde	**Marianne Schech**
Fricka	**Blanche Thebom**
Siegmund	**Ramon Vinay**
Wotan	**Hermann Uhde**
Hunding	**Norman Scott**
Helmwige	**Gloria Lind**
Gerhilde	**Carlotta Ordassy**
Ortlinde	**Heidi Krall**
Rossweisse	**Sandra Warfield**
Grimgerde	**Martha Lipton**
Waltraute	**Mariquita Moll**
Siegrune	**Rosalind Elias**
Schwertleite	**Belen Amparan**

Metropolitan Opera Orchestra
Dimitri Mitropoulos

<u>Act I</u>
After the Prelude and Siegmund's Wess' Herd dies auch sei, hier muss ich rasten, *the rest of the first scene and the entire second scene are cut completely. Recording resumes in the third scene with Siegmund's* Ein Schwert verhiess mir der Vater, ich fänd' es in höchster Not, *but after these words, there is a cut of seven measures before continuing with* ein Weib sah ich, wonnig and hehr. *After Siegmund's* tief in des Busens Berge, glimmt nur noch lichtlose Glut, *just three(!) measures are cut. After Sieglinde's* Mir zagt es vor der Wonne, die mich entzückt!, *fifty-eight measures are cut before continuing with her* So blickte der Greis grüssend auf mich.

<u>Act II</u>
After Wotan's wer büsst mir der Minne Macht?, *there is a cut of twenty-six*

measures before beginning again with Fricka's Mir schaudert das Herz. *After Fricka's* Die Betrog'ne lass auch zertreten!, *there is a cut of 133 measures before Wotan's* Was verlangst du?. *This section lasts for only six measures before there is a cut of fifty-eight measures, and recording resumes with Fricka's* Deiner ew'gen Gattin heilige Ehre *and continues to the end of the first scene. The second and third scenes are cut completely. Recording begins again with the Todesverkündigung scene in the fourth scene with Brünnhilde's* Siegmund! Sieh' auf mich!. *After Siegmund's* grüss' auch die holden Wunschesmädchen: zu ihnen folg' ich dir nicht!, *there is a cut of 117 measures before resuming with Brünnhilde's* Ich sehe die Not, die das Herz dir zernagt. *After Siegmund's* Sollte die grimmige Wal nicht schrecken ein gramvolles Weib?, *there is a cut of seventy-five measures before beginning again with Hunding's* Wehwalt! Wehwalt! Steh' mir zum Streit. *After Wotan's* Zurück vor dem Speer! In Stücken das Schwert!, *there is a cut of forty-two measures before resuming with his* Doch Brünnhilde! Weh' der Verbrecherin!.

Act III

The scene of the Ride of the Valkyries is abbreviated with several cuts. After's Brünnhilde's first appeal to her sisters, there is yet another cut before finally resuming with Brünnhilde's Der wilde Jäger. *After Wotan's* wie ihren Wert von sich sie warf!, *there is a cut of sixty-three measures before beginning again with his* Hörst du's, Brünnhilde?. *After Brünnhilde's* Hier bin ich, Vater: gebiete die Strafe!, *there is a cut of fifty-six measures before resuming with Wotan's* Nicht send' ich dich mehr aus Walhall. *From where Brünnhilde should have begun singing* Nimmst du mir alles, was einst du gabst?, *there is a cut of forty-eight measures before beginning again with Wotan's* Aus eurer Schar. *After Brünnhilde's* dass Siegmund Schutz du versagtest, *there is a cut of ninety-four measures before resuming with Wotan's* So tatest du, was so gern zu tun ich begehrt. *After Wotan's* als mir göttlicher Not nagende Galle gemischt, *there is a cut of 136 measures before resuming with his* Doch fort muss ich jetzt. *The recording continues from this point to the conclusion without any breaks.*

33⅓ rpm	**Metropolitan Opera Record Club MO 728**

<u>Selections from this set were also released as follows:</u>

722. **WAGNER:** *Die Walküre—Ein Schwert verhiess mir der Vater.*
    Cassette   **MET 519-C** / released 1993 to ?
    CD   **MET 519-CD** / released 1993 to ?

723. **WAGNER:** *Die Walküre—Winterstürme wichen dem Wonnemond ... Du bist der Lenz ... Siegmund heiß' ich und Siegmund bin ich!*
    CD   **MET 258** / released 2006 to ?

724. **WAGNER:** *Die Walküre—Walkürenritt.* *("Ride of the Valkyries")*
     CD   **MET 258** / released 2006 to ?

725. **WAGNER:** *Die Walküre—War es so schmählich, was ich verbrach.*
     CD   **MET 258** / released 2006 to ?

726. **WAGNER:** *Die Walküre—Loge hör! lausche hieher! ... Feuerzauber.* *("Magic Fire Music")*
     CD   **MET 258** / released 2006 to ?

Session of 9 February 1956, Midnight to 3:00 A.M.; Carnegie Hall, NYC.

[Thanks to the midnight starting time of this session, the artists assembled at Carnegie Hall for this session on 8 February 1956, but when the session began, it had just become 9 February 1956.]

Max Rudolf has written to the compiler of this discography: "Of the nightly session for the Ravel Concerto I recall that we had trouble with the subway noises which could be heard in Carnegie Hall. Certain passages had to be repeated and 'sliced.' Besides, Wittgenstein was quite nervous, which also made repeats necessary. The solo passages were recorded at another time and then sliced in, meaning that we had to record no more than 15 minutes of orchestral music. Incidentally the Met Orchestra came to Carnegie Hall after having played a performance of *Aïda*."

727. **RAVEL:** *Concerto for the Left Hand for Piano and Orchestra in D Major.*
     Paul Wittgenstein & Metropolitan Opera Orchestra – Max Rudolf.
     33⅓ rpm   **Period SPL 742**
                      Orion ORS-7028

This ends the section which began at item 647 of twenty recordings made from 1955 through 1957 for which there is little official information.

The chronological listing by session resumes here.

Sessions of 23 February, 7 & 10 April 1958; Manhattan Center, NYC.
[Information from Victor archives.]

During these three sessions a complete recording of _Vanessa_ was made.

728.   **BARBER: _Vanessa_**

Vanessa	**Eleanor Steber**
Erika	**Rosalind Elias**
The Old Baroness	**Regina Resnik**
Anatol	**Nicolai Gedda**
The Old Doctor	**Giorgio Tozzi**
Nicholas	**George Cehanovsky**
A Footman	**Robert Nagy**

Metropolitan Opera Chorus
(Kurt Adler, chorus master)
Metropolitan Opera Orchestra
Dimitri Mitropoulos
(Ignace Strasfogel, assistant conductor)

Act I	7 April 1958
Act II	23 February 1958
Act III	7 & 10 April 1958
Act IV, Scene 1	23 February 1958
Act IV Intermezzo	7 & 10 April 1958
Act IV, Scene 2	23 February 1958

33⅓ rpm	**RCA Victor LM-6138** _mono_ / released August 1958 to ?
	RCA Victor LSC-6138 _stereo_ / released August 1958 to ?
	RCA Red Seal ARL2-2094 / released February 1977 to ?
	RCA RL02094
Cassette	**RCA Victor Gold Seal 7899-4-RG**
_CD_	**RCA Victor Gold Seal 7899-2-RG**
	RCA Victor Gold Seal GD 87899
	RCA Red Seal 88697446172

Selections from this set were also released as follows:

729. **BARBER: _Vanessa – Excerpts._**
     33⅓ rpm   **RCA Victor LM-6062** _mono_ / released January 1959 to ?
                       RCA Victor LSC-6062 _stereo_ / released January 1959 to ?

730. **BARBER: _Vanessa—Must the winter come so soon?_**
     33⅓ rpm   **RCA Victor SP-33-21** _mono_

731. **BARBER:** *Vanessa—Do not utter a word, Anatol.*
  CD   **RCA Victor Red Seal 09026-63860-2** / released 2001 to ?
                       MET 211-CD

732. **BARBER:** *Vanessa—To leave, to break.* *("Quintet")*
  33⅓ rpm   **RCA Red Seal CRM8-5177** / released 1984 to ?
                       MET 405 / released 1985 to ?
  Cassette   **RCA Red Seal CRK8-5177** / released 1984 to ?
                       RCA Victor 09026-62689-4 / released 1995 to ?
                       MET 405-C / released 1985 to ?
  CD   **RCA Victor Red Seal 09026-61580-2** / released 1993 to ?
                       RCA Victor 09026-62689-2 / released 1995 to ?

Session of 15 April 1958, 12:00 to 6:00 P.M.; Symphony Hall, Boston.
[Information from Victor archives.]

733.   **SAINT-SAËNS:** *Samson et Dalila – Excerpts*

Delilah	**Risë Stevens**
Samson	**Mario Del Monaco**
High Priest of Dagon	**Clifford Harvuot**
Abimelech	**Ezio Flagello**

Metropolitan Opera Chorus
(Kurt Adler, chorus master)
Metropolitan Opera Orchestra
Fausto Cleva

Arrêtez, ô mes frères!
Amour! viens aider ma faiblesse.
En ces lieux
Mon cœur s'ouvre à ta voix.
Vois ma misère, hélas!
Gloire à Dagon vainqueur!

  33⅓ rpm   **RCA Victor LM-2309** *mono* / released June 1959 to ?
                       RCA Victor LSC-2309 *stereo* / released June 1959 to ?

Sessions of 1, 2, 3, 4, 8, 9, 10, 11 & 12 September 1958; Manhattan Center, NYC.
[Information from Victor archives.]

734.   **ROSSINI:** *Il Barbiere di Siviglia*

Figaro	**Robert Merrill**
Rosina	**Roberta Peters**
Count Almaviva	**Cesare Valletti**
Don Basilio	**Giorgio Tozzi**
Dr. Bartolo	**Fernando Corena**
Berta	**Margaret Roggero**
Fiorello	**Calvin Marsh**
A Sergeant	**Calvin Marsh**
Ambrogio	**Carlo Tomanelli**

Metropolitan Opera Chorus
(Kurt Adler, chorus master)
Metropolitan Opera Orchestra
Erich Leinsdorf
(Victor Trucco, assistant conductor)

33⅓ rpm	**RCA Victor LM-6143** *mono* / released July 1959 to ?
	RCA Victor LSC-6143 *stereo* / released July 1959 to ?
	RCA Victrola VICS-6102
Cassette	**RCA Victor 6505-4-RG** / released 1987 to ?
	RCA VKS 43543
CD	**RCA Victor 6505-2-RG** / released 1987 to ?
	RCA Victor 09026-68552-2 / released 1996 to ?
	RCA GD 86505

Selections from this set were also released as follows:

736. **ROSSINI:** *Il Barbiere di Siviglia – Excerpts.*

33⅓ rpm	**RCA Victor LM-6071** *mono* / released November 1959 to ?
	RCA Victor LSC-6071 *stereo* / released November 1959 to ?
	RCA GL 42776 / released 1979 to ?
Cassette	**RCA Victor 60188-4-RG** / released 1990 to ?
CD	**RCA Victor Gold Seal 60188-2-RG** / released 1990 to ?
	RCA Victor Red Seal 09026-63494-2 / released 1999 to ?

736. **ROSSINI:** *Il Barbiere di Siviglia—Ecco ridente in cielo.*

33⅓ rpm	**RCA Red Seal CRM8-5177** / released 1984 to ?
Cassette	**RCA Red Seal CRK8-5177** / released 1984 to ?
	MET 508-C / released 1990 to ?

<u>CD</u>   **RCA Victor Red Seal 09026-61580-2** / released 1993 to ?
                     MET 508-CD / released 1990 to ?

737. **ROSSINI:** *Il Barbiere di Siviglia—Largo al factotum.*
   Cassette   **RCA Victor 09026-68080-4** / released 1995 to ?
                     RCA Victor Red Seal 09026-61440-4 / released 1992 to ?
                     RCA Victor 09026-62689-4 / released 1995 to ?
   CD   **RCA Victor 09026-68080-2** / released 1995 to ?
                     RCA Victor Red Seal 09026-61440-2 / released 1992 to ?
                     RCA Victor 09026-62689-2 / released 1995 to ?
                     RCA Victor Red Seal 09026-68921-2 / released 1997 to ?

738. **ROSSINI:** *Il Barbiere di Siviglia—Una voce poco fa.*
   33⅓ rpm   **MET 50** / released 1985 to ?
   Cassette   **RCA Victor 60841-4-RG** / released 1991 to ?
                     MET 50-C / released 1985 to ?
   CD   **RCA Victor 60841-2-RG** / released 1991 to ?

739. **ROSSINI:** *Il Barbiere di Siviglia—Contro un cor.*
   CD   **MET 230**

740. **ROSSINI:** *Il Barbiere di Siviglia—Alfine eccoci quà.*
   33⅓ rpm   **RCA Victor LM-6171** *mono* / released September 1966 to 1 March 1967
                     RCA Gold Seal AGM3-4805 / released 1983 to ?
   Cassette   **RCA Gold Seal CGK2-4805** / released 1983 to ?

741. **ROSSINI:** *Il Barbiere di Siviglia—Di sì felice innesto.*
   Cassette   **MET 508-C** / released 1990 to ?
   CD   **MET 508-CD** / released 1990 to ?

<u>***Sessions of 12, 13, 15 & 16 February, 1 & 4 March 1959; Manhattan Center, NYC.***</u>
[Information from Victor archives.]

742.   **VERDI:** *Macbeth*

Macbeth	**Leonard Warren**
Lady Macbeth	**Leonie Rysanek**
Banquo	**Jerome Hines**
Macduff	**Carlo Bergonzi**
Malcolm	**William Olvis**
Lady-in-Attendance	**Carlotta Ordassy**
A Physician	**Gerhard Pechner**

A Murderer	**Osie Hawkins**
A Warrior	**Calvin Marsh**
A Bloody Child	**Emilia Cundari**
A Crowned Child	**Mildred Allen**
A Manservant	**Harold Sternberg**

Metropolitan Opera Chorus
(Kurt Adler, chorus master)
Metropolitan Opera Orchestra
Erich Leinsdorf
(Victor Trucco, assistant conductor)

33⅓ rpm	**RCA Victor LM-6147** *mono* / released January 1960 to ?
	RCA Victor LSC-6147 *stereo* / released January 1960 to ?
	RCA Victrola VICS- 6121 / released October 1969 to ?
	RCA Gold Seal AGL3-4516 / released 1982 to ?
	RCA Victrola VICS- 6147
	RCA RE 25006-8
Cassette	**RCA Gold Seal AGK2-4516** / released 1982 to ?
CD	**RCA Victor Gold Seal 4516-2-RG** / released 1987 to ?
	RCA GD 84516 / released 1987 to ?

Selections from this set were also released as follows:

743. VERDI: *Macbeth – Excerpts.*
| *33⅓ rpm* | **RCA Victor LM-6076** *mono* / released January 1960 to 1 September 1961 ? |
| | **RCA Victor LSC-6076** *stereo* / released January 1960 to 1 September 1961 ? |

744. VERDI: *Macbeth—Vieni! t'afretta! accendere.*
| *CD* | **RCA Victor 09026-68920-2** / released 1997 to ? |
| | **Musical Heritage Society 515055X** |

745. VERDI: *Macbeth—Mi si affaccia un pugnal?!*
| *33⅓ rpm* | **RCA Special Products DPL1-0216** |

746. VERDI: *Macbeth—Fatal mia donna! un murmure.*
| *33⅓ rpm* | **MET 405** / released 1985 to ? |
| *Cassette* | **MET 405-C** / released 1985 to ? |

747. VERDI: *Macbeth—La luce langue.*
Cassette	**RCA Victor 09026-62689-4** / released 1995 to ?
CD	**RCA Victor 09026-62689-2** / released 1995 to ?
	RCA Victor 09026-68920-2
	Musical Heritage Society 515055X

748. **VERDI:** *Macbeth—Come dal ciel precipita.*
    33⅓ rpm   **RCA Red Seal CRM8-5177** / released 1984 to ?
                              MET 405 / released 1985 to ?
    Cassette   **RCA Red Seal CRK8-5177** / released 1984 to ?
                              MET 405-C / released 1985 to ?
    CD   **RCA Victor Red Seal 09026-61580-2** / released 1993 to ?

749. **VERDI:** *Macbeth—Sangue a me.*
    33⅓ rpm   **MET 50** / released 1985 to ?
    Cassette   **MET 50-C** / released 1985 to ?

750. **VERDI:** *Macbeth—Patria oppressa!*
    33⅓ rpm   **MET 408** / released 1986 to ?
    Cassette   **MET 408-C** / released 1986 to ?

751. **VERDI:** *Macbeth—Ah, la paterna mano.*
    33⅓ rpm   **RCA Red Seal LSC-3084**
                              RCA Red Seal CRM8-5177 / released 1984 to ?
    Cassette   **RCA Red Seal CRK8-5177** / released 1984 to ?
                              RCA Victor 09026-62689-4 / released 1995 to ?
    CD   **RCA Victor Red Seal 09026-61580-2** / released 1993 to ?
                              RCA Victor 09026-62689-2 / released 1995 to ?

752. **VERDI:** *Macbeth—Una macchia è qui tuttora.*
    33⅓ rpm   **RCA Red Seal CRM8-5177** / released 1984 to ?
    Cassette   **RCA Red Seal CRK8-5177** / released 1984 to ?
    CD   **RCA Victor Red Seal 09026-61580-2** / released 1993 to ?

753. **VERDI:** *Macbeth—Pietà, rispetto, amore.*
    33⅓ rpm   **RCA Victor LM-2453** / released March 1960 to ?
                              RCA Victrola PVM 1-9048 / released 1976 to ?
    Cassette   **RCA Victor 09026-62689-4** / released 1995 to ?
    CD   **RCA Victor 09026-62689-2** / released 1995 to ?
                              VAI LWC-1—LWC-2 / released 2000 to ?

__Performance of 22 April 1972; Metropolitan Opera House, Lincoln Center, NYC.__
[Information from published recording.]

754.   ***Highlights from the***
            Metropolitan Opera Gala Honoring
                     Sir Rudolf Bing.

VERDI: *Il Trovatore—Tacea la note placida.*
   Martina Arroyo & Metropolitan Opera Orchestra – Richard Bonynge.

PUCCINI: *Manon Lescaut—Tu, tu amore?*
   Montserrat Caballé, Plácido Domingo & Metropolitan Opera Orchestra – James Levine.

RICHARD STRAUSS: *Salome—Ah! Du wolltest mich nicht deinem Mund küssen lassen.*
("Final Scene") [Herod's words are omitted.]
   Birgit Nilsson & Metropolitan Opera Orchestra – Karl Böhm.

MOZART: *Le Nozze di Figaro—Dove sono.*
   Leontyne Price & Metropolitan Opera Orchestra – Francesco Molinari-Pradelli.

JOHANN STRAUSS, II: *Die Fledermaus—Ich lade gern mir Gäste ein.*
(in English to a special text by John Gutman as *"Chacun à Bing's goût"*)
   Regina Resnik & Metropolitan Opera Orchestra – Kurt Adler.

VERDI: *La Forza del Destino—Invano Alvaro.*
   Richard Tucker, Robert Merrill & Metropolitan Opera Orchestra – Francesco Molinari-Pradelli.

VERDI: *Otello—Già nella notte densa.*
   Teresa Zylis-Gara, Franco Corelli & Metropolitan Opera Orchestra – Karl Böhm.

   33⅓ rpm   **Deutsche Grammophon 2530 260** [This edition was labeled as being "Volume I"
                        but no later volumes were released.]
   Open Reel Tape, 4 Track, 7½ ips.   **Deutsche Grammophon DGG L 2260**
   CD   **Deutsche Grammophon 00289 477 6540**
                 Deutsche Grammophon 459 201-2 / released 1998 to ?

                  Selections from this set were also released as follows:

755. **PUCCINI:** *Manon Lescaut—Tu, tu amore?*
   Cassette   **Deutsche Grammophon 447 270-4** / released 1996 to ?
   CD   **Deutsche Grammophon 447 270-2** / released 1996 to ?
                    Deutsche Grammophon 449 229-2

756. **RICHARD STRAUSS:** *Salome—Ah! Du wolltest mich nicht deinem Mund*
   küssen lassen. *("Final Scene")* [Herod's words are omitted.]
   CD   **Deutsche Grammophon 431 1072**

757. **JOHANN STRAUSS, II:** *Die Fledermaus—Ich lade gern mir Gäste ein.*
   (in English to a special text by John Gutman as *"Chacun à Bing's goût"*)
   33⅓ rpm   **MET 50** / released 1985 to ?
   Cassette   **MET 50-C** / released 1985 to ?

758. **VERDI:** *Otello—Già nella notte densa.*
   CD   **London/Decca 289 467 918-2** / released 2001 to ?

[Information from Deutsche Grammophon.]

759.

BIZET: *Carmen*

Carmen	**Marilyn Horne**
Don José	**James McCracken**
Escamillo	**Tom Krause**
Micaëla	**Adriana Maliponte**
Frasquita	**Colette Boky**
Mercédès	**Marcia Baldwin**
Zuniga	**Donald Gramm**
Dancaïre	**Russell Christopher**
Lillas Pastia	**Russell Christopher**
Remendado	**Andrea Velis**
Moralès	**Raymond Gibbs**

Manhattan Opera Chorus
(John Mauceri, chorus director)
Metropolitan Opera Children's Chorus
(David Stivender, children's chorus director)
Metropolitan Opera Orchestra
Leonard Bernstein
(John Mauceri, assistant to Leonard Bernstein)

33⅓ rpm	**Deutsche Grammophon 2709 043**
Cassette	**Deutsche Grammophon 413 279-4**
CD	**Deutsche Grammophon 427 440-2**
	Deutsche Grammophon 289 471 750-2

Selections from this set were also released as follows:

760. **BIZET:** *Carmen – Excerpts.*
33⅓ rpm	**Deutsche Grammophon 2530 534**
Cassette	**Deutsche Grammophon 3300 478**

761. **BIZET:** *Carmen—Prelude.*
CD	**Deutsche Grammophon 289 469 322-2** / released 2001 to ?
	Deutsche Grammophon 457 691-2 / released 1998 to ?

762. **BIZET:** *Carmen—Habañera.* *("L'amour est un oiseau rebelle")*
CD	**Deutsche Grammophon 289 472 179-2**
	Deutsche Grammophon 457 691-2 / released 1998 to ?

763. **BIZET:** *Carmen—Act III Finale.*
     Cassette   **MET 502-C** / released 1988 to ?
     _CD_   **MET 502-CD** / released 1988 to ?

764. **BIZET:** *Carmen—Act IV Entr'acte.*
     33⅓ rpm   **MET 408** / released 1986 to ?
     Cassette   **MET 408-C** / released 1986 to ?

Performance of 28 March 1982; Metropolitan Opera House, Lincoln Center, NYC.
[Information from published recording.]

765.   ***In Concert at the Met.***

Leontyne Price, Marilyn Horne
Metropolitan Opera Orchestra
James Levine

MOZART: *Così Fan Tutte—Ah, guarda sorella.*
   Leontyne Price, Marilyn Horne & Metropolitan Opera Orchestra – James Levine.

MOZART: *Le Nozze di Figaro—Dove sono.*
   Leontyne Price & Metropolitan Opera Orchestra – James Levine.

HANDEL: *Rodelinda—Vivi, tiranno!*
   Marilyn Horne & Metropolitan Opera Orchestra – James Levine.

HANDEL: *Rinaldo—Fermati! No, crudel!*
   Leontyne Price, Marilyn Horne & Metropolitan Opera Orchestra – James Levine.

VERDI: *Les Vêpres Siciliennes—Overture.*
   Metropolitan Opera Orchestra – James Levine.

VERDI: *Aïda—Silenzio! Aïda verso noi s'avanza.*
   Leontyne Price, Marilyn Horne & Metropolitan Opera Orchestra – James Levine.

ROSSINI: *L'Assedio di Corinto—Non temer, d'un basso affetto.*
   Marilyn Horne & Metropolitan Opera Orchestra – James Levine.

VERDI: *La Forza del Destino—Pace, pace, mio Dio.*
   Leontyne Price & Metropolitan Opera Orchestra – James Levine.

BELLINI: *Norma—Overture.*
   Metropolitan Opera Orchestra – James Levine.

BELLINI: *Norma—Mira, O Norma!*
  Leontyne Price, Marilyn Horne & Metropolitan Opera Orchestra – James Levine.

MEYERBEER: *Les Huguenots—Non, non, non … vous n'avez jamais, je gage.*
  Marilyn Horne & Metropolitan Opera Orchestra – James Levine.

PUCCINI: *La Rondine—Chi il bel sogno di Doretta.*
  Leontyne Price & Metropolitan Opera Orchestra – James Levine.

PUCCINI: *Madama Butterfly—Scuoti quella fronda di ciliegio.* *("Flower Duet")*
  Leontyne Price, Marilyn Horne & Metropolitan Opera Orchestra – James Levine.

33⅓ rpm	**RCA Red Seal CRC2-4609** / released 1983 to ?	
	RCA Red Seal RL 04609 / released 1983 to ?	
Cassette	**RCA Red Seal CRE2-4609** / released 1983 to ?	
CD	**RCA Red Seal RCD2-4609** / released 1983 to ?	

<u>Selections from this set were also released as follows:</u>

766. **MOZART:** *Così Fan Tutte—Ah, guarda sorella.*
  <u>*CD*</u>   **RCA Victor Gold Seal 09026-68152-2** / released 1996 to ?

767. **HANDEL:** *Rodelinda—Vivi, tiranno!*
  <u>*CD*</u>   **RCA Victor Red Seal 09026-68921-2** / released 1997 to ?

768. **HANDEL:** *Rinaldo—Fermati! No, crudel!*
  33⅓ rpm   **Metropolitan Opera MO-1** / released 1984 to ?

769. **VERDI:** *Les Vêpres Siciliennes—Overture.*
  33⅓ rpm   **RCA Red Seal ARL1-4856** / released 1983 to ?
                        RCA Gold Seal AGL1-7138
  Cassette   **RCA Red Seal ARK1-4856** / released 1983 to ?

770. **VERDI:** *Aïda—Ebben, qual nuovo fremito.* [This is a heavily cut version of the *Aïda* selection listed above in item #765.]
  33⅓ rpm   **MET 50** / released 1985 to ?
  Cassette   **MET 50-C** / released 1985 to ?

771. **PUCCINI:** *Madama Butterfly—Scuoti quella fronda di ciliegio.* *("Flower Duet")*
  Cassette   **RCA Red Seal 09026-62699-4** / released 1994 to ?
  <u>*CD*</u>   **RCA Red Seal 09026-62699-2** / released 1994 to ?

Sessions of April 1987; Manhattan Center, NYC.

[In addition to the recording session information from the published recording given above, files at the Metropolitan Opera list the more specific dates of 20 through 30 April 1987.]

772.   **WAGNER:** *Die Walküre*

Siegmund	**Gary Lakes**
Hunding	**Kurt Moll**
Wotan	**James Morris**
Sieglinde	**Jessye Norman**
Brünnhilde	**Hildegard Behrens**
Fricka	**Christa Ludwig**
Gerhilde	**Marita Napier**
Ortlinde	**Marilyn Mims**
Waltraute	**Reinhild Runkel**
Schwertleite	**Ruthild Engert**
Helmwige	**Linda Kelm**
Siegrune	**Diane Kesling**
Grimgerde	**Meredith Parsons**
Rossweisse	**Anne Wilkens**

Metropolitan Opera Orchestra
James Levine
(Max Epstein, musical assistant)

33⅓ rpm	**Deutsche Grammophon 423 389-1**
Cassette	**Deutsche Grammophon 423 389-4**
CD	**Deutsche Grammophon 423 389-2**
	Deutsche Grammophon 445 354-2
	Deutsche Grammophon 471 678-2

Selections from this set were also released as follows:

773. **WAGNER:** *Die Walküre – Excerpts.*
     CD   **Deutsche Grammophon 427 359-2**

774. **WAGNER:** *Die Walküre—Der Männer Sippe sass hier im Saal.*
     CD   **Deutsche Grammophon 437 825-2**

775. **WAGNER:** *Die Walküre—Du bist der Lenz.*
     Cassette   **Deutsche Grammophon 439 153-4**
     CD   **Deutsche Grammophon 439 153-2**

776. **WAGNER:** *Die Walküre—Walkürenritt.* *("Ride of the Valkyries")*
     CD   **Deutsche Grammophon 437 825-2**

Deutsche Grammophon 449 229-2
Deutsche Grammophon 457 440-2 / released 1997 to ?

777. **WAGNER:** *Die Walküre—Nicht sehre dich Sorge um mich.*
 Cassette **MET 519-C** / released 1993 to ?
 CD   **Deutsche Grammophon 449 229-2**
     MET 519-CD / released 1993 to ?

778. **WAGNER:** *Die Walküre—Leb' wohl, du kühnes herrliches Kind!*
 CD   **Deutsche Grammophon 449 229-2**

779. **WAGNER:** *Die Walküre—Der Augen leuchtendes Paar ... Feuerzauber.* *("Magic Fire Music")*
 CD   **Deutsche Grammophon 437 825-2**

780. **WAGNER:** *Die Walküre—Feuerzauber.* *("Magic Fire Music")*
 Cassette **Deutsche Grammophon 445 769-4**
     MET 519-C / released 1993 to ?
 CD   **Deutsche Grammophon 445 769-2**
     MET 519-CD / released 1993 to ?

Sessions of April & May 1988; Manhattan Center, NYC.

[In addition to the recording session information from the published recordings given above, files at the Metropolitan Opera list the more specific dates of 18 April through 6 May 1988.]

781.   **WAGNER:** *Das Rheingold*

Wotan	**James Morris**
Donner	**Siegfried Lorenz**
Froh	**Mark Baker**
Loge	**Siegfried Jerusalem**
Alberich	**Ekkehard Wlaschiha**
Mime	**Heinz Zednik**
Fasolt	**Kurt Moll**
Fafner	**Jan-Hendrik Rootering**
Fricka	**Christa Ludwig**
Freia	**Mari Anne Häggander**
Erda	**Birgitta Svendén**
Woglinde	**Hei-Kyung Hong**
Wellgunde	**Diane Kesling**
Flosshilde	**Meredith Parsons**

Metropolitan Opera Orchestra
James Levine
(Max Epstein, musical assistant)

33⅓ rpm	**Deutsche Grammophon 427 607-1**
Cassette	**Deutsche Grammophon 427 607-4**
CD	**Deutsche Grammophon 427 607-2**
	Deutsche Grammophon 445 295-2
	Deutsche Grammophon 445 354-2
	Deutsche Grammophon 471 678-2

Selections from this set were also released as follows:

782. **WAGNER: *Das Rheingold—Lugt Schwestern! Die Weckerin lacht in den Grund.***
  CD   **Deutsche Grammophon 437 825-2**

783. **WAGNER: *Das Rheingold—Wotan! Gemahl! erwache!***
  Cassette   **MET 519-C** / released 1993 to ?
  CD   **MET 519-CD** / released 1993 to ?

784. **WAGNER: *Das Rheingold—Immer ist Undank Loges Lohn!***
  Cassette   **MET 519-C** / released 1993 to ?
  CD   **MET 519-CD** / released 1993 to ?

785. **WAGNER: *Das Rheingold—Zur Burg führt die Brücke.*** *("Einzug der Götter in Walhall"*
  "Entrance of the Gods into Valhalla")
  CD   **Deutsche Grammophon 437 825-2**

786.   **WAGNER: *Siegfried***

Siegfried	**Reiner Goldberg**
Mime	**Heinz Zednik**
The Wanderer	**James Morris**
Alberich	**Ekkehard Wlaschiha**
Fafner	**Kurt Moll**
Erda	**Birgitta Svendén**
Brünnhilde	**Hildegard Behrens**
Forest Bird	**Kathleen Battle**

Metropolitan Opera Orchestra
James Levine
(Max Epstein, musical assistant)

CD   **Deutsche Grammophon 429 407-2**
              Deutsche Grammophon 429 402-2
              Deutsche Grammophon 445 354-2
              Deutsche Grammophon 471 678-2

<u>Selections from this set were also released as follows:</u>

787. **WAGNER:** *Siegfried—Aber, wie sah meine Mutter wohl aus? ("Waldweben"*
"Forest Murmurs")
CD   **Deutsche Grammophon 437 825-2**

788. **WAGNER:** *Siegfried—Nun sing! Ich lausche dem Gesang.*
CD   **Deutsche Grammophon 437 825-2**

789. **WAGNER:** *Siegfried—Heil dir, Sonne! Heil dir, Licht!*
CD   **Deutsche Grammophon 437 825-2**

Performance of 4 June 1988; Tokyo Bunka Kaikan, Japan.
[Information from published recording.]

790.   *Live in Tokyo 1988.*

                Kathleen Battle, Plácido Domingo
                Metropolitan Opera Orchestra
                James Levine
                (Max Epstein, musical assistant)

VERDI: *La Forza del Destino—Overture.*
   Metropolitan Opera Orchestra – James Levine.

VERDI: *La Traviata—Signora! … Che t'accadde? … Parigi, o cara.*
   Kathleen Battle, Plácido Domingo, Margaret Jane Wray & Metropolitan Opera Orchestra – James Levine.

DONIZETTI: *Don Pasquale—Quel guardo il cavaliere.*
   Kathleen Battle & Metropolitan Opera Orchestra – James Levine.

DONIZETTI: *Lucia di Lammermoor—Tombe degl'avi miei … Fra poco a me ricovero.*
   Plácido Domingo & Metropolitan Opera Orchestra – James Levine.

DONIZETTI: *L'Elisir d'Amore—Caro elisir … Trallarallera … Esulti pur la barbara.*
   Kathleen Battle, Plácido Domingo & Metropolitan Opera Orchestra – James Levine.

ROSSINI: *L'Italiana in Algeri—Overture.*
   Metropolitan Opera Orchestra – James Levine.

GOUNOD: *Roméo et Juliette—Va! je t'ai pardonné ... Nuit d'hyménée.*
Kathleen Battle, Plácido Domingo & Metropolitan Opera Orchestra – James Levine.

MOZART: *Don Giovanni—Là ci darem la mano.*
Kathleen Battle, Plácido Domingo & Metropolitan Opera Orchestra – James Levine.

LEHÁR: *Die Lustige Witwe—Lippen schweigen.* (in English as *"Love unspoken"*)
Kathleen Battle, Plácido Domingo & Metropolitan Opera Orchestra – James Levine.

33⅓ rpm	**Deutsche Grammophon 427 686-1** [This edition had the title *"Live in Tokyo 1988."*]
Cassette	**Deutsche Grammophon 427 686-4** [This edition had the title *"Live in Tokyo 1988."*]
CD	**Deutsche Grammophon 427 686-2** [This edition had the title *"Live in Tokyo 1988."*]
	Deutsche Grammophon 445 552-2 [This edition had the title *"Battle & Domingo Live."*]

<u>Selections from this set were also released as follows:</u>

791. **VERDI:** *La Forza del Destino—Overture.*
    CD   **Deutsche Grammophon 449 229-2**

792. **DONIZETTI:** *Lucia di Lammermoor—Fra poco a me ricovero.*
    Cassette   **Deutsche Grammophon 439 517-4**
    CD   **Deutsche Grammophon 439 517-2**
                 Deutsche Grammophon 449 229-2

793. **ROSSINI:** *L'Italiana in Algeri—Overture.*
    CD   **Deutsche Grammophon 449 229-2**

794. **LEHÁR:** *Die Lustige Witwe—Lippen schweigen.* (in English as *"Love unspoken"*)
    CD   **Deutsche Grammophon 289 459 155-2**

Sessions of April 1989; Manhattan Center, NYC.
[In addition to the recording session information from the published recording given above, files at the Metropolitan Opera list the more specific dates of 12 through 13 April 1989.]

795. **SCHOENBERG:** *Erwartung, Op. 17.*
    Jessye Norman & Metropolitan Opera Orchestra – James Levine.
    CD   **Philips 426 261-2**
                 Philips B0005512-02

<u>Sessions of May 1989; Manhattan Center, NYC.</u>

[In addition to the recording session information from the published recording given above, files at the Metropolitan Opera list the more specific dates of 8 through 19 May 1989.]

796.   **WAGNER:** *Götterdämmerung*

Siegfried	**Reiner Goldberg**
Gunther	**Bernd Weikl**
Hagen	**Matti Salminen**
Alberich	**Ekkehard Wlaschiha**
Brünnhilde	**Hildegard Behrens**
Gutrune	**Cheryl Studer**
Waltraute	**Hanna Schwarz**
First Norn	**Helga Dernesch**
Second Norn	**Tatiana Troyanos**
Third Norn	**Andrea Gruber**
Woglinde	**Hei-Kyung Hong**
Wellgunde	**Diane Kesling**
Flosshilde	**Meredith Parsons**

Metropolitan Opera Chorus
(David Stivender, chorus master)
Metropolitan Opera Orchestra
James Levine
(Max Epstein, musical assistant)

<u>CD</u>   **Deutsche Grammophon 429 385-2**
               Deutsche Grammophon 445 354-2
               Deutsche Grammophon 471 678-2

Selections from this set were also released as follows:

797. **WAGNER:** *Götterdämmerung – Excerpts.*
    <u>CD</u>   **Deutsche Grammophon 435 489-2**

798. **WAGNER:** *Götterdämmerung—Welches Unhold's List.*
    <u>Cassette</u>   **MET 520-C** / released 1993 to ?
    <u>CD</u>   **MET 520-CD** / released 1993 to ?

799. **WAGNER:** *Götterdämmerung—Trauermarsch.* *("Funeral March")*
    <u>Cassette</u>   **Deutsche Grammophon 445 769-4**
    <u>CD</u>   **Deutsche Grammophon 437 825-2**
                 Deutsche Grammophon 449 229-2
                 Deutsche Grammophon 445 769-2

800. **WAGNER:** *Götterdämmerung—Fliegt heim, ihr Raben.* *("Brünnhilde's Immolation Scene")*
    Cassette   **Deutsche Grammophon 439 153-4**
    CD   **Deutsche Grammophon 437 825-2**
           Deutsche Grammophon 449 229-2
           Deutsche Grammophon 439 153-2

801. **WAGNER:** *Götterdämmerung—Finale.*
    Cassette   **MET 520-C** / released 1993 to ?
    CD   **MET 520-CD** / released 1993 to ?

Sessions of May & September 1989; Manhattan Center, NYC.

[In addition to the recording session information from the published recording given above, files at the Metropolitan Opera list the first recording date as 1 May and the last as 9 September 1989.]

802.   **DONIZETTI:** *L'Elisir d'Amore*

Adina	**Kathleen Battle**
Nemorino	**Luciano Pavarotti**
Belcore	**Leo Nucci**
Dr. Dulcamara	**Enzo Dara**
Giannetta	**Dawn Upshaw**

Metropolitan Opera Chorus
(David Stivender, chorus master)
Metropolitan Opera Orchestra
James Levine
(Craig Rutenberg, musical assistant and fortepiano)

    33⅓ rpm   **Deutsche Grammophon 429 744-1**
    Cassette   **Deutsche Grammophon 429 744-4**
    CD   **Deutsche Grammophon 429 744-2**

Selections from this set were also released as follows:

803. **DONIZETTI:** *L'Elisir d'Amore – Excerpts.*
    CD   **Deutsche Grammophon 435 880-2**

804. **DONIZETTI:** *L'Elisir d'Amore—Quanto è bella, quanto è cara!*
    Cassette   **Deutsche Grammophon 439 517-4**
    CD   **Deutsche Grammophon 439 517-2**

805. **DONIZETTI:** *L'Elisir d'Amore—Saria possible?*
    <u>CD</u>   **Deutsche Grammophon 449 229-2**

806. **DONIZETTI:** *L'Elisir d'Amore—Una furtive lagrima.*
    <u>Cassette</u>   **Deutsche Grammophon 437 636-4**
                  Deutsche Grammophon 439 514-4
                  Deutsche Grammophon 439 517-4
    <u>CD</u>   **Deutsche Grammophon 437 636-2**
                  Deutsche Grammophon 439 514-2
                  Deutsche Grammophon 439 517-2
                  Deutsche Grammophon 457 444-2
                  Deutsche Grammophon 289 453 848-2
                  Deutsche Grammophon 289 459 362-2
                  Deutsche Grammophon 289 463 783-2
                  Deutsche Grammophon 445 900-2
                  Deutsche Grammophon 449 229-2

Sessions of May 1990; Manhattan Center, NYC.

[In addition to the recording session information from the published recording given above, files at the Metropolitan Opera list the more specific dates of 8 through 15 May 1990.]

807.   **MOZART:** *Le Nozze di Figaro*

Count Almaviva	**Thomas Hampson**
Countess Almaviva	**Kiri Te Kanawa**
Susanna	**Dawn Upshaw**
Figaro	**Ferruccio Furlanetto**
Cherubino	**Anne Sofie von Otter**
Marcellina	**Tatiana Troyanos**
Bartolo	**Paul Plishka**
Basilio	**Anthony Laciura**
Don Curzio	**Michael Forest**
Antonio	**Renato Capecchi**
Barbarina	**Heidi Grant**
Two Countrywomen	**Joyce Guyer**
	Stella Zambalis

Metropolitan Opera Chorus
(John Keenan, chorus master)
Metropolitan Opera Orchestra
James Levine
(Max Epstein, musical assistant)

**(Basso continuo: Craig Rutenberg, hammerklavier;
Jerry Grossman, cello; Laurence Glazener, double bass)**

<u>CD</u>   **Deutsche Grammophon 431 619-2**
                     Deutsche Grammophon 00289 477 5614

<u>Selections from this set were also released as follows:</u>

808. **MOZART:** *Le Nozze di Figaro – Excerpts.*
      <u>CD</u>   **Deutsche Grammophon 435 488-2**

809. **MOZART:** *Le Nozze di Figaro—Overture.*
      <u>Cassette</u>   **Deutsche Grammophon 439 150-4**
                             Deutsche Grammophon 439 514-4
      <u>CD</u>   **Deutsche Grammophon 439 150-2**
                             Deutsche Grammophon 439 514-2

810. **MOZART:** *Le Nozze di Figaro—Non so più, cosa son.*
      <u>CD</u>   **Deutsche Grammophon 449 229-2**
                             Deutsche Grammophon 289 445 085-2

811. **MOZART:** *Le Nozze di Figaro—Porgi, amor.*
      <u>Cassette</u>   **Deutsche Grammophon 439 153-4**
      <u>CD</u>   **Deutsche Grammophon 439 153-2**
                             Deutsche Grammophon 289 445 085-2

812. **MOZART:** *Le Nozze di Figaro—Voi che sapete.*
      <u>Cassette</u>   **Deutsche Grammophon 437 636-4**
      <u>CD</u>   **Deutsche Grammophon 437 636-2**
                             Deutsche Grammophon 289 445 085-2

813. **MOZART:** *Le Nozze di Figaro—Venite, inginocchiatevi.*
      <u>Cassette</u>   **Deutsche Grammophon 439 153-4**
      <u>CD</u>   **Deutsche Grammophon 439 153-2**

814. **MOZART:** *Le Nozze di Figaro—Vedrò mentr'io sospiro.*
      <u>CD</u>   **Deutsche Grammophon 449 229-2**

815. **MOZART:** *Le Nozze di Figaro—Dove sono.*
      <u>Cassette</u>   **Deutsche Grammophon 437 636-4**
      <u>CD</u>   **Deutsche Grammophon 437 636-2**
                             Deutsche Grammophon 449 229-2
                             Deutsche Grammophon 289 445 085-2

816. **MOZART:** *Le Nozze di Figaro—Che soave zeffiretto.*
     <u>CD</u>   **Deutsche Grammophon 289 445 085-2**

817. **MOZART:** *Le Nozze di Figaro—Deh vieni, non tardar.*
     <u>Cassette</u>   **Deutsche Grammophon 437 636-4**
     <u>CD</u>   **Deutsche Grammophon 437 636-2**
                         Deutsche Grammophon 449 229-2
                         Deutsche Grammophon 289 445 085-2
                         Deutsche Grammophon 289 453 848-2

**Sessions of 18 through 26 May 1990; Manhattan Center, NYC.**
[Information from published recording.]

818.   **VERDI:** *Aïda*

Aïda	**Aprile Millo**
Radamès	**Plácido Domingo**
Amneris	**Dolora Zajick**
Amonasro	**James Morris**
Ramfis	**Samuel Ramey**
The King	**Terry Cook**
The High Priestess	**Hei-Kyung Hong**
A Messenger	**Charles Anthony**

Metropolitan Opera Chorus
(John Keenan, choral preparation)
Metropolitan Opera Orchestra
James Levine
(Max Epstein, musical assistant)

     <u>Cassette</u>   **Sony Classical S3T 45973**
     <u>CD</u>   **Sony Classical S3K 45973**
                         Sony Classical 88697527722

Selections from this set were also released as follows:

819. **VERDI:** *Aïda – Excerpts.*
     <u>CD</u>   **Sony Classical SMK 53506**

820. **VERDI:** *Aïda—Celeste Aïda.*
     <u>Cassette</u>   **Sony Classical MLT 66707**

CD   **Sony Classical MLK 66707**
                  Sony Classical S2K 92845

821. **VERDI:** *Aïda—Ritorna vincitor!*
    Cassette   **Sony Classical MLT 64070**
    CD   **Sony Classical MLK 64070**

822. **VERDI:** *Aïda—Grand March.*
    Cassette   **Sony Classical MLT 64070**
                  Sony Classical MLT 66707
    CD   **Sony Classical MLK 64070**
                  Sony Classical MLK 66707

Sessions of April 1991 & June 1992; Manhattan Center, NYC.

[In addition to the recording session information from the published recording given above, files at the Metropolitan Opera list the more specific dates of 8 through 23 April 1991 and 9 through 15 June 1992.]

823.   **WAGNER:** *Parsifal*

Amfortas	**James Morris**
Titurel	**Jan-Hendrik Rootering**
Gurnemanz	**Kurt Moll**
Parsifal	**Plácido Domingo**
Klingsor	**Ekkehard Wlaschiha**
Kundry	**Jessye Norman**
Knights of the Grail	**Allan Glassman**
	Julien Robbins
Esquires	**Heidi Grant-Murphy**
	Jane Bunnell
	Paul Groves
	Anthony Laciura
Flower Maidens	**Heidi Grant-Murphy**
	Kaaren Erickson
	Jane Bunnell
	Korliss Uecker
	Joyce Guyer
	Wendy White
Voice from above	**Hitomi Katagiri**

Metropolitan Opera Chorus
(Norbert Balatsch, chorus master)

Metropolitan Opera Orchestra
James Levine
(Dennis Giauque, musical assistant)

<u>CD</u>   **Deutsche Grammophon 437 501-2**

<u>Selections from this set were also released as follows:</u>

824. **WAGNER:** *Parsifal – Excerpts.*
  <u>CD</u>   **Deutsche Grammophon 445 868-2**

825. **WAGNER:** *Parsifal—Prelude.*
  <u>CD</u>   **Deutsche Grammophon 289 469 226-2**

826. **WAGNER:** *Parsifal—Ich sah' das Kind.*
  <u>CD</u>   **Philips B0005513-02**

827. **WAGNER:** *Parsifal—Wehe! Wehe! Was tat ich? Wo war ich?*
  <u>CD</u>   **Philips B0005513-02**

828. **WAGNER:** *Parsifal—Grausamer! Fühlst du im Herzen.*
  <u>CD</u>   **Philips B0005513-02**

829. **WAGNER:** *Parsifal—Charfreitagszauber.* *("Good Friday Spell")*
  <u>CD</u>   **Deutsche Grammophon 289 445 085-2**
                    Deutsche Grammophon 289 469 226-2
                    Deutsche Grammophon 449 229-2

830. **WAGNER:** *Parsifal—Nur eine Waffe taugt.*
  <u>CD</u>   **Philips B0007191-02**

Sessions of May 1991; Manhattan Center, NYC.
[In addition to the recording session information from the published recording given above, files at the Metropolitan Opera list the more specific and additional dates of 29 May through 1 June 1991.]

831. **WAGNER:** *Rienzi—Overture.*
  The Met Orchestra – James Levine.
  <u>CD</u>   **Deutsche Grammophon 435 874-2**

832. **WAGNER:** *Tannhäuser—Overture and Venusberg Music.*
  The Met Orchestra – James Levine.
  <u>CD</u>   **Deutsche Grammophon 435 874-2**
                    Deutsche Grammophon 459 071-2

833. WAGNER: *Die Meistersing von Nürnberg—Prelude.*
    The Met Orchestra – James Levine.
    <u>Cassette</u>   **Deutsche Grammophon 445 769-4**
    <u>CD</u>   **Deutsche Grammophon 435 874-2**
              Deutsche Grammophon 445 769-2

834. WAGNER: *Lohengrin—Prelude to Act III.*
    The Met Orchestra – James Levine.
    <u>Cassette</u>   **Deutsche Grammophon 445 769-4**
    <u>CD</u>   **Deutsche Grammophon 435 874-2**
              Deutsche Grammophon 445 769-2

835. WAGNER: *Der Fliegende Holländer—Overture.*
    The Met Orchestra – James Levine.
    <u>CD</u>   **Deutsche Grammophon 435 874-2**

<u>***Sessions of 2, 4, 6, 8, 9, 10, 11 & 18 May 1991; Manhattan Center, NYC.***</u>
[Information from published recording.]

836.   **VERDI:** *Luisa Miller*

Count Walter	**Jan-Hendrik Rootering**
Rodolfo	**Plácido Domingo**
Duchess Federica	**Florence Quivar**
Wurm	**Paul Plishka**
Miller	**Vladimir Chernov**
Luisa	**Aprile Millo**
Laura	**Wendy White**
A Peasant	**John Bills**

Metropolitan Opera Chorus
(John Keenan, chorus master)
Metropolitan Opera Orchestra
James Levine
(Jane Klaviter, musical assistant)

    <u>CD</u>   **Sony Classical S2K 48073**

<u>Selections from this set were also released as follows:</u>

837. VERDI: *Luisa Miller – Excerpts.*
    <u>CD</u>   **Sony Classical SMK 53508**

838. **VERDI:** *Luisa Miller—Quando le sere al placido.*
    Cassette   **Sony Classical MLT 64070**
                   Sony Classical MLT 66707
    CD   **Sony Classical MLK 64070**
                   Sony Classical MLK 66707
                   Sony Classical S2K 92845

Sessions of 6 through 18 May 1991; Manhattan Center, NYC.

[In addition to the recording session information from the published recording given above, files at the Metropolitan Opera list an additional recording date of 1 April 1992.]

839.   **VERDI:** *Il Trovatore*

Count di Luna	**Vladimir Chernov**
Leonora	**Aprile Millo**
Azucena	**Dolora Zajick**
Manrico	**Plácido Domingo**
Ferrando	**James Morris**
Inez	**Sondra Kelly**
Ruiz	**Anthony Laciura**
An Old Gypsy	**Glenn Bater**
A Messenger	**Tim Willson**

Metropolitan Opera Chorus
(John Keenan, chorus master)
Metropolitan Opera Orchestra
James Levine
(Jane Klaviter, musical assistant)

    CD   **Sony Classical S2K 48070**

Selections from this set were also released as follows:

840. **VERDI:** *Il Trovatore—Vedi! le fosche notturne spoglie.* *("Anvil Chorus")*
    Cassette   **Sony Classical MLT 66707**
    CD   **Sony Classical MLK 66707**

841. **VERDI:** *Il Trovatore—Di quella pira.*
    Cassette   **Sony Classical MLT 66707**
    CD   **Sony Classical MLK 66707**
                   Sony Classical S2K 92845

Sessions of June 1991; Manhattan Center, NYC.
[In addition to the recording session information from the published recording given above, files at the Metropolitan Opera list the additional and more specific dates of 30 May through 7 June 1991.]

842.   **VERDI:** _La Traviata_

Violetta Valery	**Cheryl Studer**
Flora Bervoix	**Wendy White**
Annina	**Sondra Kelly**
Alfredo Germont	**Luciano Pavarotti**
Giorgio Germont	**Juan Pons**
Gastone	**Anthony Laciura**
Baron Douphol	**Bruno Pola**
Marquis d'Obigny	**Jeffrey Wells**
Dr. Grenvil	**Julien Robbins**
Giuseppe	**John Hanriot**
Flora's Servant	**Ross Crolius**
A Messenger	**Mitchell Sendrowitz**

Metropolitan Opera Chorus
(John Keenan, chorus master)
Metropolitan Opera Orchestra
James Levine
(John Keenan, musical assistant)

_CD_   **Deutsche Grammophon 435 797-2**

Selections from this set were also released as follows:

843. **VERDI:** _La Traviata – Excerpts._
     _CD_   **Deutsche Grammophon 437 726-2**

844. **VERDI:** _La Traviata—Prelude._
     _CD_   **Deutsche Grammophon 449 229-2**

845. **VERDI:** _La Traviata—Libiamo, libiamo ne' lieti calici._ _("Brindisi")_
     Cassette   **Deutsche Grammophon 445 774-4**
     _CD_   **Deutsche Grammophon 445 774-2**
                  Deutsche Grammophon 449 229-2

846. **VERDI:** _La Traviata—Sempre libera._
     Cassette   **Deutsche Grammophon 439 153-4**
     _CD_   **Deutsche Grammophon 445 900-2**
                  Deutsche Grammophon 439 153-2
                  Deutsche Grammophon 445 774-2

847. **VERDI:** *La Traviata—De' miei bollenti spiriti.*
    Cassette   **Deutsche Grammophon 439 517-4**
    CD   **Deutsche Grammophon 289 459 362-2**
                  Deutsche Grammophon 289 462 783-2
                  Deutsche Grammophon 439 517-2

848. **VERDI:** *La Traviata—Che fai? Nulla! … Amami, Alfredo.*
    Cassette   **Deutsche Grammophon 439 514-4**
    CD   **Deutsche Grammophon 439 514-2**

849. **VERDI:** *La Traviata—Parigi, o cara.*
    Cassette   **Deutsche Grammophon 445 774-4**
    CD   **Deutsche Grammophon 445 774-2**
                  Deutsche Grammophon 449 229-2

__Performance of 10 November 1991; Avery Fisher Hall, Lincoln Center, NYC.__
[Information from published recording.]

850.   *A Salute to American Music.*
                    The Richard Tucker Music Foundation – Gala XVI

                        Soloists
                        Collegiate Chorale
                    (Robert Bass, director)
       Members of the Metropolitan Opera Orchestra
                     James Conlon
       (Leontyne Price, mistress of ceremonies)

America the Beautiful (Samuel A. Ward).
    Leontyne Price & Members of the Metropolitan Opera Orchestra – James Conlon.

MENOTTI: *Amelia al Ballo—Overture.*
    Members of the Metropolitan Opera Orchestra – James Conlon.

WEILL: *Street Scene—Ice-Cream Sextet.*
    Maureen O'Flynn, Phyllis Pancella, Jerry Hadley, Paul Groves, Daniel Smith, Jeff Mattsey & Members of the Metropolitan Opera Orchestra – James Conlon.

VIRGIL THOMSON: *Songs from William Blake—Tiger, Tiger.*
    Sherrill Milnes & Members of the Metropolitan Opera Orchestra – James Conlon.

GRIFFES: *Poems by Fiona MacLeod—Lament of Ian the Proud.*
    Renée Fleming & Members of the Metropolitan Opera Orchestra – James Conlon.

[Ah, May the Red Rose Live Alway (Stephen Foster).
Karen Holvik with Steven Blier at the piano.]

BERNSTEIN: *Chichester Psalms—Psalm No. 1.*
Collegiate Chorale & Members of the Metropolitan Opera Orchestra – James Conlon.

COPLAND: *Old American Songs—At the River.*
Tatiana Troyanos & Members of the Metropolitan Opera Orchestra – James Conlon.

BOLCOM: *Songs of Innocence and Experience—The Tyger.*
Collegiate Chorale & Members of the Metropolitan Opera Orchestra – James Conlon.

MOORE: *The Devil and Daniel Webster—I've got a ram, Goliath.*
Sherrill Milnes & Members of the Metropolitan Opera Orchestra – James Conlon.

BLITZSTEIN: *Regina—Rain Quartet.*
Maureen O'Flynn, Renée Fleming, Denise Woods, Samuel Ramey, Jeff Mattsey, Collegiate Chorale & Members of the Metropolitan Opera Orchestra – James Conlon.

GERSHWIN: *Porgy and Bess—Leavin' for the promise' lan'.*
Denise Woods, Collegiate Chorale & Members of the Metropolitan Opera Orchestra – James Conlon.

STRAVINSKY: *The Rake's Progress—Prelude.*
Members of the Metropolitan Opera Orchestra – James Conlon.

LEVY: *Mourning Becomes Electra—Too weak to kill the man I hate.*
Sherrill Milnes & Members of the Metropolitan Opera Orchestra – James Conlon.

BARBER: *Vanessa—Must the winter come so soon?*
Frederica von Stade & Members of the Metropolitan Opera Orchestra – James Conlon.

FLOYD: *Susannah—Hear me, O Lord.*
Samuel Ramey & Members of the Metropolitan Opera Orchestra – James Conlon.

BARBER: *Antony and Cleopatra—Give me my robe.*
Carol Vaness & Members of the Metropolitan Opera Orchestra – James Conlon.

Night and Day (Cole Porter).
Samuel Ramey & Members of the Metropolitan Opera Orchestra – James Conlon.

Prelude to a Kiss (Duke Ellington).
Renée Fleming & Members of the Metropolitan Opera Orchestra – James Conlon.

WEILL: *Knickerbocker Holiday—September Song.*
Robert Merrill & Members of the Metropolitan Opera Orchestra – James Conlon.

BERNSTEIN: *West Side Story—Maria.*
Jerry Hadley & Members of the Metropolitan Opera Orchestra – James Conlon.

RODGERS: *Carousel—If I loved you.*
Carol Vaness, Jeff Mattsey & Members of the Metropolitan Opera Orchestra – James Conlon.

God Bless America (Irving Berlin).
  Marilyn Horne & Members of the Metropolitan Opera Orchestra – James Conlon.

BERNSTEIN: *Candide—Make our garden grow.*
  Renée Fleming, Jerry Hadley, Collegiate Chorale & Members of the Metropolitan Opera Orchestra – James Conlon.

  <u>CD</u>   **RCA Victor Red Seal 09026-61508-2**

          <u>Selections from this set were also released as follows:</u>

851. *A Salute to American Music – Excerpts.*
     <u>Cassette</u>   **RCA Victor Red Seal 09026-61509-4**
     <u>CD</u>   **RCA Victor Red Seal 09026-61509-2**

852. *God Bless America* (Irving Berlin).
     <u>CD</u>   **RCA Victor 09026-61545-2**

<u>**Sessions of 20 through 24 April & 11 through 14 May 1992; Manhattan Center, NYC.**</u>
[Information from published recording.]

853.   **VERDI:** *Don Carlos*
[Complete edition of 5 acts in Italian (including unpublished Verdian excerpts) by Ursula Günther. Revision according
        to the original manuscript by Ursula Günther and Luciano Petazzoni.]

Philip II	**Ferruccio Furlanetto**
Don Carlos	**Michael Sylvester**
Rodrigo	**Vladimir Chernov**
The Grand Inquisitor	**Samuel Ramey**
A Monk	**Paul Plishka**
Elisabeth of Valois	**Aprile Millo**
The Princess Eboli	**Dolora Zajick**
Thibault	**Jane Bunnell**
A Voice from Heaven	**Kathleen Battle**
The Count of Lerma	**Dwayne Croft**
A Royal Herald	**John Horton Murray**
A Woodman	**Kevin Short**

Metropolitan Opera Chorus
(Raymond Hughes, chorus master)
Metropolitan Opera Orchestra
James Levine
(Jane Klaviter, John Keenan, musical assistants)

_CD_	**Sony Classical S3K 52500**
	Sony Classical 88697527732

<u>Selections from this set were also released as follows:</u>

854. **VERDI:** _Don Carlos – Excerpts._
    _CD_   **Sony Classical SMK 53507**

855. **VERDI:** _Don Carlos—Dio, che nell' alma infondere._
    Cassette   **Sony Classical MLT 64070**
    _CD_   **Sony Classical MLK 64070**

856. **VERDI:** _Don Carlos—O don fatale._
    Cassette   **Sony Classical MLT 64070**
    _CD_   **Sony Classical MLK 64070**

Sessions of 24 April, 15 & 16 May 1992; Manhattan Center, NYC.
[Information from published recording.]

857. **VERDI:** _Les Vêpres Siciliennes—Les Quatre Saisons._
    The MET Orchestra – James Levine.
    _CD_   **Sony Classical SK 52489**

858. **VERDI:** _Macbeth—Ballabile._
    The MET Orchestra – James Levine.
    _CD_   **Sony Classical SK 52489**

859. **VERDI:** _Don Carlos—Le Ballet de la Reine._
    The MET Orchestra – James Levine.
    _CD_   **Sony Classical SK 52489**

860. **VERDI:** _Otello—Ballabile._
    The MET Orchestra – James Levine.
    _CD_   **Sony Classical SK 52489**

861. **VERDI:** _Aïda—Danza di piccolo schiavi mori._
    The MET Orchestra – James Levine.
    _CD_   **Sony Classical SK 52489**

862. **VERDI:** _Aïda—Ballabile._
    The MET Orchestra – James Levine.
    _CD_   **Sony Classical SK 52489**

Sessions of May 1992; Manhattan Center, NYC.

[In addition to the recording session information from the published recording given above, files at the Metropolitan Opera list the more specific dates of 19 through 20 May 1992.]

863. **MUSSORGSKY:** *Pictures at an Exhibition.*
   The MET Orchestra – James Levine.
   CD   **Deutsche Grammophon 437 531-2**
                 Deutsche Grammophon 457 895-2
                 Deutsche Grammophon G2-37531

864. **MUSSORGSKY:** *Pictures at an Exhibition—The Great Gate of Kiev.* (from the above work)
   The MET Orchestra – James Levine.
   CD   **Deutsche Grammophon 449 229-2**

865. **STRAVINSKY:** *Le Sacre du Printemps.* *("The Rite of Spring")*
   The MET Orchestra – James Levine.
   CD   **Deutsche Grammophon 437 531-2**
                 Deutsche Grammophon Galleria 457 895-2
                 Deutsche Grammophon G2-37531
                 Deutsche Grammophon 474 485-2

Sessions of August 1992; Manhattan Center, NYC.

[In addition to the recording session information from the published recording given above, files at the Metropolitan Opera list the more specific dates of 24 through 31 August 1992.]

866.   **PUCCINI:** *Manon Lescaut*

Manon	**Mirella Freni**
Des Grieux	**Luciano Pavarotti**
Lescaut	**Dwayne Croft**
Geronte	**Giuseppe Taddei**
Edmondo	**Ramón Vargas**
The Innkeeper	**Federico Davia**
The Dancing Master	**Anthony Laciura**
Musician	**Cecilia Bartoli**
Madrigal Singers	**Heidi Grant Murphy**
	Korliss Uecker
	Jane Bunnell
	Jane Shaulis
Sergeant of the Archers	**James Courtney**
A Lamplighter	**Paul Groves**
A Ship's Captain	**Federico Davia**

Metropolitan Opera Chorus
(Raymond Hughes, chorus master)
Metropolitan Opera Orchestra
James Levine
(Jane Bakken Klaviter, John Keenan, musical assistants)

<u>CD</u>   **London 440 200-2**
            Musical Heritage Society 524497X

<u>Selections from this set were also released as follows:</u>

867. **PUCCINI:** *Manon Lescaut—Tra voi, belle, brune e bionde.*
     <u>Cassette</u>   **London/Decca 458 000-4**
     <u>CD</u>   **London/Decca 458 000-2**
               London/Decca 289 470 050-2
               Decca B0010170-02

868. **PUCCINI:** *Manon Lescaut—Donna non vidi mai.*
     <u>Cassette</u>   **London/Decca 458 000-4**
     <u>CD</u>   **London/Decca 450 000-2**
               London/Decca 470 000-2
               London/Decca 289 470 050-2
               Decca B0010170-02

869. **PUCCINI:** *Manon Lescaut—In quelle trine morbide.*
     <u>Cassette</u>   **London/Decca 443 819-4**
     <u>CD</u>   **London/Decca 443 819-2**

870. **PUCCINI:** *Manon Lescaut—Madrigal: Sulla vetta tu del monte.*
     <u>CD</u>   **Deutsche Grammophon 449 229-2**

871. **PUCCINI:** *Manon Lescaut—No! pazzo son!*
     <u>CD</u>   **London/Decca 289 470 050-2**

872. **PUCCINI:** *Manon Lescaut—Sola, perduta, abbandonata.*
     <u>CD</u>   **Deutsche Grammophon 449 229-2**

Sessions of April 1993; Abyssinian Baptist Church, NYC.
[In addition to the recording session information from the published recording given above, files at the Metropolitan Opera list the more specific dates of 16 through 26 April 1993.]

873. **MOZART:** *Le Nozze di Figaro—Porgi amor.*
    Kathleen Battle & Metropolitan Opera Orchestra – James Levine.
    <u>CD</u> **Deutsche Grammophon 439 949-2**
        Universal B0003495-02

874. **MOZART:** *Die Entführung aus dem Serail—Welche Wonne, welche Lust.*
    Kathleen Battle & Metropolitan Opera Orchestra – James Levine.
    <u>CD</u> **Deutsche Grammophon 439 949-2**
        Deutsche Grammophon 289 472 179-2
        Universal B0003495-02

875. **MOZART:** *Die Entführung aus dem Serail—Traurigkeit ward mir zum Lose.*
    Kathleen Battle & Metropolitan Opera Orchestra – James Levine.
    <u>CD</u> **Deutsche Grammophon 439 949-2**

876. **MOZART:** *Zaïde—Ruhe sanft, mein holdes Leben.*
    Kathleen Battle & Metropolitan Opera Orchestra – James Levine.
    <u>CD</u> **Deutsche Grammophon 439 949-2**

877. **MOZART:** *Così Fan Tutte—Una donna a quindici anni.*
    Kathleen Battle & Metropolitan Opera Orchestra – James Levine.
    <u>CD</u> **Deutsche Grammophon 439 949-2**
        Universal B0003495-02

878. **MOZART:** *La Clemenza di Tito—S'altro che lacrime.*
    Kathleen Battle & Metropolitan Opera Orchestra – James Levine.
    <u>CD</u> **Deutsche Grammophon 439 949-2**
        Universal B0003495-02

879. **MOZART:** *Le Nozze di Figaro—Deh vieni, non tardar.*
    Kathleen Battle & Metropolitan Opera Orchestra – James Levine.
    <u>CD</u> **Deutsche Grammophon 439 949-2**

880. **MOZART:** *Don Giovanni—Batti, batti, o bel Masetto.*
    Kathleen Battle & Metropolitan Opera Orchestra – James Levine.
    <u>CD</u> **Deutsche Grammophon 439 949-2**

881. **MOZART:** *Don Giovanni—Vedrai, carino.*
    Kathleen Battle & Metropolitan Opera Orchestra – James Levine.
    <u>CD</u> **Deutsche Grammophon 439 949-2**

882. **MOZART:** *Die Entführung aus dem Serail—Ach ich liebte.*
    Kathleen Battle & Metropolitan Opera Orchestra – James Levine.
    <u>CD</u> **Deutsche Grammophon 439 949-2**

883. **MOZART:** *Le Nozze di Figaro—Non so più, cosa son.*
     Kathleen Battle & Metropolitan Opera Orchestra – James Levine.
     <u>CD</u>   **Deutsche Grammophon 439 949-2**

884. **MOZART:** *Die Zauberflöte—Ach, ich fühl's.*
     Kathleen Battle & Metropolitan Opera Orchestra – James Levine.
     <u>CD</u>   **Deutsche Grammophon 439 949-2**

885. **MOZART:** *Die Zauberflöte—Bald prangt, den Morgen zu verkünden.*
     Kathleen Battle, Joel Evans, Eric Sadkin, Gregory Rodriguez (Elena Doria, Metropolitan Opera Children's Chorus director) & Metropolitan Opera Orchestra – James Levine.
     <u>CD</u>   **Deutsche Grammophon 439 949-2**

<u>*Sessions of June 1993; Manhattan Center, NYC.*</u>

[In addition to the recording session information from the published recordings given above, files at the Metropolitan Opera list the more specific dates of 28 through 30 June 1993 for the Beethoven and Schubert symphonies. For the Verdi opera, the additional and more specific dates of 16 through 29 June 1993 and 2 through 3 September 1994 are listed.]

886. **BEETHOVEN:** *Symphony No. 3 in E-Flat Major, Op. 55.* *("Eroïca")*
     The MET Orchestra – James Levine.
     <u>CD</u>   **Deutsche Grammophon 439 862-2**

887. **SCHUBERT:** *Symphony No. 8 in B Minor, D. 759.* *("Unfinished")*
     The MET Orchestra – James Levine.
     <u>CD</u>   **Deutsche Grammophon 439 862-2**
                          Deutsche Grammophon 437 691-2

888.   **VERDI:** *Rigoletto*

The Duke of Mantua	**Luciano Pavarotti**
Rigoletto	**Vladimir Chernov**
Gilda	**Cheryl Studer**
Sparafucile	**Roberto Scandiuzzi**
Maddalena	**Denyce Graves**
Giovanna	**Jane Shaulis**
The Count of Monterone	**Ildebrando D'Arcangelo**
Marullo	**Dwayne Croft**
Borsa	**Paul Groves**
The Count of Ceprano	**Yannis Yannissis**
The Countess of Ceprano	**Heidi Grant Murphy**
Usher	**Robert Maher**
Page of the Duchess	**Elyssa Lindner**

Metropolitan Opera Chorus
(Raymond Hughes, chorus master)
Metropolitan Opera Orchestra
James Levine
(Jane Bakken Klaviter, musical assistant)

_CD_   **Deutsche Grammophon 447 064-2**

A selection from this set was also released as follows:

889. **VERDI:** *Rigoletto—La donna è mobile.*
     _CD_   **Deutsche Grammophon 289 463 783-2**

Sessions of 2 & 3 July 1993; Manhattan Center, NYC.
[Information from published recording.]

890. **BERG:** *Three Fragments from "Wozzeck."*
     Renée Fleming & The MET Orchestra – James Levine.
     _CD_   **Sony SK 53959**

891. **BERG:** *Three Orchestral Pieces, Op. 6.*
     The MET Orchestra – James Levine.
     _CD_   **Sony SK 53959**

892. **BERG:** *Lulu-Suite.*
     Renée Fleming & The MET Orchestra – James Levine.
     _CD_   **Sony SK 53959**

Sessions of March & April 1994; Manhattan Center, NYC.
[In addition to the recording session information from the published recording given above, files at the Metropolitan Opera list the additional and more specific dates of 31 March through 20 April 1994, 1 September 1994, 3 through 8 March 1995 and 5 July 1996.]

893.   **MOZART:** *Idomeneo, Re di Creta*

Idomeneo	**Plácido Domingo**
Idamante	**Cecilia Bartoli**
Ilia	**Heidi Grant Murphy**
Elettra	**Carol Vaness**
Arbace	**Thomas Hampson**

High Priest of Neptune	**Frank Lopardo**
The Voice (Oracle)	**Bryn Terfel**
Two Cretan Women	**Joyce Guyer**
	Jane Bunnell
Two Trojans	**Paul Groves**
	Yanni Yannissis

Metropolitan Opera Chorus
(Raymond Hughes, chorus master)
Metropolitan Opera Orchestra
James Levine
(Martin Isepp, musical assistance and harpsichord continuo)
(Kevin Murphy, additional musical assistance;
Jerry Grossman, cello; Laurence Glazener, double bass)

CD   **Deutsch Grammophon 447 737-2**

A selection from this set was also released as follows:

894. **MOZART:** *Idomeneo, Re di Creta—Fuor del mar.*
      CD   **Decca B0005733-02**

Sessions of 28 and 29 April & 3 through 7 May 1994; Manhattan Center, NYC.
[Information from published recording.]

895.   **WAGNER:** *Der Fliegende Holländer*

The Dutchman	**James Morris**
Senta	**Deborah Voigt**
Erik	**Ben Heppner**
Daland	**Jan-Hendrik Rootering**
Helmsman	**Paul Groves**
Mary	**Birgitta Svendén**

Metropolitan Opera Chorus
(Raymond Hughes, chorus master)
Metropolitan Opera Orchestra
James Levine
(Jane Klaviter, musical assistant)

CD   **Sony Classical S2K 66342**
            Sony Classical 88697448222

<u>Selections from this set were also released as follows:</u>

896. **WAGNER:** *Der Fliegende Holländer – Excerpts.*
   <u>*CD*</u>   **Sony Classical SK 61969**

Sessions of August & September 1994; Manhattan Center, NYC.
[In addition to the recording session information from the published recording given above, files at the Metropolitan Opera list the more specific dates of 31 August through 2 September 1994.]

897. **MOZART:** *Le Nozze di Figaro—Non più andrai.*
   Bryn Terfel & Metropolitan Opera Orchestra – James Levine.
   <u>*CD*</u>   **Deutsche Grammophon 445 866-2**
                    Deutsche Grammophon 289 445 085-2

898. **MOZART:** *Don Giovanni—Deh, vieni alla finestra.*
   Bryn Terfel & Metropolitan Opera Orchestra – James Levine.
   <u>*CD*</u>   **Deutsche Grammophon 445 866-2**
                    Deutsche Grammophon 289 445 085-2

899. **MOZART:** *Don Giovanni—Madamina, il catalogo.*
   Bryn Terfel & Metropolitan Opera Orchestra – James Levine.
   <u>*CD*</u>   **Deutsche Grammophon 445 866-2**
                    Deutsche Grammophon 289 445 085-2

900. **ROSSINI:** *La Cenerentola—Miei rampolli femminini.*
   Bryn Terfel & Metropolitan Opera Orchestra – James Levine.
   <u>*CD*</u>   **Deutsche Grammophon 445 866-2**

901. **GOUNOD:** *Faust—Vous qui faites l'endormie.* *("Sérénade")*
   Bryn Terfel & Metropolitan Opera Orchestra – James Levine.
   <u>*CD*</u>   **Deutsche Grammophon 445 866-2**

902. **VERDI:** *Falstaff—L'Onore! Ladri!*
   Bryn Terfel & Metropolitan Opera Orchestra – James Levine.
   <u>*CD*</u>   **Deutsche Grammophon 445 866-2**

903. **VERDI:** *Macbeth—Perfidi! All'anglo contra me v'unite!*
   Bryn Terfel & Metropolitan Opera Orchestra – James Levine.
   <u>*CD*</u>   **Deutsche Grammophon 445 866-2**

904. **WAGNER:** *Tannhäuser—O du mein holder Abendstern.* *("Evening Star")*
   Bryn Terfel & Metropolitan Opera Orchestra – James Levine.
   <u>*CD*</u>   **Deutsche Grammophon 445 866-2**

905. WAGNER: *Der Fliegende Holländer—Die Frist ist um.*
   Bryn Terfel & Metropolitan Opera Orchestra – James Levine.
   <u>CD</u>   **Deutsche Grammophon 445 866-2**

Sessions of May 1995; Manhattan Center, NYC.

[In addition to the recording session information from the published recordings given above, files at the Metropolitan Opera list the more specific dates of 25 through 26 May 1995 for the Strauss works and 23 through 27 May 1995 for the Wagner works.]

906. RICHARD STRAUSS: *Don Quixote, Op. 35.*
   Jerry Grossman (cello), Michael Ouzounian (viola), Raymond Gniewek (violin) & The MET Orchestra – James Levine.
   <u>CD</u>   **Deutsche Grammophon 447 762-2**
                  Deutsche Grammophon 459 071-2

907. RICHARD STRAUSS: *Tod und Verklärung, Op. 24.* *("Death and Transfiguration")*
   The MET Orchestra – James Levine.
   <u>CD</u>   **Deutsche Grammophon 447 762-2**
                  Deutsche Grammophon 474 485-2

908. WAGNER: *Lohengrin—Prelude.*
   The MET Orchestra – James Levine.
   <u>CD</u>   **Deutsche Grammophon 447 764-2**

909. WAGNER: *Die Walküre—Walkürenritt.* *("Ride of the Valkyries")*
   The MET Orchestra – James Levine.
   <u>CD</u>   **Deutsche Grammophon 447 764-2**

910. WAGNER: *Siegfried—Waldweben.* *("Forest Murmurs")*
   The MET Orchestra – James Levine.
   <u>CD</u>   **Deutsche Grammophon 447 764-2**

911. WAGNER: *Götterdämmerung—Trauermarsch.* *("Funeral March")*
   The MET Orchestra – James Levine.
   <u>CD</u>   **Deutsche Grammophon 447 764-2**

912. WAGNER: *Tristan und Isolde—Prelude and Liebestod.*
   The MET Orchestra – James Levine.
   <u>CD</u>   **Deutsche Grammophon 447 764-2**

913. WAGNER: *Die Meistersinger von Nürnberg—Prelude to Act III.*
   The MET Orchestra – James Levine.
   <u>CD</u>   **Deutsche Grammophon 447 764-2**

914. **WAGNER:** *Parsifal—Charfreitagszauber.* *("Good Friday Spell")*
     The MET Orchestra – James Levine.
     <u>CD</u>   **Deutsche Grammophon 447 764-2**

Sessions of September 1995; Manhattan Center, NYC.
[In addition to the recording session information from the published recording given above, files at the Metropolitan Opera list the more specific dates of 29 through 30 September 1995.]

915. **MOZART:** *Così Fan Tutte—Rivolgete a lui lo sguardo.*
     Bryn Terfel & Metropolitan Opera Orchestra – James Levine.
     <u>CD</u>   **Deutsche Grammophon 445 866-2**

916. **MOZART:** *Die Zauberflöte—Der Vogelfänger bin ich ja.*
     Bryn Terfel & Metropolitan Opera Orchestra – James Levine.
     <u>CD</u>   **Deutsche Grammophon 445 866-2**
                     Deutsche Grammophon 289 445 085-2

917. **DONIZETTI:** *Don Pasquale—Bella siccome un angelo.*
     Bryn Terfel & Metropolitan Opera Orchestra – James Levine.
     <u>CD</u>   **Deutsche Grammophon 445 866-2**

918. **OFFENBACH:** *Les Contes d'Hoffmann—Scintille, diamant.*
     Bryn Terfel & Metropolitan Opera Orchestra – James Levine.
     <u>CD</u>   **Deutsche Grammophon 445 866-2**

919. **BORODIN:** *Prince Igor—No sleep, no rest.* *("Aria of Prince Igor, Act II")*
     Bryn Terfel & Metropolitan Opera Orchestra – James Levine.
     <u>CD</u>   **Deutsche Grammophon 445 866-2**

Performance of 27 April 1996; Metropolitan Opera House, Lincoln Center, NYC.
[Information from published recording.]

920.   *James Levine's 25ᵗʰ Anniversary*
                          Metropolitan Opera Gala.

                          Soloists
                  Metropolitan Opera Orchestra
                          James Levine

     BIZET: *Les Pêcheurs de Perles—Au fond du temple saint.*
     Roberto Alagna, Bryn Terfel & Metropolitan Opera Orchestra – James Levine.

CHARPENTIER: *Louise—Depuis le jour.*
Renée Fleming & Metropolitan Opera Orchestra – James Levine.

GOUNOD: *Faust—Mais ce Dieu, que peut-il pour moi?*
Plácido Domingo, Samuel Ramey & Metropolitan Opera Orchestra – James Levine.

LEHÁR: *Giuditta—Meine Lippen sie küssen so heiss.*
Ilena Cotrubas & Metropolitan Opera Orchestra – James Levine.

VERDI: *Don Carlos—O don fatale!*
Dolora Zajick & Metropolitan Opera Orchestra – James Levine.

MOZART: *Don Giovanni—Sola, sola, in buio loco.*
Renée Fleming, Kiri Te Kanawa, Hei-Kyung Hong, Jerry Hadley, Bryn Terfel, Julien Robbins & Metropolitan Opera Orchestra – James Levine.

GOUNOD: *Roméo et Juliette—Je veux vivre.*
Ruth Ann Swenson & Metropolitan Opera Orchestra – James Levine.

JOHANN STRAUSS, II: *Die Fledermaus—Dieser Anstand, so manierlich.*
Karita Mattila, Håkan Hagegård & Metropolitan Opera Orchestra – James Levine.

MASSENET: *Werther—Pourquoi me réveiller.*
Alfredo Kraus & Metropolitan Opera Orchestra – James Levine.

SAINT-SAËNS: *Samson et Dalila—Mon cœur s'ouvre à ta voix.* *("My heart at thy sweet voice")*
Grace Bumbry & Metropolitan Opera Orchestra – James Levine.

WAGNER: *Tannhäuser—Dich, teure Halle.*
Deborah Voigt & Metropolitan Opera Orchestra – James Levine.

OFFENBACH: *La Périchole—Ah, quel dîner.*
Frederica von Stade & Metropolitan Opera Orchestra – James Levine.

RICHARD STRAUSS: *Der Rosenkavalier—Hab mir's gelobt.*
Renée Fleming, Anne Sofie von Otter, Heidi Grant Murphy & Metropolitan Opera Orchestra – James Levine.

[A Tribute to James Levine by Birgit Nilsson.]

<u>CD</u>   **Deutsch Grammophon 449 177-2**

<u>A selection from this set was also released as follows:</u>

921. **BIZET:** *Les Pêcheurs de Perles—Au fond du temple saint.*
     <u>CD</u>   **Deutsche Grammophon 289 471 717-2**

Sessions of 28 May through 1 June & 24 and 25 September 1996; Manhattan Center, NYC.

[In addition to the recording session information from the published recording given above, files at the Metropolitan Opera list the following dates of 25 May through 1 June 1996 and 25 through 26 September 1996 for this recording.]

922.   **VERDI:** *I Lombardi*

Arvino	**Richard Leech**
Pagano	**Samuel Ramey**
Viclinda	**Patricia Racette**
Giselda	**June Anderson**
Pirro	**Ildebrando D'Arcangelo**
A Prior of Milan	**Anthony Dean Griffey**
Acciano	**Yanni Yannissis**
Oronte	**Luciano Pavarotti**
Sofia	**Jane Shaulis**

Violin Solo by Raymond Gniewek
Metropolitan Opera Chorus
(Raymond Hughes, chorus master)
Metropolitan Opera Orchestra
James Levine
(Jane Klaviter, musical assistant)

CD   **London 455 287-2**

Selections from this set were also released as follows:

923. **VERDI:** *I Lombardi—La mia letizia infondere.*
      CD   **London/Decca 289 470 050-2**
                    London/Decca 470 000-2

924. **VERDI:** *I Lombardi—Come poteva un angelo.*
      CD   **London/Decca 470 000-2**

Sessions of 26 through 30 May 1998; Manhattan Center, NYC.

[Information from published recording.]

925. **HERRMANN:** *Wuthering Heights—I have dreamt.*
      Renée Fleming & Metropolitan Opera Orchestra – James Levine.
      CD   **London/Decca 289 460 567-2**

926. **MOORE:** *The Ballad of Baby Doe—The Letter Song.*
     Renée Fleming & Metropolitan Opera Orchestra – James Levine.
     <u>CD</u>   **London/Decca 289 460 567-2**

927. **MENOTTI:** *The Medium—Monica's Waltz.*
     Renée Fleming & Metropolitan Opera Orchestra – James Levine.
     <u>CD</u>   **London/Decca 289 460 567-2**

928. **GERSHWIN:** *Porgy and Bess—Summertime.*
     Renée Fleming & Metropolitan Opera Orchestra – James Levine.
     <u>CD</u>   **London/Decca 289 460 567-2**

929. **GERSHWIN:** *Porgy and Bess—My man's gone now.*
     Renée Fleming, New York Voices (Teddy Swarrer, director) & Metropolitan Opera Orchestra –
     James Levine.
     <u>CD</u>   **London/Decca 289 460 567-2**

930. **BERNSTEIN:** *Candide—Glitter and be gay.*
     Renée Fleming & Metropolitan Opera Orchestra – James Levine.
     <u>CD</u>   **London/Decca 289 460 567-2**

931. **FLOYD:** *Susannah—Ain't it a pretty night!*
     Renée Fleming & Metropolitan Opera Orchestra – James Levine.
     <u>CD</u>   **London/Decca 289 460 567-2**

932. **FLOYD:** *Susannah—The trees on the mountains.*
     Renée Fleming & Metropolitan Opera Orchestra – James Levine.
     <u>CD</u>   **London/Decca 289 460 567-2**

933. **STRAVINSKY:** *The Rake's Progress—No word from Tom.*
     Renée Fleming & Metropolitan Opera Orchestra – James Levine.
     <u>CD</u>   **London/Decca 289 460 567-2**

934. **BARBER:** *Vanessa—Do not utter a word, Anatol.*
     Renée Fleming & Metropolitan Opera Orchestra – James Levine.
     <u>CD</u>   **London/Decca 289 460 567-2**

935. **PREVIN:** *A Streetcar Named Desire—I want magic!*
     Renée Fleming & Metropolitan Opera Orchestra – James Levine.
     <u>CD</u>   **London/Decca 289 460 567-2**

Additional Recordings

Here are listed commercial recordings which do not fit into the main discography.

1. Leeds & Catlin. In a perfect world the recordings in this section would have begun the discography, but it is doubtful if any of these recordings are still in existence. David Hamilton kindly provided photocopies from the very rare catalogue of Leeds & Catlin recordings that had been discovered by Steven Smolian. This is the *1902 Catalogue of the Famous L. & C. Records* that were manufactured by the Leeds & Catlin Co., 53 East Eleventh Street, New York City, which listed their wax cylinders on sale for sixty cents each.

On pages twelve and thirteen of this catalogue are listed the recordings of the Metropolitan Opera House String Orchestra conducted by Nahan Franko. Franko, whose first name is misspelled as Nathan in the catalogue, was concertmaster and conductor of the orchestra during his many years with the opera company. It is probable that the name of the orchestra included the word "string" to emphasize that strings were used in these recordings unlike most ensemble instrumental recordings of the period that relied solely on wind instruments.

Here is a transcription of the listings for these recordings from the 1902 catalogue with Nahan Franko's first name wrongly given along with a number of unique examples of spelling just as they appear on the pages. This is quite an impressive list considering that these would have been just two minute cylinders.

METROPOLITAN OPERA HOUSE
STRING ORCHESTRA.

This is to certify that the full Orchestra of the Metropolitan Opera House have played the following selections, under my leadership, for the Leeds & Catlin Co.

NATHAN FRANKO,
**Concertmeister of the Metropolitan Opera
House Orchestra, New York City.**

These Records are not loud, but as a musical treat they are unsurpassed.

8005. Ballet Music from Faust No. 1.
8000. Ballet Music from Faust No. 2.
8011. Brahms' Hungarian Dances, No. 1.
8015. Brahm's Hungarian Dances, No. 2.
8013. Handel's Largo.
8012. Hunting Horns, from Tannhauser.
8002. Kamennoi Ostrow.
8006. Liebestode, from Tristan and Isolde.
8007. Liszt Hungarian Rhapsodie No. 3.
8017. Lohengrin, Introduction to 3d Act.
8009. Magic Fire Scene from Walkure.
8003. Meistersinger. Overture.
8016. Procession of Bacchus, from Sylvia.
8008. Rakszky. March.
8004. Rienzi. Overture.
8014. Rubenstein's Wedding Procession.
8010. Sailors' Chorus, from Flying Dutchman.
8001. Seranade, by Moszkowski.
8018. Traumerei.

It is of interest to note that the back page of the catalogue contains an endorsement of Leeds and Catlin recordings by the Metropolitan Opera's librarian Lionel Mapleson, who made the famous series of in house cylinder recordings from Metropolitan Opera performances during the years 1901-1904. On stationary of the Maurice Grau Opera Co., The Metropolitan Opera House, he writes:

New York, Jan 14, 1902.

LEEDS & CATLIN Co.,

Gentlemen:—I am simply *astounded* at the tone you have succeeded in producing with your new system Records. I have been just listening to the Serenade, Faust (sung by Sig. Franciso), and all that have heard it, here at the Opera House, agree with me that these records are the very finest they have ever heard, and we have tried all kinds of Phonograph Records, and your Records are easily the first in the race.

I prefer listening *through tubes,* and the Serenade I speak of above, is a wonder when so heard.

Wishing you the success you deserve, believe me,

Faithfully yours,

LIONEL S. MAPLESON

2. Vocal Ensemble of the Metropolitan Opera. Although it did not use either the Metropolitan Opera Chorus or Orchestra, the following recording was advertised as employing a "Vocal Ensemble of the Metropolitan Opera."

Sessions of 15, 18 & 22 May 1945; Carnegie Hall, NYC.

WAGNER: *Die Walküre—Act III*

Brünnhilde	**Helen Traubel**
Wotan	**Herbert Janssen**
Sieglinde	**Irene Jessner**
Helmwige	**Doris Doree**
Gerhilde	**Maxine Stellman**
Ortlinde	**Irene Jessner**
Rossweisse	**Doris Doe**
Grimgerde	**Martha Lipton**
Waltraute	**Jeanne Palmer**
Siegrune	**Hertha Glaz**
Schwertleite	**Anna Kaskas**

Philharmonic-Symphony Orchestra of New York
Artur Rodzinski

matrices: **XCO 34729/35**	15 May 1945	Beginning
matrices: **XCO 34747/50**	18 May 1945	Ich wusste den Zwiespalt
matrices: **XCO 34802/5**	22 May 1945	Leb wohl, du kühnes

78 rpm	**Columbia M-581** (12171/8-D) *manual sequence* / released 15 October 1945 to ?
	Columbia MM-581 (12179/86-D) *automatic sequence* / released 15 October 1945 to ?
	Columbia LX 955/62
	Columbia 15906/13
33⅓ rpm	**Columbia SL-5** (ML 4242/3) *manual sequence*
	Columbia SL-105 (ML 4244/5) *automatic sequence*
	Odyssey 32 26 0018 (32 16 0306/ 32 16 0308) (synthetic stereo)
	CBS 61452
CD	**Retrospective Recordings RET 007**

3. The Zeffirelli *La Traviata* film. While the soundtrack of this 1983 film was released on sound recordings, it was made for use with the film and makes its greatest impact with the visual element. Notes by James Levine with the sound recordings state, "This recording reproduces the music track of the film exactly as it is heard in the movie theater," and further that it produces "an effect very different from a complete opera recording produced under studio conditions." The film is available on DVD as Universal 20326.

VERDI: *La Traviata*

Violetta	**Teresa Stratas**
Alfredo	**Plácido Domingo**
Germont	**Cornell MacNeal**
Baron Douphol	**Allan Monk**
Flora	**Axelle Gall**
Annina	**Pina Cei**
Gaston	**Maurizio Barbacini**
Dr. Grenvil	**Robert Sommer**
Marquis	**Richard Oneto**
Young Porter	**Renato Cestiè**
Alfredo's Sister	**Dominique Journet**
Giuseppe	**Luciano Brizi**
Messenger	**Tony Ammirati**

The Voices of:	**Ariel Bybee**
	Geraldine Decker
	Ferruccio Furlanetto
	Russell Christopher
	Michael Best
	Richard Vernon
	Charles Anthony

Metropolitan Opera Chorus
Metropolitan Opera Orchestra
James Levine

33⅓ rpm	**Elektra 60267-1-T**
	WEA 25-0072-1
Cassette	**Elektra 60267-4-T**
	WEA 25-0072-4

4. Metropolitan Opera Radio Broadcasts. While there may be pirate recordings available, the only authorized recordings of Metropolitan Opera radio broadcasts are those available from the Metropolitan. Beginning in 1974 these historic recordings were made available in beautifully illustrated sets with extensive notes and librettos. While earlier releases were on 33⅓ rpm long playing discs and later cassettes, recent releases have been on compact discs. All of these recordings are presented without any of the original announcer's commentary. Please check the Metropolitan's website at www.metopera.org for current availability and format. Those recordings that were available in 2009 are preceded by an asterisk.

* 17 April 1937. **BIZET:** *Carmen* / Ponselle, Maison, Huehn, Burke; conducted by Papi.

7 January 1939. **R. STRAUSS:** *Der Rosenkavalier* / Lehmann, Stevens, List, Farell, Schorr; conducted by Bodanzky.

21 January 1939. **VERDI:** *Simon Boccanegra* / Tibbett, Rethberg, Martinelli, Pinza, Warren; conducted by Panizza.

24 February 1940. **VERDI:** *Otello* / Martinelli, Rethberg, Tibbett; conducted by Panizza.

7 December 1940. **MOZART:** *Le Nozze di Figaro* / Pinza, Albanese, Rethberg, Brownlee, Novotna, Baccaloni, Petina; conducted by Panizza.

* 14 December 1940. **VERDI:** *Un Ballo in Maschera* / Milanov, Björling, Sved, Castagna, Andreva; conducted by Panizza.

* 4 January 1941. **WAGNER:** *Tannhäuser* / Melchior, Flagstad, Thorborg, Janssen, List; conducted by Leinsdorf.

8 February 1941. **WAGNER:** *Tristan und Isolde* / Flagstad, Melchior, Thorborg, Kipnis, Huehn; conducted by Leinsdorf.

22 February 1941. **BEETHOVEN:** *Fidelio* / Flagstad, Maison, Kipnis, Farell, Huehn, Janssen; conducted by Walter.

2 December 1944. **WAGNER:** *Die Walküre* / Traubel, Bampton, Melchior, Janssen; conducted by Szell.

19 January 1946. **PUCCINI:** *Madama Butterfly* / Albanese, Melton, Brownlee; conducted by Cimara.

* 16 March 1946. **PONCHIELLI:** *La Gioconda* / Milanov, Stevens, Harshaw, Tucker, Warren, Vaghi; conducted by Cooper.

1 February 1947. **GOUNOD: *Roméo et Juliette*** / Sayão, Björling, Brownlee, Moscona; conducted by Cooper.

10 December 1949. **PUCCINI: *Manon Lescaut*** / Kirsten, Björling, Valdengo, Baccaloni; conducted by Antonicelli.

24 February 1951. **R. STRAUSS: *Der Rosenkavalier*** / Steber, Novotná, Berger, Baum, Thompson, Krenn; conducted by Reiner.

* 19 January 1952 & 23 February 1952. **R. STRAUSS: *Salome & Elektra*** / Welitsch, Höngen, Svanholm, Hotter, Sullivan & Varnay, Wegner, Höngen, Svanholm, Schöffler; both conducted by Reiner.

* 4 December 1954. **GIORDANO: *Andrea Chénier*** / Milanov, del Monaco, Warren; conducted by Cleva.

* 3 December 1955. **OFFENBACH: *Les Contes d'Hoffmann*** / Tucker, Singher, Peters, Stevens, Amara; conducted by Monteux.

7 January 1956. **PUCCINI: *Tosca*** / Tebaldi, Tucker, Warren; conducted by Mitropoulos.

8 March 1958. **VERDI: *Otello*** / del Monaco, de los Angeles, Warren, Elias, Moscona; conducted by Cleva.

* 14 February 1959. **MOZART: *Don Giovanni*** / London, Steber, Della Casa, Hurley, Valletti, Flagello, Uppman, Wildermann; conducted by Böhm.

4 March 1961. **PUCCINI: *Turandot*** / Nilsson, Moffo, Corelli, Giaiotti; conducted by Stokowski.

* 30 March 1963. **BELLINI: *La Sonnambula*** / Sutherland, Gedda, Flagello; conducted by Varviso.

* 9 March 1974. **VERDI: *I Vespri Siciliani*** / Caballé, Gedda, Milnes, Diaz, Munzer, Ahlstedt; conducted by Levine.

* 20 April 1985. **WAGNER: *Parsifal*** / Vickers, Rysanek, Estes, Moll, Mazura, Robbins; conducted by Levine.

* *The First Texaco Season 1940-41: Highlights.*

* *Met Centennial Collection 1935-59.*

James Levine 25th Anniversary Collection.

Bibliography

Annand, Major H. H. *The Catalogue of the United States Everlasting Indestructible Cylinders, 1908-1913.* Second edition. Bournemouth, England: The Talking Machine Review – International, 1973.

Arnold, Claude Graveley. *The Orchestra on Record, 1896-1926: an Encyclopedia of Orchestra Recordings Made by the Acoustical Process.* Westport, CT: Greenwood Press, 1997.

Bolig, John R. *The Victor Red Seal Discography. Volume I: Single-Sided Series (1903-1925).* Denver: Mainspring Press, 2004.

———. *The Victor Red Seal Discography. Volume II: Double-Sided Series to 1930.* Denver: Mainspring Press, 2006.

———. *The Victor Discography: Green, Blue, and Purple Labels (1910-1926).* Denver: Mainspring Press, 2006.

Clough, Francs F., and G. J. Cuming. *The World's Encyclopædia of Recorded Music.* London: Sidgwick & Jackson Limited in association with The Decca Record Company Limited and in the U.S.A., Canada, and South America: The London Gramophone Corporation, 1952.

Clough, Francs F., and G. J. Cuming, E. A. Hughes. *The World's Encyclopædia of Recorded Music.* Second Supplement (1951-1952). London: London Records Inc. in association with Sidgwick & Jackson Limited, 1953.

Clough, Francs F. and G. J. Cuming, E. A. Hughes, Angela Noble. *The World's Encyclopædia of Recorded Music.* Third Supplement (1953-1955). London: Sidgwick & Jackson Limited in association with The Decca Record Company Limited and in the U.S.A., Canada, and South America: London Records Inc., 1957.

Copeland, George A., and Ronald Dethlefson. *Pathé Records and Phonographs in America, 1914-1922.* Revised Second Edition. Los Angeles: Mulholland Press, 2001.

Darrell, R. D. *The Gramophone Shop Encyclopedia of Recorded Music.* New York: The Gramophone Shop, Inc., 1936.

Deakins, Duane D., and Elizabeth Deakins, Thomas Grattelo. *U. S. Everlasting Records.* Murphys, CA: Duane D. Deakins, May 1961.

Encyclopedic Discography of Victor Recordings. Available online at: http://victor.library.ucsb.edu/index.php (22 Oct. 2009).

Fagan, Ted, and William R. Moran. *The Encyclopedic Discography of Victor Recordings. Matrix Series: 1 through 4999.* New York: Greenwood Press, 1986.

Gray, Michael H. *The "World's Greatest Music" and "World's Greatest Opera" Records: a Discography.* ARSC Journal, vol. VII, no. 1/2 (1975): 33-55.

———. *The "World's Greatest Music" Records.* Le Grand Baton, vol. 11, no. 4 (Number 30; December 1974): 33-38.

Hamilton, David. "A Metropolitan Opera Discography." ARSC Journal, vol. XVI, no. 3 (1984): 59.

Kelly, Alan. *His Master's Voice/Die Stimme seines Herrn.* Westport, CT: Greenwood Press, 1994. (Also additions and corrections [30 April 2004] on CD-ROM available from Alan Kelly, 64 Alms Hill Road, Sheffield, S11 9RS, United Kingdom. email: akark@dsl.pipex.com.)

————. *His Master's Voice/La Voce del Padrone.* New York: Greenwood Press, 1988. (Also 2nd edition [26 February 2004] on CD-ROM available from Alan Kelly, 64 Alms Hill Road, Sheffield, S11 9RS, United Kingdom. email: akark@dsl.pipex.com.)

————. *His Master's Voice/La Voix de son Maître.* New York: Greenwood Press, 1990. (Also additions and corrections [26 February 2004] on CD-ROM available from Alan Kelly, 64 Alms Hill Road, Sheffield, S11 9RS, United Kingdom. email: akark@dsl.pipex.com.)

Laird, Ross. *Brunswick Records: a Discography of Recordings, 1916-1931.* Westport, CT: Greenwood Press, 2001.

Leslie, George Clark. *The Gramophone Shop Encyclopedia of Recorded Music.* New and completely revised 1942 edition. New York: Simon and Schuster, 1942.

O'Connell, Charles. *The Other Side of the Record.* New York: Alfred A. Knopf, 1947.

Phillips, Harvey E. *The Carmen Chronicle: the Making of an Opera.* New York: Stein and Day, 1973.

Reid, Robert H. *The Gramophone Shop Encyclopedia of Recorded Music.* Third edition, revised and enlarged. New York: The Gramophone Shop, Inc., 1948.

Rust, Brian. *The American Record Label Book.* New Rochelle, NY: Arlington House, 1978.

Rust, Brian, and Tim Brooks. *The Columbia Master Book Discography.* Westport, CT: Greenwood Press, 1999.

Sherman, Michael W., and William R. Moran, Kurt R. Nauck III. *The Collector's Guide to Victor Records.* Dallas: Monarch Record Enterprises, 1992.

Sherman, Michael W., and Kurt R. Nauck III. *Note the Notes: an Illustrated History of the Columbia 78 rpm Record Label, 1901-1958.* New Orleans: Monarch Record Enterprises, 1998.

Sooy, Raymond. *Memoirs of My Recording and Traveling Experiences for the Victor Talking Machine Company, 1898-1925.* Available online at the David Sarnoff Library at: http://www.davidsarnoff.org/soo.html (18 Oct. 2009).

Sutton, Allan, and CD-ROM by Kurt Nauck. *American Record Labels and Companies: an Encyclopedia (1891-1943).* Denver: Mainspring Press, 2000.

The Victor (Victrola) Book of the Opera. For anyone interested in historical vocal recordings, the various editions of this work provide a necessary and entertaining resource with their abundant photographs, plot synopses in the vernacular of their periods, and recording details. Some of the information provided about Victor recordings is not now available elsewhere. The earlier editions are particularly rich in evocative photographs.

The Victor Book of the Opera: Stories of Seventy Grand Operas with Three Hundred Illustrations & Descriptions of Seven Hundred Victor Opera Records. Camden, NJ: Victor Talking Machine Co., 1912. 375 pages.

This is the first edition of the work and there were at least three printings of this first edition with minor typographical changes. The second and third printings still had 1912 copyrights but were given the confusing labels of being the second and third "editions." This is confusing because there were true second and third editions which appeared in 1913 and 1915.

The Victor Book of the Opera: Stories of One-Hundred Operas with Five-Hundred Illustrations & Descriptions of One-Thousand Victor Opera Records. Camden, NJ: Victor Talking Machine Co., 1913. 480 pages.

This was called the "Revised Edition" with a 1913 copyright and is the real second edition.

The Victor Book of the Opera: Stories of One-Hundred and Ten Operas with Seven-Hundred Illustrations and Descriptions of Twelve-Hundred Victor Opera Records. Camden, NJ: Victor Talking Machine Company, 1915. 558 pages.

This was the "Third Revised Edition."

Rous, Samuel Holland. *The Victrola Book of the Opera: Stories of One-Hundred and Twenty Operas with Seven-Hundred Illustrations and Descriptions of Twelve-Hundred Victor Opera Records.* Camden, NJ: Victor Talking Machine Company, 1917. 553 pages.

This was the "Fourth Revised Edition," and the first edition to give the name of the author who was probably also the author of the earlier editions. Samuel Holland Rous used the name S. H. Dudley when he sang small rôles with touring opera companies and in the making of many popular recordings in the 1890s and first years of the twentieth century. He was the editor of the Victor Catalogues and monthly supplements for many years.

————. *The Victrola Book of the Opera: Stories of the Operas with Illustrations and Descriptions of Victor Opera Records.* Camden, NJ: Victor Talking Machine Company, 1919. 436 pages.
> This was the "Fifth Revised Edition."

The Victrola Book of the Opera: Stories of the Operas with Illustrations & Descriptions of Victor Opera Records. Camden, NJ: Victor Talking Machine Company, 1921. 433 pages.
> This was the "Sixth Edition, Rewritten and Revised." The number of photographs is lessened from this edition onward.

The Victrola Book of the Opera: Stories of the Operas with Illustrations & Descriptions of Victor Opera Records. Camden, NJ: Victor Talking Machine Company, 1924. 447 pages.
> This was the "Seventh Edition, Rewritten and Revised."

The Victrola Book of the Opera: Stories of the Operas with Illustrations & Descriptions of Victor Opera Records. Camden, NJ: Victor Talking Machine Company, 1929. 428 pages.
> This was the "Eighth Edition, Rewritten and Revised."

O'Connell, Charles. *The Victor Book of the Opera: Stories of the Operas with Illustrations and Descriptions of Victor Opera Records.* Camden, NJ: RCA Manufacturing Company, 1936. 526 pages.
> This was the "Ninth Edition," and was revised by Charles O'Connell.

————. *The Victor Book of the Opera: Stories of the Operas with Illustrations and Descriptions of Victor Opera Records.* Camden, NJ: RCA Manufacturing Company, 1936. 535 pages.
> This was the "Tenth Edition," and was revised by Charles O'Connell. It had the same copyright date as the ninth edition but appeared in 1939 according to the Publisher's Preface to the 1949 edition.

Biancolli, Louis, and Robert Bagar. *The Victor Book of Operas.* New York: Simon and Schuster, 1949. 596 pages.
> Although not listed as such, this was the "Eleventh Edition."

————. *The Victor Book of Operas.* New York: Simon and Schuster, 1953. 628 pages.
> This was the "Newly Revised Edition," and did not mention that it was really the "Twelfth Edition." Bart Winer added the histories and descriptions of nine operas.

Simon, Henry W. *The Victor Book of the Opera: the Historical Background and Act-by-act Summaries of 120 Operatic Masterworks—and Complete Listings of the Best Available Recordings, an Outline History of Opera, and Over 400 Illustrations of the Great Composers, the Great Singers and the Great Scenes of Grand Opera in All Its Historic Splendor.* New York: Simon and Schuster, 1968.
> This was correctly called the "Thirteenth Edition" and also had Gerald Fitzgerald as picture editor. This edition listed recordings by all companies and not just those by "Victor."

Composer Index

Classical compositions are listed under the names of the composers. Individual arias, scenes, and other parts from a work are listed in the order in which they appear in that work. The word *Excerpts* following a title refers to recordings that are called, among other titles, *Highlights, Excerpts, Brani Scelti, Abridged, Extraits, Great Moments,* and *Querschnitt.* The word *Selections* following a title refers to orchestral arrangements without voices which are sometimes called *Fantasias* and *Potpourris.*

BARBER, Samuel
Antony and Cleopatra—Give me my robe. 850
Vanessa. 728
Vanessa—Excerpts. 729
Vanessa—Must the winter come so soon? 730, 850
Vanessa—Do not utter a word, Anatol. 731, 934
Vanessa—To leave, to break. ("Quintet") 732

BEETHOVEN, Ludwig van
Egmont—Die Trommel geruhret. 411
Egmont—Freudvoll und Leidvoll. 412
Fidelio—O welche Lust! ("Prisoners' Chorus") 186
Symphony No. 3 in E-Flat Major, Op. 55. ("Eroïca") 886

BELLINI, Vincenzo
Norma—Overture. 765
Norma—Ite sul colle, o Druidi! 138, 425
Norma—Casta Diva. 164, 165, 401
Norma—Deh! proteggimi, o dio! ("Preghiera") 402
Norma—Oh! rimembranza! 403
Norma—Dolci qual arpa armonica. 416
Norma—Deh! con te, con te li prendi ... Mira, o Norma! ... Sì, fino all'ore estreme. 417
Norma—Mira, O Norma! 166, 765
Norma—Non parti? 136
Norma—Ah! del Tebro. 178

235

Title Index

Individual arias, scenes, and other parts from a work are listed alphabetically both by the name of the complete work followed by the excerpt [*e.g., Rigoletto—Questo o quella*] and also by the excerpt followed by name of the complete work [*e.g., Questo o quella (Rigoletto)*]. Initial articles (Il, die, der, L', *etc.*) are ignored in the alphabetization. The word *Excerpts* following a title refers to recordings that are called, among other titles, *Highlights, Excerpts, Brani Scelti, Abridged, Extraits, Great Moments* and *Querschnitt.* The word *Selections* following a title refers to orchestral arrangements without voices, which are sometimes called *Fantasias* and *Potpourris.* Popular songs and the names of special concerts are listed in this sequence.

Artist Index

Since every item in this discography refers to the Metropolitan Opera Chorus and Orchestra either together or separately, the Chorus and Orchestra are not indexed here. The only Metropolitan Opera ensemble listed in this index is the Metropolitan Opera Children's Chorus.

Adler, Kurt. 496-497, 523, 556, 567, 574, 587-588, 597, 609, 618, 627, 647, 655, 663, 672, 681, 685, 687, 690, 692, 700, 709, 713, 716, 718, 728, 733-734, 742, 754
Alagna, Roberto. 920
Alberghetti, Anna Maria. 581-583
Alcock, Merle. 154
Alda, Frances. 17, 74
Alessandroni, Cesare. 56-57
Allen, Mildred. 742
Alvary, Lorenzo. 268, 313, 325, 335-336, 350, 364, 597
Amara, Lucine. 574, 647, 663, 667, 672, 685, 690, 709, 713
Amato, Pasquale. 44-47, 51, 54-55, 65-67, 70
Amparan, Belen. 655, 709, 721
Anderson, June. 922
Anderson, Marian. 640
Anthony, Charles. 652, 663, 685, 687, 818
Anthony, Grace. 128-130, 134, 150, 158
Antonicelli, Giuseppe. 511
Antonini, Alfredo. 581-583
Arroyo, Martina. 754
Baccaloni, Salvatore. 511, 652, 667, 700
Bada, Angelo. 46-47, 142
Baker, John. 523
Baker, Mark. 781
Balatsch, Norbert. 823
Baldwin, Marcia. 759
Bamboschek, Giuseppe. 96-101
Bampton, Rose. 201, 204, 227-231, 233-235, 238-239, 249, 251, 256, 259-260, 262-263, 268, 272-273, 310-313
Barbieri, Fedora. 549-552
Barbini, Ernesto. 567
Barioni, Daniele. 690, 692, 700, 716
Bartoli, Cecilia. 866, 893
Bass, Robert. 850

About the Author

In the early 1950s when **Frederick P. Fellers** was seven years old, an elderly relative gave him a collection of old 78 rpm recordings. Among these magical discs was one that became a favorite—the 1922 recording of the "Zampa Overture" and the "Polovtsian Dances" played by the Metropolitan Opera House Orchestra. A few years later, Fellers discovered the weekly Metropolitan Opera radio broadcasts. Here was the same orchestra from the old recording along with its own chorus and many superb solo singers. In listening to these broadcasts, it was always a pleasure to hear the voice of Milton Cross as he explained the action and talked about the singers. His voice consisted of nobility along with real affection for the Metropolitan Opera, and it included that most rare substance—sincerity. In fact, his voice was of a quality that sometimes matched that of the singers on the stage. The excellent intermission features produced by Geraldine Souvaine were consistently entertaining and yet always informative. These broadcasts, which were an exciting weekly event, encouraged Fellers to find more of the Metropolitan Opera's recordings.

Frederick Fellers received his bachelor's degree in German from Wright State University and his master's degree in library science from Kent State University. These were separated by an interlude of four year's military service which included a year in Vietnam. Fellers was employed for nearly three decades as a librarian at the Indianapolis-Marion County Public Library. Fellers has also enjoyed aiding the Archives of the Indianapolis Symphony Orchestra. Now happily retired, he continues to look forward to the Metropolitan Opera's broadcasts and recordings as he has for more than fifty years. In thanks, Fellers is donating all his royalties for this book to the *Support the Met Broadcasts Campaign* and asks readers to also consider making a donation.